Penguin Education
Social Science and Public Policy

Martin Rein

Social Science
and Public Policy

Penguin Education

Penguin Books Ltd,
Harmondsworth, Middlesex, England
Penguin Books,
625 Madison Avenue, New York, New York 10022, U.S.A.
Penguin Books Australia Ltd,
Ringwood, Victoria, Australia
Penguin Books Canada Ltd,
41 Steelcase Road West, Markham, Ontario, Canada
Penguin Books (N.Z.) Ltd,
182–190 Wairau Road, Auckland 10, New Zealand

First published 1976

ISBN 0 14 08.0367 X

Printed in the United States of America by
Offset Paperback Mfrs., Inc., Dallas, Pennsylvania

Set in Monotype Times

Contents

To Lisa and Glen

Acknowledgements

Many people have contributed directly and indirectly to the writing of this book. I want, in particular, to acknowledge the invaluable aid that Peter Marris and Paul Kecskemeti have given me in sorting out my muddled thoughts and also in suggesting new directions that I could follow. Peter Marris and I have shared ideas for almost a decade. Over the years, we have spent many hours together discussing the issues raised in this book, and these discussions have influenced me greatly. I am much in his debt for his support and advice. Paul Kecskemeti has made me sensitive to the philosophical roots of much of my thinking and my treatment of the chapter on the 'Fact–Value Dilemma' owes much to him. The ideas about story telling and metaphors were developed jointly in a course I taught with Don Schon at M.I.T. My work with Don Schon has been a continued source of inspiration. David Cohen, Sol Levine, S. M. Miller and Robert Weiss in the United States, and David Donnison, and John Goldthorpe in England offered not only supportive criticism, but provocatively challenged those ideas that I thought were most settled, thus pressing me to develop many new insights. Tom Burns's comments on Chapter 7 were very helpful. I have borrowed from all of these persons many ideas which I have faithfully tried to acknowledge, but some of them have become so intertwined with my own thoughts that I can no longer adequately attribute them. I hope that those who have helped me will feel that I have put their advice to good use.

Karla O'Brien, at the M.I.T.–Harvard Joint Center for Urban Studies, was extremely helpful in editing Chapters 2 and 3.

Introduction

The essays in this book were written separately. They are nevertheless tied together by a common subject and a common theme. They all attempt, from different perspectives, to examine the question of what is and what ought to be the relationship between, on the one hand, empirical research and social science theory and, on the other, the development, implementation and assessment of public policies. Essentially I deal with only one aspect of the link between social science and policy, namely the inherent cognitive and methodological criteria social scientists, as scientists, apply to the conduct of policy-oriented research. So my main emphasis is on the underlying assumptions that guide analysis, although I also discuss, to some extent, the feedback of policy-oriented research to collective learning.

Most social scientists take for granted the view that knowledge about reality influences the ideals we hold. There is no sense in valuing something which can never be implemented. To some extent, therefore, facts shape the values we pursue. And since the intellectual processes that accompany ethical deliberations are concerned with matters of fact, we must give attention to the factual aspects of value questions. A corollary to this view is that social science can reduce conflict by expanding the areas of agreement on what are the facts of the situation and how they came about. If one assumes that there is a link between what is truthful (factual) and what is right (desirable), factual analysis must also improve the quality of policy decisions. Governments should therefore invest in policy-oriented research, because such analyses can broaden consensus by expanding the factual bases on which policy is built.

I disagree with this interpretation of how policy and analysis interact. A study may be valid by internal criteria and still arouse violent opposition from people against whose interest it goes. The crucial issues in a policy debate are not so much matters of fact as questions of interpretation. Theories of why things are as they are are difficult to document and to refute. The line of causality can often be reversed with equal plausibility, and there is no easy way to choose among the conflicting interpretations which follow. As people who hold different views acquire knowledge, they can argue their positions more cogently and thereby attempt to influence others by reason. In this sense information increases power. However, more knowledge, more equitably distributed, may produce more disagreement and make it more difficult for a government to act. What is presented as an impartial theory will often strike interested people as the greatest of injustices. Research findings can sharpen the areas of disagreement, make the issues more uncertain, complex and technical; and as a result the contribution of social science to policy seems more remote. The debate about the heritability of I.Q. or the relationship between education and income are two current examples. Social science does contribute to policy and practice, but the link is neither consensual, graceful nor self-evident.

The uses of social science for social policy have interested me since I first began seriously to study, write, advise and teach that elusive and difficult-to-define field of inquiry and action.[1] After all what is the purpose of studying policy if not in some measure to influence it? In search of an answer I began exploring how the subject was dealt with in philosophy, where it is treated as a problem of the transition from factual and descriptive statements to normative and ethical propositions. I discovered, as perhaps might have been expected, that the philosophical debate was, by and large, abstract and divorced from specific policy concerns,

1. Several of the essays have been published previously; for example, 'Policy Analysis as an Interpretation of Beliefs', *Journal of the Institute of American Planners*, vol. 37, no. 5, 1971; and (with Robert Weiss) 'The Evaluation of Broad-Aim Programs: Experimental Design, Its Difficulties and an Alternative', *Administrative Science Quarterly*, vol. 15, no. 1, March 1970.

while modern social science literature was, by contrast, more concrete, but without benefit of a formal framework from which to address ethical and epistemological issues. Of course, earlier social scientists like Mannheim and Weber also agonized about the problem. Their legacy defined the sociology of knowledge as a field of inquiry, affirming that understanding of social events cannot be isolated from the values and positions in society of those who seek to analyse them. It would surely be intriguing to discover ways in which the philosophical and sociological traditions could be integrated or, at the least, in which the differences between them could be identified and analysed.

While I decided not to pursue this line of inquiry, my brief foray into these traditions did help me to formulate more explicitly the main issues that have preoccupied me. The essays in this book represent my efforts to come to terms with these problems. Briefly stated, my principal concern is to identify what alternative can be presented if we wish to reject what I call the decisionist assumptions held by the positivists. They take the view that values must be accepted as an arbitrary decision, posited by the will or by passion, while 'factual' premises are grounded in reality. There is therefore a gulf between goals and value judgements, on the one hand, and the universe of facts which can be arranged and ordered in an objective, scientific, rational and coherent fashion on the other. What implications follow when we proceed from the opposite assumption: that the two premises cannot be neatly separated and are themselves the crucial object of inquiry? Must we then always inquire precisely how valuations enter policy analysis?

These essays are an attempt to develop an approach to the analysis of policy issues which is based on value criticism and informed by the unresolved questions posed by the sociology of knowledge. A value-critical approach subjects goals and values to critical review, that is, values themselves become the object of analysis; they are not merely accepted as a voluntary choice of the will, unamenable to further debate. Most attempts at the analysis of values ask the analyst to discuss alternative means to an end which is accepted without question; or to expose these instrumental means to review by measuring, or taking account in other ways of the short- and long-term consequences of pursuing a particular purpose; or to treat the factual aspects of values and examine their distribution in the population; and/or to study shifts in values held by different groups over time. All these approaches have merit, and I do not reject the positivist tradition in which they are carried out. But I do believe that they are insufficient, for I consider the crucial task in policy review to be the analysis of goals in their own terms, in relation to: (a) the intrinsic meaning of collective values when translated into social purposes; (b) the relationship to other goals with which they may be in conflict; (c) the question of priorities which arises from the pursuit of goals which have equal attractiveness (when they cannot all achieve their maximum value at the same time); and (d) economic and political constraints which must either be accepted or redefined.

In the value-critical approach, not only are values treated as the subject of analysis, but it is assumed that analysis can never be independent of the value we hold. They constitute the framework which helps us organize, not only the problems we address and neglect, but also the inferences we draw and the advice we offer about those questions that are subjected to systematic inquiry. Information and data can never be understood in isolation from the context of ideas which give them meaning. And it is these frames, or modes, or values, or ideologies, or theories, or whatever we choose to call them, which are crucial for any creative work; for without them, we have no question to ask. Problem-setting is as important as problem-solving because the frames which organize thoughts shape the conclusions we reach.

Finally, a value-critical approach adopts a cognitive style for understanding events which are idiographic rather than nomo-thetic.[2] In the former case, analysis takes the form of a narrative or a case study and explanations are always embedded in a specific context. Hence story-telling, arguments and description, diagnostic and normative metaphors are the primary intellectual tools. In the latter, the ideal for analysis is to isolate a generalized law based on stylized or simplified facts, which are largely inde-

2. Nomothetic: 'The study of cases or events as universals, with a view to formulating general laws.'

pendent of specific situations. This book is essentially about these themes.

Chapter 1 provides a personal statement of how I approach policy questions. Some of the themes I raise are further developed in the concluding chapter.

Chapter 2, 'The Fact–Value Dilemma', elaborates the value-critical approach and criticizes the positivists' position which assumes that values are first premises of an ethical position which are not subject to further review and analysis. Accordingly, the main task of social scientists is to separate facts from values. Treating ends as 'given', the problem is how to devise and test alternative means to reach them (experimentation), to assess how means presently pursued contribute to the achievement of these aims (evaluation) and to determine the unintended consequences in the pursuit of different means. However, once facts and values are uncompromisingly separated from each other, the difficult question arises as to how they may best be put together again if we are to create a policy science. The first part of the essay reviews three ways to reintegrate the normative and the factual: mapping, code harmonization and feedback. The limitations of each approach are reviewed. I then proceed from the assumption that facts and values must be integrated at each stage of understanding and analysis. Now a new set of ethical, epistemological and pragmatic difficulties arises for a policy-relevant social science. Each perspective presents its own difficulties, and what is needed is an approach which accepts the best of both intellectual traditions.

The fact–value controversy emerges in other ways as well. Social phenomena cannot be understood in isolation from the framework of thought which organizes evidence, interprets it and infers policy decisions which are consistent with it. A better appreciation of these frameworks or ideologies is crucial to understanding how social science and policy influence each other. However, to accept this mode of thinking raises a number of difficult questions. If research appears to proceed within a framework of thought, but does not seem able to help choose among competing frameworks, how useful and independent is the contribution of social science to the development of policy, fettered and constrained as it is by preconceived beliefs? Chapter

3, 'Values, Social Science and Social Policy', deals with this difficult problem. Whereas in Chapter 2 I was concerned essentially with the philosophical problems of relating questions of values to questions of fact, I consider here the same issues but from a more pragmatic perspective. Proceeding from the belief that rational thought should inform the development of policy, I review three obstacles which seem to frustrate the potential contribution of empirical research and social science theory to policy formulation: inherent social conflict in a democracy – different people want different things; the complex and changing nature of reality – the researcher may be certain of his goals, but he cannot be certain of the means to implement them; knowledge presupposes a framework by which it may be interpreted – but in a pluralistic system there are competing frameworks, and social science findings are seldom so conclusive that they indicate a firm choice. If social science research exists within a framework of thought, then we should question whether research contributes to policy or whether policy commitments provide the frame within which research is carried out. Two possible approaches to this dilemma are reviewed: the sceptical and the cautiously optimistic. According to the sceptical approach, evidence does not help in the social choice among competing frameworks; research follows policy developments, but the process is not reciprocal. The optimistic view holds that public policy typically evolves from what is initially a common framework of thought. In the short run, research contributes to policy when findings are consistent with the established framework; and in the long run, research contributes to alterations in the framework. The usefulness of research to policy will depend on the type of research, its source of funding and its administrative relationship to the policy maker.

In Chapter 3, therefore, I show how social science research is hindered by the competing frameworks to which its results may be related. The same study can lead to different policy conclusions, and this reduces the research's influence. In the next essay I review the other side of this question: a commitment to certain ideals serves as a paradigm, shaping what the analyst perceives and what he regards as worth studying. Chapter 4, 'Policy Analysis as the Interpretation of Beliefs', asks how social policies may be analysed. I argue that social policy is concerned with the integration of values, the principles by which these values are translated into policies and programmes, the assessment of the outcomes of implementing these principles in terms of the values asserted and the search for strategies of feasible change which promise a better fit between values, principles and outcomes. One aspect without the others is not policy analysis. Yet current efforts have failed to integrate these tasks and as a result the status of social policy analysis as a legitimate discipline has been questioned. Rather than trying to force a grand synthesis among competing perspectives, this essay tries to extend our understanding of how partisan views enter policy analysis. I try to show, by specific examples, the various ways in which the claim for dispassionate and value-neutral analysis is overstated. I argue that the examination of policy issues by social scientists can most fruitfully be understood as an interpretation of their beliefs about equality as a social goal. Specifically, the essay illustrates how these beliefs intrude at each level of analysis – in the definitions of the purposes of policy, in the priorities assigned to conflicting values, in the institutional forms which translate values to programmes, and in the interpretations about what changes are politically feasible. The conclusion that there is no single true policy analysis suggests a stance that analysts might adopt.

Since beliefs about equality are crucial in the analysis of questions of policy, it seemed important to explore this theme still further. Chapter 5, 'Stratification and Social Policy', is an example of an effort to apply a value-critical perspective to an analysis of equality as a social end. A review of available evidence suggests that only very modest advances towards the equalization of income and opportunity have occurred in mature industrial societies since the Second World War. When one considers the ambiguities and conflicting principles that pervade the problem of equality and the difficulty of achieving redistribution, on what grounds can egalitarians argue their case? In the concluding section of this essay an attempt is made to identify which values are widely shared by a form of analogical reasoning that asks which basic presuppositions in our beliefs we are really committed to. The search for common areas of agreement in what appears to be a field of dispute is, of course, only one path that a value-critical approach may take. But if such agreements can be identified, an attempt can then be made to show that those who oppose a shared ideal speak in violation of their own position. This essay was originally written with Peter Marris for a conference sponsored by the Academy of Science in late 1969. The sponsor of the meeting, after a long delay, decided against publishing the proceedings. I have extensively revised the argument set out in that paper and up-dated the evidence presented in it, and I wish to thank my co-author for permission to reproduce this unpublished article here.

Chapter 6, 'Social Science and Health', considers competing interpretations of the guiding metaphors that describe how society functions and why things are as they are.[3] Our interpretation of these serves as a guide in the selection of relevant policy variables and provides a framework not only for the analysis of data, but for the design of constructive policy alternatives. A better understanding of how frameworks of belief enable us to organize and interpret evidence and to infer policy decisions, is crucial if we are to see how social science and policy influence each other. I examine this theme through an extensive review of theoretical and empirical social scientific literature in the field of health care. Three frameworks are discussed in detail – resource allocation, personal and social theory and institutional performance. Each provides a different interpretation of how the link between health and poverty occurs and what can be done about it.

Chapter 7, 'Social Science for Social Policy', describes how story-telling can draw together the factual and the normative and so is an important means by which social science can contribute to policy debates.

3. This essay is an extensive revision of an earlier one entitled, 'Social Science and the Elimination of Poverty', *The Journal of the Institute of American Planners*, vol. 33, no. 3, 1967. I wish to thank Diana Mitchell for help in revising it.

Chapter 1

Policy Analysis: A Personal Approach

Since the question of the interplay between personal values and policy analysis plays so prominent a part in these essays, I would like to make a brief statement of my own values and provide a more detailed elaboration of how they influence the way I analyse policy questions.

I approach policy questions sceptically. I believe that scepticism is valuable, essentially because it seeks to confront people with the results of their actions. Unless we are realistic, we are likely to fail, to blind ourselves to consequences, and to rationalize illusions as achievement. So, at best, there is some honesty and truthfulness in scepticism – a concern for worthwhile actions rather than noble gestures or fine words. It makes us see ourselves in context, as creatures of our time, where possibilities are largely determined by our circumstances – both as to what can be done, and how we can think about it. The risk is that it becomes a defeatist and fatalistic frame of mind. It still, then, perhaps has some virtue – as a tactic for forcing people to confront the illusions of hope. But it is vulnerable to the charge that, by questioning the optimistic claims of every policy, scepticism weakens reformers more than conservatives – since it takes more energy and faith to change things than to leave them as they are. Any choice of policy is risky – full of uncertainties and unforeseeable consequences: at some point, we have to commit ourselves for better or worse. So, I think, we must have underlying the scepticism, some faith and hope which it ultimately serves, otherwise honest scepticism degenerates into cynicism and paralyses our ability to act.

In other words, I believe that scepticism is valuable because it questions facile beliefs and facile interpretations of facts, and requires one to be serious about the practicality of ideals and their implications. This defence of scepticism presupposes an underlying commitment to ideals – otherwise why does it matter whether people are facile and impractical or not? Let me briefly state my underlying beliefs. I believe that equality is a fundamental principle in a good society but it remains an unresolved puzzle as to how this aim can best be achieved.

As a point of departure, I accept Tawney's view that democracy as a political system is unstable,

'as long as it remains only a political system and nothing more, instead of being, as it should be, not only a form of government, but a type of society, and a manner of life which is in harmony with that type. To make it a type of society requires advances along two lines ... the resolution to eliminate all forms of special privilege ... and the conversion of economic power ... into the servant of society, working within clearly defined limits, and accountable for its actions to a public authority ... To broaden [democracy's] foundations means ... to destroy plutocracy and set in its place an egalitarian society.'[1]

While Tawney's dream is quite a tall order to fill, as an ideal it sets a direction worth striving for. My views about equality and the conflict between goals of equity and equality are set out in greater detail in Chapter 5, 'Social Stratification and Social Policy'.

Given these broad concerns about equality and action, several approaches to the analysis of policy seem to follow.

1. Treat the Question of Purpose as Unresolved

The study of social policy is basically concerned with the range of human needs and the social institutions created to meet them. Yet we have no adequate definition of 'need', and much confusion prevails about the distinctions between 'need', 'preference' and 'social problems'. Moreover, the institutional arrangements meeting these 'needs' seem infinitely varied and have a rapid rate of

1. R. H. Tawney, *Equality*, Allen & Unwin, revised edition, 1952, pp. 15–16.

obsolescence. What is accepted in one decade as truth may be challenged in another. In England, for example, the welfare state was committed to the principle that economic need arising from the interruption of income should be met through the social insurance approach. Benefits were to be set at a uniform flat rate and the small residual fall-outs of this system were to be protected by a nationally financed and administered public assistance programme which allocated benefits according to a test of need. Thirty years later, each of these major lines of established policy was challenged. Flat-rate pensions gave way to wage-supplemented pensions and to the principle of continuity of life-style rather than minimum needs. The residual role of public assistance failed to materialize as the proportion of the population on welfare rose in 1973 to 8·5 per cent; and welfare and insurance schemes came increasingly to overlap because the level of social-insurance benefits fell below the welfare standard. Even the very principle of universal, comprehensive, compulsory *public* social insurance has been challenged by giving individuals the opportunity to opt out of the public sector and to secure benefits in the private market.

I am not criticizing these developments here, but present them as an illustration of the view that ideas are embedded in practice; the relationship between the means and ends of social policy is not settled, nor is it ever likely to be finally resolved. This unsettled nature of social policy derives largely from a constant redefinition of its purposes. Evolving social objectives are central to the development of social policy, and as a result the study of the interplay between social purposes and how they work out in practice must also be central to the analyst's concern.

Accordingly, in analysing a specific policy I try to search out its uncertain objectives systematically. Given my doubts about the stability of purposes, I assume that objectives in any public policy are multiple, ambiguous and conflicting. The effort to clarify the aims of social policy and the way in which conflicting objectives are reconciled by those who implement it is a useful method of formulating good questions about plans for the future. Future policy is after all partly a redefinition of either social objectives or the constraints which inhibit the implementation of objectives already held. Because this is so, it follows that it must be difficult to discover what an organization is trying to accomplish, and whether its present arrangements facilitate or inhibit the achievement of these evolving goals. We should not simply accept the goals as given; it is necessary to scrutinize both the input and the goals.

2. Attend to Practice as Well as Policy

One way of coping with ambivalent purposes is through vagueness and ambiguity. If one examines the purposes of most social legislation one usually finds that the moral and ideological objectives, the goals of social policy, are open to many interpretations. Ambiguity seems to be essential for agreement. When the purposes of policy are unclear and incompatible, each successive stage in the process of implementation provides a new context in which further clarification is sought.[2] One of the consequences of passing ambiguous and inconsistent legislation is to shift the arena of decision to a lower level. The lack of consensus is resolved at the level of everyday practice, through the concrete actions taken by administrators and practitioners. Hence an analysis of practice must be combined with the study of policy. Indeed, the goals of programmes can often be understood best not from formal statements of legislative intent, but from everyday practice. So programmes that appear different may be similar, while programmes that are similarly structured or intended may actually differ in their consequences. (It was this outlook that led S. M. Miller and me to develop the common notion of an 'aging vat' to describe the variety of training programmes for youth which, rather than providing skills, primarily served to keep youth out of the labour market until they could hold a better job when they were older.) This line of theory is similar to functionalism. Even though the stated goals are vague and ambiguous, the policy can be seen to fulfill – perhaps unconsciously – a function (removing youngsters from the labour

2. For a fuller analysis of this issue see Martin Rein and Francine Rabinovitz, 'Implementation: A Theoretical Perspective', May 1974 (mimeograph).

market as they grow up). The trouble with this approach is that you can nearly always invent a plausible function – so that the style of analysis drifts towards Panglossian conservatism: everything is functional somehow – so why should it change?

Turning next to questions of policy, I believe that one useful approach to understanding policy is to examine recurring issues in the design of social programmes. S. M. Miller and I have tried to crystallize these by a set of dichotomies: should policies directed at social change seek fundamental or incremental reform; should universal or selective principles govern the distribution of services, or both; should social objectives be primarily directed towards equality of opportunity or equality of conditions; should policy decisions be made through a centralized, élite-dominated system or through a pluralistic, competitive system with consumer sovereignty?[3]

It seems that in real life these dichotomies cannot be avoided, even though the answer we seek is typically cast in terms of Platonic ideals where all the good things in life are assumed to be mutually reinforcing and where cruel choices can be avoided. This tension between ideals and realities often leads to situations where at some later time we will accept an element we earlier rejected. This leads to my next imperative – that policies must be viewed in an historical context.

3. Examine Policy in Historical Perspective

I do not altogether accept either a dialectic or a linear theory about the historical development of social policy. That is to say, I do not believe that the fusion of opposites leads to social progress, or that the social policies of one era are necessarily an improvement over those of another. Knowledge about policy questions is not cumulative in a scientific sense, partly because the problems are intractable, and also because the environment changes so that old solutions do not fit the new circumstances.

3. For an elaboration of some of these issues of choice, see S. M. Miller, 'Criteria for Anti-Poverty Policies: A Paradigm of Choice', *Poverty and Human Resources Abstracts*, vol. 3, no. 5, September–October 1968, pp. 3–11.

Social policy is forever debating what appear to be similar issues, although the perspective changes in the light of a specific point in time and of the policies which preceded it. Consider one example. In an effort to win acceptance for the principle of the legally enforceable right to social benefit, as contrasted with the distribution of largess by charity and discretion, proponents of social insurance programmes have insisted upon a separation of cash from personal social services, such as casework. However, when the right to benefits seemed secure, the inclusion of services within an insurance framework seemed less threatening. The Social Reform Commission in Denmark argued that the principle of separating cash and services had been carried too far in the area of short-term insurance benefits for the unemployed and sick and that cash policies alone were self-defeating. The Commission recommended the re-introduction of caseworkers and other support services. In the United States also we can find examples of efforts to bring cash and services together in the insurance field, whereas in the public assistance field we find a determined effort, among some reformers, to separate them. Each position is partially valid; each position has its own inherent limitation. To pursue one principle to an extreme leaves the programme vulnerable when judged by another criterion. But to discuss the principles without examining practice is also misleading. So while there has been a vigorous debate about 'the income versus the service' strategy, with official policy in the executive office favouring the former, in practice the latter approach became dominant as expenditure on benefits in kind grew to become the primary strategy to aid the poor.

The relationship between cash and services is only one example of a general tendency in social policy to develop in a cyclic rather than a linear manner. Since the problems are in essence intractable, and can rarely be resolved without sacrificing some strongly held values, the issues tend to be recurrent. Each generation takes up the same issues again and seeks to re-define them in the light of its own political, economic and social reality.

An historical perspective is useful for yet another reason. It is widely accepted that no single programme can be successful in isolation from others. Beveridge's famous report of 1942, which ushered in the British welfare state, called attention to the principle that an adequate social insurance programme must depend upon and be buttressed by social intervention in other areas as well. He listed four: full employment, adequate housing at low cost, children's allowances and comprehensive health care. Yet, as many critics have pointed out, little was done in the post-Beveridge period in the areas of housing and wage differentials.[4] As a result the income-maintenance programme became inadequate.

I believe that we shall continue to approach policy in a fragmented way. Although we accept the interrelationship of the sectors of social policy, we seldom develop a comprehensive and integrated national social plan to embrace them all. Political, administrative and economic constraints lead to the development of some services and the neglect of others. Even if these constraints were not strong, the intellectual difficulties of establishing priorities among conflicting claims and subordinating them to a single purpose without internal contradictions would remain. So social policies tend to develop in an almost faddist manner; first one then another fashion is pursued.

4. Distrust Orthodoxy

Conflicting objectives, political, economic, and administrative constraints, and changing circumstances, inhibit the development of permanent policies. Moreover, policy develops from compromise among contending interests, ideals and purposes so that an accepted pattern contains the contradictions and limitations which make it politically acceptable. As a result, I always try to question the orthodox and established pattern, trying to discover where it is vulnerable and what alternative approaches are required. Some concrete illustrations may be helpful. In the early 1960s, the dominant criticism of the social services was that organizations had disengaged themselves from the poor. Professionals were preoccupied with good clients and neglected the

4. See, for example, Eveline M. Burns, 'Social Security in Britain – Twenty Years After Beveridge', *Industrial Relations*, vol. 2, no. 1, October 1962, pp. 15–32.

hard-to-reach cases. Rigidity and a lack of relevance reinforced each other, creating an urgent need for the structural reform of social services. While this analysis was reasonable, it was incomplete and therefore misleading. Part of the reason why social services could not function effectively was that they lacked the resources to carry out their mandate. Rationing devices are used to exclude individuals from services partly because of the realities of scarcity. So even the new poverty programmes soon came to take on the very characteristics they had been launched to cure.

Let me offer another illustration from the field of mental health. It is now widely accepted that mental health services should be organized geographically to service individuals and families who reside in specific geographic sections, called catchment areas. Since this is accepted policy, I think it is important to consider the limitations of this approach and to examine those situations in which services could be organized by function rather than location. For example, services to college students in a university-saturated area such as Boston may be better organized by clientele than by where students live.

When long-term treatment is the orthodox and accepted model, the importance of short-term services needs to be re-emphasized. When a good deal of attention is paid to diagnosis, one should balance this by stressing concrete services. When community care and de-institutionalization become the accepted ideology of the helping professions, the benefits of institutional care need to be reassessed. All these examples stress the value of running counter to the prevailing trends.

5. *Approach Social Policy as a Moral Critic*

Peter Townsend's *The Last Refuge*[5] is perhaps the prototype of the sort of study which tries to act as moral witness of how society neglects its own established values. It is a moving account of the

5. The term moral witness was coined by Peter Marris. For a study in this tradition, see Peter Townsend, *The Last Refuge: A Survey of Residential Institutions and Homes for the Aged in England and Wales*, abridged edition, Routledge & Kegan Paul, 1964.

aged in English and Welsh institutions, ignored and mistreated in outdated buildings and without adequate resources and facilities. Although English society has committed itself to the abolition of the almshouse and to the break-up of the Poor Law, their influence remains pervasive. Townsend offers a graphic indictment of a society which has failed to implement its own ideals. It is an eloquent, well-documented plea for social justice. In this sense, Townsend argues his position by appealing to common values which are also accepted in law.

In contrast, I tend to approach policy analysis by questioning morality rather than by asserting it. Three lines of investigation are typical of this kind of analysis:

(a) People often hold and act upon a set of beliefs of which they are not fully aware. Therefore, like Townsend, I attempt to highlight the difference between what men of action say they believe in and what they actually do. For there is a disparity between one's espoused theory of action and the actual theory in use.[6] For example, some social workers see their mission as promoting self-determination. Yet the history of social work suggests that from its inception it has been more concerned with supporting a work ethic, constricting and reducing freedoms for some groups in society rather than expanding them. Keith Lucas's *Decisions About People in Need*,[7] and Alvin Schorr's study of the trend towards proscription[8] illustrate the tendency of public-assistance policy to hold welfare clients to a higher standard of moral behaviour than generally prevails in the community. The caseworker's actual behaviour must be recognized as a series of constraints and pressures that are necessarily the expression of his or her espoused professional creed.

(b) Examine the consequences in action of principles which are widely shared. For example, in a study of the Planned Parenthood Federation and its local affiliates, I discovered that one of the consequences of the organization's quest for respectability and

6. For a detailed elaboration of this discrepancy see Chris Argyris and Donald A. Schon, *Theories in Action*, San Francisco, Jossey-Bass, 1974.

7. Keith Lucas, *Decisions About People in Need*, North Carolina University Press, 1957.

8. Alvin Schorr, 'The Trend to Rx', *Social Work*, vol. 7, January 1962.

legitimacy was to ensure a condition of paralysis and inaction.[9] This arose because Planned Parenthood affiliates followed a co-operative rationality in which clients and finance were sought from local agencies, and formal affiliation with local Health and Welfare Councils was valued.

(c) I try to show that all interventions may be regarded both as a way of doing something and as a process that forsakes some other action. To examine a problem from one perspective is to neglect considering it from another. This is to say that all programmes have hidden costs. For example, the Job Corps served for many youngsters as a 'second chance' institution to reintegrate them into the world of work. However, the costs to young people exposed to the programme may be seen from several angles. There are those who failed to be accepted and those who, once accepted, were unable to graduate. Both groups might be especially vulnerable to a sense of double defeat. We might consider also what are the social costs to those graduates who were still unable to get adequate jobs. Whenever attention is focused on success, I find myself almost instinctively concerned about failure and, in this example, especially about the double and triple failures of those who are repeatedly rejected or unable to cope.

In sociology this attention to self and organizational deception, to the consequences of pursuing specific policies and to the neglect of other relevant policies is known as latent functional analysis rather than muck-raking. But whatever the terminology the broad approaches set out above can be translated into more familiar questions about ends and means and their interrelationship. To these we turn.

At the centre of my concern is the question of social objectives, the purposes of policy, and the goals of welfare organizations. I start with the premise that defining coherent social purposes in public policy is an endemic problem. While governments develop social programmes, they rarely if ever develop social policy in the singular. Rather, when the various different programmes designed to achieve similar purposes are examined in detail, we see multiple policies which are often in conflict.

9. Martin Rein, 'Organization for Social Change', *Journal of Social Work*, vol. 9, no. 2, April 1964.

To understand goals we need to consider them not as philosophical abstractions of the common weal, but as a reflection of the interest of specific social groups. It is therefore useful to view goals concretely in terms of the actors who cherish them and of what is at stake for them when they forsake, compromise on, or achieve their ends.

Social scientists feel most at ease in the analysis of alternative means to achieve a stated aim, and the current conception of political process assigns to the social scientist the task of dispassionately assessing the social costs of alternative methods of achieving specific goals. In this way the expert usurps no political prerogatives. In practice, however, the analysis of means is seldom a merely technical question; it characteristically masks a more fundamental debate about ends. Consider the advice given by social scientists on the choice between two road-building schemes, only one of which can be included in a given national budget. Each scheme costs about the same amount, but one produces a net present value of 10 per cent above the other. The Cabinet member in charge of transport is thus advised by the social scientists to choose the road which yields the most favourable benefit ratio. But such a decision might be inappropriate. In a thoughtful analysis of this situation, an economist offers this observation:

But the figures may hide the following reality: Scheme A, let us say, has the higher present value but 90% of the benefits are time-savings, and 10% represent the value of accident-savings; whereas in the case of Scheme B, with the lower present value, 40% of the benefits accrue because of accident reduction and only 60% from time-savings. When the minister inquires further into the actual valuation of accidents, he may find the values put upon them, as compared with the valuation of time, not quite in accord with his own prejudices, particularly if he finds that the death on the roads of old people has a positive economic value (as follows from one convention for measuring the values of human life).[10]

I am inclined therefore to treat debate about means as masked ideology and try to make explicit, as in the above quotation, the

10. Denys Mumby, 'The Assessment of Priorities in Public Expenditures', *Political Quarterly*, vol. 39, no. 4, October–December 1968, p. 381.

fact that a review of alternative means can also embrace conflicting goals. Consider another example. The recent debate of alternative income maintenance programmes was not a neutral assessment of the costs and benefits of children's allowances and negative income tax, or, more generally, means-tested or universal schemes; it was also about the relative importance given to the issues of social stigma, work requirements, benefit adequacy, and income redistribution.

I am especially interested in questions of distribution and redistribution. I assume that a primary objective of using public funds for social services is to bring about a redistribution across an individual's lifetime, or among different income groups, or between those who retire or are active in the labour market, or between different geographic areas, etc. Who gets what is, after all, one crucial aspect of what politics and government is all about. By and large, these distributional outcomes of public intervention have not been a central concern of either economists or sociologists in their research on social policy, although there is an increasing number of exceptions to this generalization.[11]

6. Consider the Political Reception of Policy Studies

These essays are primarily concerned with the logic of social analysis and the role of values in such an inquiry; they have not explicitly dealt with the political reception of these ideas. But something should be said also about how social science knowledge is likely to be used in the policy process. To pursue this question in a meaningful way, we need to be clear about the meaning of knowledge and the use of the term policy. We start by distinguishing types of knowledge. Of course we should not mindlessly invent typologies independent of their use. Meaningful classifications are always embedded in context. For example, I have found it useful elsewhere to examine the kind of social

11. See, for example, Burton Weisbrod's treatment of distributional effects, 'Income Redistribution Effect and Benefit Cost Analysis', in S. B. Chase, *Problems in Public Expenditure Analysis*, Washington, D.C., The Brookings Institution, 1968.

science knowledge which contributed to the development of negative income-tax policy in the United States.[12] Here I was able to distinguish three types of knowledge: programmatic knowledge, that is, knowledge about the actual operation of specific governmental programmes; social knowledge, which calls for information on social relationships and family behaviour; and economic knowledge, that is, information on material incentives, economic needs, and work relationships. These distinctions are helpful because they remind us that social science knowledge is not all of a piece. Information on social behaviour, for example, is not the same as an economic model based on presumed responses to material incentives. Social science knowledge is also relevant to a review of programmatic concerns, especially the question of how policies are translated from law into practice, although this area tends to be neglected by academic social science.

We then need to isolate the different arenas in which these types of knowledge might be used. For simplicity's sake let us identify the following arenas: the administrative agency responsible for carrying out the welfare programme and overseeing its cost; the political operations within the executive office which is responsible for setting policy initiative, based at least in part on the information provided for it by the operating bureaucracies; and, finally, Congress reacting to that initiative. We also need to differentiate the various processes of policy making. Among the processes are ferment (those activities which call for sensitizing policy makers to the need for action and then conceptualizing the alternatives), bargaining (about the different elements of cost and beneficiaries), and, finally, design (where a specific programmatic proposal is submitted for decision). These do not take place serially over time and so should not be confused with stages. These processes go on within each arena, even though some arenas take more initiative than others with respect to some of them.

Now, armed with at least a primitive vocabulary which enables us to differentiate types of knowledge, arenas of decision and policy processes, we can approach the question of the reception of

12. For a fuller discussion see 'Social Science and the Negative Income Tax', a paper prepared for O.E.C.D., 1975 (with Hugh Heclo).

social science knowledge into the political process more realistically. In the case of welfare reform in the United States, several generalizations seem appropriate. First, we can identify the committed motivation of social science research. This finding is, of course, at odds with a purist's model of inquiry, which posits that disinterested analysis generates knowledge which in turn impels action. Instead, the reverse seems true. A commitment to some sort of action is the force which inspires the analysis in the first place and later guides its development. It is true that social scientific inquiry can modify and redirect the initial commitment, but it is moral, political and other attachments, rather than research findings, which determine when something is investigated and how it is handled.

Secondly, different types of knowledge tend to be used in different arenas. For example, economic knowledge was used largely by the political executive to initiate the view that altering marginal tax rates would affect work incentives. Programmatic knowledge was later used to refute this thesis, by pointing out first that many local welfare programmes actually operated with even lower marginal tax rates than those proposed by the reforms, and then showing from the experience in implementing these programmes that low tax rates do not significantly increase welfare recipients' participation in the labour force. Most important was the obvious, but neglected, fact that no one programme, such as public assistance, can be understood in isolation from the family of income-tested programmes of which it is a part. Seen in this broader perspective of complementary and competitive programmes, it became absurd to lower the marginal tax rate of one programme when the effect of other social programmes would be to raise it quite substantially. So knowledge about the way public assistance operated and the way in which the whole family of income-tested programmes performed led to an assault on the initial reform idea the executive had proposed. Finally, some members of Congress were most concerned about the problems of parental responsibility for child support and the effect of welfare on fertility and family relationships. That is to say, they were concerned with the sociological as well as the economic dimension of welfare programmes. Eventually the Joint Economic

Committee launched an intensive study of these social dimensions, but by this time inflation and high unemployment had altered the context of debate and the initiative for reform passed. From this concrete example, I wish to draw several conclusions about the way in which social science knowledge might be used in policy making.

We have seen that different types of knowledge are used competitively to support previously held political views. I believe that it is important for more than one type to be used in each arena. However, to introduce competing analyses which arise from different knowledge orientations in the same arena of decision, also diminishes and moderates the contribution of social science knowledge to policy-making. Certainly no one sector of the social science community has a monopoly on useful knowledge, but even so a more competitive use of social science, over a wider range of orientations, with overlap across arenas and processes, is likely to produce substantial argument and increase confusion as the issues become more complex. Besides, disagreement among the experts will also give greater prominence to the political policy makers' responsibility for choices, at the same time reducing the claim of the social scientist to be a policy adviser. Policy makers and administrators are therefore likely to discount what is said by social scientists who cannot agree among themselves. Even so, I believe that, given the present state of social science knowledge, it is probably better to recognize how conflicting and uncertain its interpretations are than to assign a very high value to a particular orientation, which is narrowly distributed in the policy-making process and has not the benefit of competition from alternative views.

In addition it is important to recognize that it is not only academic knowledge generated by social science which is useful in the policy-making process, but also the judgement and experience of social scientists acting as advocates for, and advisers on, different points of view. There is much to be said for the opinion that it is social scientists, rather than social science *per se*, that play the most prominent role in policy making. And when a social scientist employs policy analysis in an effort to redirect a policy debate, he is likely to have to make some sort of political accommodation if he hopes to be useful. He becomes embedded in a political struggle and cannot, therefore, deny the legitimate claims of groups other than social scientists to have a say in policy also. Advisors to governments must be prepared to have their initial concepts redirected in the course of the political struggle. The evolution of the concept of negative income tax (N.I.T.) is a case in point. The social science concept was redirected in the course of the debate. At first social scientists hoped that the welfare reform discussed during the Nixon Administration would serve as an anti-poverty strategy designed primarily as a way of minimizing disincentive by permitting people to keep a portion of their earnings. Slowly the N.I.T. was transformed into a programme whose primary aim was to reduce welfare dependency by maximizing work incentives through lower rates of tax.

Many social scientists hoped that such incentives would by themselves be sufficient to encourage work. They rejected policies which compelled people to work. Nevertheless, as the debates on welfare reform evolved, some of them found themselves in the position of having to support a policy of work requirements as a result of their active participation in trying to get welfare reform passed by Congress.

Knowledge is not used simply to influence policy actively. The process is more complex; as policy evolves, knowledge is used selectively to justify actions reached on other grounds. Moreover, knowledge and policy are interactive, being as much influenced by as influencing the current agenda for reform. While the active role is accepted as the dominant model, in practice social science both justifies policy decisions and interacts with them.

I hope these remarks help to illustrate what I mean by a value-critical approach to policy analysis. In the short run, an analysis which proceeds from these assumptions is likely to be greeted by policy makers with either exasperation or indifference, but it may make a more enduring contribution to policy in the long run.

Conclusion

I have reviewed a number of different approaches to inter-relationships between ideals and events. These may briefly be restated as follows: one approach seeks to discover what the values 'really' are, by seeing what the policy actually does. This research style exposes the hypocrisy or self-deception of policies. Another is synthesis, tracing the consistency of values by looking at the interaction of related problems. (The broader the boundaries of the system, the more powerful the insights of the synthesis – but the more difficult to comprehend it all.) Richard Titmuss's great skill was, I think, his ability to relate policies which were conventionally treated separately.[13] A third approach is learning: learning being a process of adopting what might be called 'structures of meaning' – and these structures are made up of sets of purposes interpreted in the context of a particular organization of reality. Hence, as the organization of reality changes, so does the interpretation of purposes – and vice versa – in a continued dialectic, where the solution advanced to cope with other problems itself becomes the object of reform. So, an historical perspective is important. A final approach fulfils a simpler role as moral witness – showing up inconsistency between ideals and practice without attempting to explain much about how this happens.

Before concluding, I want to comment on some of the implications of a sceptical view of policy analysis. How can the principles I use to guide my work ultimately serve my ideals? Consider for instance the continual dilemma in social policy between liberty and care. Liberty respects the right of people to make their own choices, to control their own circumstances – it tends to favour

13. Titmuss's great insight, which he first expressed in his inaugural lecture in 1955, was into the shared relationships of occupation, fringe benefits acquired through work, forgiveness of burdens by tax exemption and the direct provision of social services through government initiative or private charity. His last lectures showed that he was still preoccupied with working out the implications of this insight. See Richard Titmuss (edited by Brian Abel Smith and Kay Titmuss), *Social Policy: An Introduction*, Allen & Unwin, and New York, Pantheon Books, 1974.

universal rights, benefits in cash rather than in kind, decentralization and community control, and market mechanisms as a means of expressing personal choice. I have called this the universal-formalist perspective.[14] But if we care for people and want to protect them from hardship, we become more concerned with the quality of service we provide them and less with their right to control these services. And this in turn leads to a preoccupation with questions of efficiency of organization, social services rather than purchasing power and selection of help by professional standards. This I have called a selective-discretionary approach. Simple dichotomies are misleading for reality is always more subtle and complex. We may, for example, want to extend freedom of choice when professional services fail to provide care for those who most need it. Or we may advocate more central control to redistribute freedom of choice. Still, it is useful to accept two competing perspectives to help us clarify what is at issue. But how do we proceed if we believe in both, and they do indeed tend in opposite directions? A value-critical approach to policy does need to be sensitive to this dilemma and to question the claims of each. The concept of a pendulum swinging between irreconcilable ideals is insufficient. We need to search for better accommodation between them. The ideal is a form of compassion which both cares and respects the autonomy of each person – and so is profoundly egalitarian. But since the ideas conflict, we have to believe, as an act of faith, that we can get closer to such an accommodation. We need to be sceptical of scepticism. We cannot proceed without a working normative universe or, as Weber puts it, an ethic of principles, but neither can such principles give the whole answer.

14. Martin Rein, 'Decentralization and Citizen Participation in Social Services', *Public Administration Review* (Special Issue), vol. 32, October 1972.

Chapter 2

The Fact–Value Dilemma

Separating Facts and Values

Robert Lynd's challenge and implicit admonishment 'Knowledge for what?' was both timely and appropriate, for sociologists of the 1940s and the 1950s who were often indifferent to the practical uses of their findings. By contrast, social scientists of the 1970s are anxious that the practical implications of their inquiries shall not be neglected. And while many academics remain sceptical about the scientific value of policies adopted under outside political influences, policy makers and administrators have increasingly used empirical evidence to support the view they themselves hold, or to criticize the view that others recommend to them.

It is now widely accepted that social science has something to offer, either as a source of dispassionate reason, or as a means of influence and persuasion, or both; for it is believed that scientific knowledge can help towards making better policy decisions. Some people claim that social science, at the least, can clarify moral choices, and, at the most, can lift all but the most fundamental moral issues out of ideological debate. Others believe that in the relationship between social science and social policy each has something to gain. For example, the Marxist tradition holds that one of the best ways to understand social reality is to try to reform it, because concealed sources of power and privilege come to the fore when their position is threatened. Experience with doing and undoing policy yields knowledge about society, just as knowledge informs policy. Sadly this promise of reciprocity between know-

ledge and action has been as disappointing in practice as the hope
that impartial social scientific findings could be placed in the
service of moral choice.

In this chapter I shall try to define more precisely what is
involved in the assertion that social science can contribute to
social policy. Since the claims for an influential role must depend
on how one views the relationship between dispassionate scientific
facts and the choice of a morally 'right' course of action, I am
concerned here essentially with the interrelationship between
values, theory and research. *Values* refer to ends or objectives,
and to the legitimate means that inform public intervention.
Values comprise the normative propositions that affirm what our
social policy ought to be, and the normative and moral assumptions that underlie present practice. *Theory* specifies the way in
which events are causally related to one another. Policy-oriented
theory specifies the underlying processes that shape the outcomes
we seek to reach. Both implicitly and explicitly, theory interprets
how the world works and also draws on this interpretation to
influence how it might work. *Research* provides factual information, that is, empirical evidence in the form of quantitative estimates and/or qualitative experience which can be organized to
relate the values we hold, and to confirm or repudiate our beliefs
about the functioning of society, institutions, and people.

Although there is general agreement about the necessity to
distinguish between values, theory, and research, there is sharp
disagreement about their relationship to each other. And this
disagreement is central to our understanding of the way in which
we relate the knowledge about society which has been obtained
through social science inquiry to the larger issues of value. In the
first place it is essential to distinguish between 'fact' statements
and 'value' statements, for only then can we discuss our disagreements about how and why policies or conditions are favoured or
disfavoured and about how they can be truthfully described and
explained. And clearly value-neutral empirical statements cannot
fully express all the views and beliefs that we hold. Nor can value-
neutral empirical premises, on their own, lead to value-charged
conclusions. By definition, empirical information cannot provide
a complete foundation for policy choices; it can only do so in

conjunction with other criteria. How then can fact statements and value judgements be linked together?

We shall begin by examining the positivist tradition and the applied-social-science framework of thought which is derived from it. 'Positive' knowledge, in contrast to 'speculative' knowledge, claims to provide cognitive stability which goes beyond ideological bias and subjective outlooks, because it is solidly established in reality (that is, in controlled observation and logical analysis of reality) and is therefore safe from destructive attack. According to this view, the only effective way to manage the difficulties presented by man's social environment is through the systematic application of the 'scientific method'. We know that this method has been used effectively in the natural sciences to win control over the physical environment. If social science can apply these techniques of analysis to social understanding, it may also acquire some of the powerful predictive capabilities of the natural sciences. The influence of social science, therefore, depends on its ability to discover general laws of social processes which will eventually enable man to control his social environment. Indeed, social science deserves to be influential in the management of social policy only to the extent that it can provide a better understanding of the laws which govern social processes. If social science, following the positivist view, is to fulfil its proper role – which is to develop an understanding of the underlying societal processes so that it can be used to predict future events and to formulate policies based upon understanding – then normative and factual questions must be separated from each other. The method of the natural sciences seems to require neutrality about values as a condition of objectivity. 'Science concerns itself with matters of fact. It excludes the determination of value.'[1] The proper conduct of scientific inquiry requires that knowledge, if it is to be useful later, must be built on theory and evidence which are neutral or indifferent to individual and collective intentions and purposes. 'It is only when we have built up our "theory" in completely disinterested terms that we can hope to build a really

1. John McMurry, *Religion, Art and Science*, Liverpool University Press, 1961, p. 11, as quoted in T. S. Simey, *Social Science and Social Purpose*, Constable, 1968, p. 4.

satisfactory "practice" on them. This is the paradox underlying the specifically modern concept of "policy science".[2]

This is a rationalist view of the world, seeking an orderly separation of facts, theory, and values. It proceeds from the assumption that values can be formulated into clear and identifiable goals, and policy-oriented research is to be preoccupied solely with measuring the extent to which these goals are, in fact, achieved. The scientist does not 'formulate' values, in the sense of making value judgements in his or her own name; he makes only fact statements about the values that are held and the objectives that are pursued by people and groups in society. The positivists assume that one can only sort out the factual consequences of pursuing different goals, the values themselves being created by the will or passion. Since they are solely expressions of desire, the values are not objectively grounded, are not amenable to proof or disproof but must be accepted or rejected as given. We are concerned with the cognitive basis of value judgements, the value characteristics of objects being assigned to them through some exercise of the will or the passion of the judges. So value judgements must be treated as arbitrarily posited rather than as statements with some objective basis: statements that are affirmed or rejected by personal decision. I decide that equality is good. It is useless to debate the merits of the case because these are merely a question of taste or personal opinion. Fact statements alone can be validated; value statements neither need nor permit validation. Instrumental values have a value component when they assert 'I desire this aim', and a fact component when they declare that such an act will bring about the state of affairs which I, independent of the fact statement, judge desirable. We can also make a factual inventory of desires, treating values as the object of someone's desires. Indeed policy recommendations are by their nature based upon verified fact statements as well as arbitrary value judgements, and they will naturally be accepted by those who agree with both. The problem is how to link the factual and arbitrary components.

Within this framework, positivists search for universally valid

2. Paul Kecskemeti, 'The Policy Sciences; Aspirations and Outlook', *World Politics*, vol. 4, no. 4, October 1951, p. 523.

generalizations. It is assumed that the basic concepts which are to be drawn upon for these generalizations can be formulated to be 'single-valued ... reproducible, separated from calendar time, and independent of place, of ambient conditions, or unnatural influences'.[3] This view about the stability of the ideas that describe social events provides the basis on which a strategy for implementing goals and overcoming problems can be built. Broad policy and specific programmes are derived from such concepts and the theory that integrates them. Interventions based on such theory lead, in turn, to the achievement of the values sought. Techniques of analysis must then be applied to the assessment of alternative strategies of intervention. Here the criteria of cost efficiency and programme effectiveness provide decision rules for choice among the range of possible options. (Considerations of equity and equality are less often used in such decision rules because it is more difficult to give effect to them and they tend to conflict with efficiency and political acceptability.) The ideal way to judge the relative merits of alternative approaches, when the ends are given, is through the social experiment, in which there is a random assignment of individuals to control and experimental groups. Research gathers evidence to determine the facts in such an experiment.

The positivist view further assumes that knowledge is cumulative and hence convergent over time. There is a clear progression from understanding to solving problems. Alternative designs are derived from a dispassionate assessment of the causes of a difficulty. The designs are then evaluated in terms of their efficiency and effectiveness in reducing the problems, and appropriate modifications in the initial design are made as required. When this procedure is followed, the problem can in principle be solved. When knowledge is cumulative, and 'meaningful' factual questions admit definitive solutions, we are continually making progress in our understanding and, hence, in our ability to achieve the aims we seek.

3. Raymond M. Hainer, 'Rationalism, Pragmatism, and Existentialism: Perceived but Undiscovered Multicultural Problems', in Evelyn Glatt and Maynard Shelly, eds., *The Research Society*, New York, Gordon and Breach Science Publishers, 1968, p. 19.

For the moment we wish to leave aside the two questions of whether the positivist view is valid and whether it is possible to use the methods of the natural sciences in social science and discuss instead how we can relate this kind of objective science to questions of valuation, that is, to judgements about values. The difficulty arises when we acknowledge that there is no logical way to derive an 'ought' from an 'is' proposition, because statements of fact are logically independent of statements of value. One language is factual and descriptive, dealing with spatial, temporal, and other measurable states. The other is a value language expressing judgements of desirability and undesirability, approval and disapproval. If we hold that scientific rigour must depend on value neutrality, we take the risk of winning objectivity at the cost of usefulness, unless we can find a way to reintegrate descriptive analysis with questions of normative value. Science would, of course, still be relevant – the problem is how it can ever be prescriptive or evaluative.

If we do not establish a link between objective description and normative understanding, there can be no policy-oriented social science. How do the policy analysts, who view themselves primarily as scientists, bridge the gulf between facts on the one hand, and values and ideals on the other? How, in other words, can facts and values be reintegrated so that social science analysis can serve to inform, to discipline, or, as some hope, to determine – or at least to influence – the decisions we take in social policy? This is the crucial question.

If we wish to develop a social science capable of taking a position on policy, we must have a framework of principles which can encompass questions of what is good, and bad, or better and worse. The idea, of course, of a value-encompassing science raises basic epistemological and methodological issues.

The main intellectual techniques or procedures by which policy-orientated social scientists appear to make the normative leap between the world of facts and the world of values are mapping, coding (code harmonization) and feedback. Each is a different aspect of the practical application of social science knowledge. *Mapping* describes a procedure to link manipulable events and their 'effects' with values about the 'ends' that one favours, and then to treat the known causes of these effects as the means to achieve the desired ends. *Coding* is concerned with establishing congruity among different values by the clarification and systematization of the value framework. *Feedback* describes the process by which we check our actions against our values to determine if we are achieving what we intend. The different techniques depend on what one accepts as given and problematic. However, all three techniques make the end that is valued coincident or identical with some consequence for which the cause is both known and manipulable by public intervention.

In the case of *mapping*, the end that is valued is given and not subject to inquiry. But it remains unclear which events within our control may function as a cause in relation to the desired end. Mapping is an attempt to discover regularities that may have practical applications. If the cause-and-effect relationship in the world of fact can be isolated, it can be mapped readily onto the normative world of ends and ideals. In *code harmonization*, the cause-and-effect relationship is taken as given. It is assumed that the passing of a law can coerce a certain kind of behaviour and produce a desired end; what is called into question is the compatability of that end with others that are socially desirable. When we acknowledge conflicting values it becomes necessary to decide which have to be sacrificed, and to what extent. One way to resolve this question is to consider whether the desired end is congruent, or in harmony with, other accepted values. In both mapping and coding we have been speaking as though the key relationships that connect known 'causes' with desired 'ends' are fully established prior to the intervention. *Feedback* comes into play when for some reason that knowledge is doubted; that is, if we lose confidence in our understanding, then we can take a second-order position and specify the process for learning.

Mapping

Our first approach to bridge-building between the two separate domains of understanding is to transpose, or map, the V or value language upon the F or factual language. To do this, we first identify an end that can be viewed as a consequence in a cause–

effect relationship, and then activate the 'cause' that we have recognized in theory as a means to achieve that end. Each language can be mapped on the other when some general or formal code defines which elements of one language correspond to which elements of the other. When there is such a code, then the F language statements can be read as equivalent or synonymous to the V statements, and a graceful transition between the two discourses is possible.

In other words, we posit a correspondence between 'means–ends,' on the one hand, and 'cause-and-effect' relationships, on the other. This is the application of social science to practical problems. But 'we must be able to see the identity of what we entertain as "end" with what the theory predicts as "effect"'.[4] In practice, the demanding requirement of an exact fit is relaxed and we ask only that effects and ends are broadly congruent; then public policy can turn to social science for guidance in selecting the best means to yield the desired effects. In the pursuit of scientific understanding about causal relationships,

one's *approval or disapproval of the object studied is held temporarily in abeyance*, subordinate to the aim of predicting as much about it as possible. In that way scientific knowledge is made available for forwarding many different and divergent aims ... Evaluation ... is not pure science but sciences applied and organized for the special purposes of altering attitudes.[5]

There are, of course, innumerable difficulties involved in getting this formula to work properly. If the known 'causes' in our equation cannot be manipulated by policy, then they are of little practical application; but even if they can be manipulated, they may also be morally offensive and politically unacceptable. Alternatively, the causes may be both manipulable and ethically neutral, and yet their implementation may conflict with other ends of public policy. For example, social science may develop an empirically verifiable theory that links family circumstances to

4. Kecskemeti, op. cit., p. 524.
5. Charles L. Stevenson, *Ethics and Language*, New Haven, Yale University Press, 1944, pp. 254–5. (Emphasis added.)

later educational achievement. This theory may then be invoked to remove from their natural families children who have failed to meet prescribed educational standards of achievement and to place them with other families who are presumed to provide the conditions for helping the children to learn more effectively. In this illustration, the causes of educational disadvantage are manipulable; but they also require the destruction of family life, and this is regarded as ethically unacceptable in most situations. Even if, under special circumstances, such a policy is judged morally acceptable, it may still conflict with other policy objectives, for example, the achievement of public aims at a reasonable cost. We are thus quickly forced to come to grips with the difficult questions of conflicting values, acceptable costs, and the establishment of priorities, because this, indeed, is how 'ends' have to be evaluated in deliberations about policy. In applied (technological) science, one does not deal with objectives (values) as such, but always with objectives weighted in terms of cost effectiveness. The question of weighting can never be fully resolved but in mapping we can at least appreciate how empirical knowledge and moral purpose may be tied together.

Code Harmonization

Society works with various legal, religious, and moral codes that are to some extent independent of one another. Code diversity becomes a problem because each code has its own internal requirements, and these invariably produce conflicts and create insuperable contradictions. For example, if the law is not to serve as an instrument of privilege it should be uniformly applicable, with identical consequences for every member of society. If this is to be so, the law cannot forbid actions in those areas of life where evasion is easy for some members of society, for this will sacrifice the principle of even-handedness. If we insist upon uniform enforceability as an absolute requirement, then we must give up, for example, puritanical laws repressing sexual licence as part of our operative code. To maximize the doctrine of uniformity, we must abate the principle that legal practice is informed by the moral code. Society is powerless to enforce these moral requirements uniformly because the conditions for evading the law are so unequal. There is a widely shared, though often unstated, belief that severe inconsistencies should not exist between the different codes on fundamental matters, for a sharp contradiction between the feeling of what is morally right and what the legal code prescribes is not acceptable. By code harmonization we therefore mean the elimination of any direct contradiction between codes, and we typically seek harmonization by changing the legal code.

Although the legal code is only one among many codes, it is nevertheless called upon to play this integrative role. The principle of the law as a seamless web implies that nothing that affects human well-being is left indeterminate, whether it is legally prescribed, prohibited or discretionary; and it is supposed that the 'science' of law deals with an all-encompassing, unified set of propositions embracing whatever human phenomena have practical significance, with no question legally undefined. Even so, acts can be immoral without being illegal, and vice versa. Indeed many acts affecting human well-being must be treated as legally indifferent, even though immoral, because of the practical impossibility of legislating for morality. So law, as an ordering system of value priorities, has a strategic position in society, because potentially it can intervene in every area of human experience. Moreover, decisions about what is legally relevant change over time. This happens especially when the courts attempt to clarify legal norms so as to eliminate flagrant inconsistencies between the moral and legal codes. For example, in the past, employers were free to impose on their employees whatever hours of labour they wanted to, if the other party 'freely' accepted the terms of employment. This is the principle of freedom of contract. The uncompromising pursuit of free contract produced inhumanity and suffering, undesirable on ethical grounds. The humanitarian or moral code calls for the relief of suffering. In a clash between legal and moral codes, the legal is necessarily dominant, and will be enforced even if it leads to inhuman consequences, unless the clash is resolved through the introduction of moral considerations into the body of the law.

Brandeis's brief of 1908 provides a concrete illustration of the way in which the Supreme Court can achieve code harmonization

when inconsistencies between moral and legal norms appear.[6]
Much legal argument attempts to reach conclusions from premises
through syllogistic reasoning. Brandeis took a different course.
He made a case for the regulation of working conditions through
a detailed, descriptive account of the effect of unregulated conditions. The specific case involved the ten-hour day for women.
Brandeis's description of the working conditions of these women
made it self-evident that their employment was dehumanizing and
should be changed. He questioned the proposition that the legal
principle of contract must always be dominant, arguing that what
is conducive to human well-being must also be taken into account.
Legally he tried to establish only that regulations would not be in
violation of the due process of law. Here, and in other comparable
cases, for example the Supreme Court decision on school desegre-
gation, the social, moral, and political merits of the law came up
for adjudication and the court engaged in 'code harmonization'.

I do not wish to stretch the argument too far. These examples
represent an approach to reform which is constrained by constitutional issues, that is to say, the arguments must be related to
constitutional principles. There is no tendency to 'harmonize'
codes across the board. Indeed, it appears that the American
system of law is formalistic, the courts rather avoiding the issue of
'harmonizing' conflicting moral and legal rules. As a result, the
moral sense of the community is frequently outraged by formally
correct legal decisions that fail to 'harmonize' moral norms.

There have been many other efforts to integrate facts and values.
Searle, for example, distinguishes between statements of brute
fact and statements of institutional fact. 'That a man has a bit of
paper with green ink on it is a brute fact, that he has $5 is an
institutional fact. It is often a matter of fact that one has certain
obligations, commitments, rights and responsibilities but it is a
matter of institutional, not brute fact.'[7] 'Ought' statements can
be derived from 'is' statements by appealing to a common

6. For a discussion of this type of brief, see Robert E. Cushman and
Robert F. Cushman, *Cases in Constitutional Law*, Appleton-Century-Crofts,
1958, p. 580.
7. John R. Searle, 'How to Derive "Ought" from "Is"', *The Philosophical Review*, vol. LXXIII, January 1964, pp. 55–6.

understanding of the obligations, commitments and responsibilities that institutional forms require. Actions are judged in the context of conventional practice; institutions offer a guide to social expectations by their actions and ideals. In Brandeis's ten-hour brief, it was implicitly understood that men should organize institutions of employment so that they were not dehumanizing. Thus, if we could demonstrate a lack of humanity in the work environment, we could also argue that the institution failed to function according to the implicit rules governing its behaviour.

Feedback

When the starting body of knowledge is fragmentary and no systematic theory is available, social science can still contribute to policy by feeding back new information from experience into the decision-making process. We then hope to acquire, through a procedure of systematic exploration by trial and error, the information that was initially lacking.

One way to begin the search is to take a set of value preferences that have already been translated into programme choices. Research can then help policy by measuring the gap between ideals and practice (evaluation) and by examining alternative means for more effectively and efficiently narrowing the gap (experimentation). At this later stage fresh insights about cause-and-effect relationships are needed to generate new ideas for the development of alternative policies. To measure the gap in achievement, to design or to invent alternative policies based on a theoretical understanding of social laws, and then to test them, requires new forms of social organization which will promote collective learning through the orderly integration of these closely related stages of understanding. Some centralized research and development operation is usually cited as the appropriate strategy.

Feedback is, of course, a universal principle of how people learn from experience, and it is not limited to the kind of formal evaluation and experimentation we have briefly sketched out. When applied to questions of public policy, it is necessary to define the group for whose well-being the various events and policies should be evaluated. It is not sufficient to take our own preferences as our reference system, nor can we always accept the preferences of the decision-maker. This is an area in which there are really difficult problems to consider; however, I do not wish to pursue them here. I want, instead, to mention another factor that is also central to the process, namely, that there must be a sufficient continuity of events, purposes, commitment and action if lessons are to be learned from the weight of evidence acquired in coping with a given problem. The positivists' approach to feedback implies an incrementalist view of policy change.

Can the learning acquired in one setting be transferred to a variety of different contexts? If learning is transferable, then inferences from a particular study may have a high degree of generality and independence of particular policy assumptions. On the other hand, feedback may show that the goals were misstated, the wrong policy questions reviewed, and that a radically new approach should be pursued. Since policy analysis as a 'science' ideally rests on an experimental model of learning, experimentation requires that we vary one by one the elements of a programme, proceeding slowly and consistently until we can determine which elements relate to success or failure and we can discern which are the causal relations in the given context. To the positivists, feedback, if it is to be really valuable, needs to isolate and determine the influence of each discrete variable. This implies a highly controlled situation in which there is sufficient continuity of policy and purpose to enable an experimental intervention to be fulfilled. If, however, we are looking for precise feedback inferences in a narrow context, it is impossible to generalize with a high degree of confidence except in relation to other events with a very similar form. Although we can derive quite precise inferences about the relationships between abstract aspects of supposed events, we cannot then say with confidence how, or whether, these relationships hold for complex, real events. Social events are too complex and unstable to allow us to apply general laws away from their narrow context.

This concept of learning through feedback presupposes that two conditions prevail in society. First, although the policy goal itself may be indeterminate, and the means to bring it about are held in suspense, we must assume that a dynamic situation prevails and that some groups with the capacity to act are interested in change. This means that the established profile of power or some new power coalition is prepared to move from one situation to another in response to the facts it receives. Second, we must assume that there is a general understanding of the direction in which we want to go, and that the outcome of a study justifies the effort. Although no exact body of information is available, there is nevertheless a general sense of appreciation about the drift of change. Of course, when a radical change has, for whatever reason, already taken place, feedback is still essential because revolutionary actions occur in situations of imperfect knowledge. Revolutionary action without feedback is doomed to failure and disaster.

In the positivist tradition, the feedback model is not one of revolution. Those who subscribe to this model will be committed to a line of action reflecting the power gradients in society and in tune with the general direction that power will go, or at least will accept. Change can only reflect the expression of power. Nevertheless, under conditions of continuity, feedback mechanisms in society will work more or less satisfactorily on the accumulated record. Feedback is always problematic in the presence of major discontinuous change. The positivists are mostly concerned with feedback of the continuous type, since the prime emphasis of their philosophy is on action based on available scientific evidence. It is obviously difficult to make scientific predictions about social processes when the distribution of power in the society changes rapidly and new coalitions may emerge at any time. Such circumstances are not conducive to cumulative learning.

If we are to realize the hopes of cumulative learning through experimentation and feedback, we must assume a general orientation and commitment to change. A detailed understanding of the kinds of changes which are needed, as discovered by the social scientists, will then be accepted. But there is a risk that inaction and paralysis will follow if the evaluation or the experiment fails to fulfil the predetermined criteria of success, the expected results having failed to materialize. And what happens when analysis consistently reacts against the normative ideas that inspired the study? After all, social analysis does seem to play the largely negative role of exploding conventional wisdom. Its long-range effect on policy questions may be 'to make choice more complex, dilemmas more baffling, and conflicts more stark'.[8] Faced with such a grim prognosis, the fallback position may be either goal development, that is, to pursue other imminent goals which can be implemented effectively, or to accept that the purpose is not subject to change in the short run and assume that a second and third programme will be tried until a better way is found to achieve the desired ends. But this hope of learning from experience presumes that, no matter what, the social scientist responsible for programme development and evaluation will continue to be in charge, or at the least that he will play a major role in influencing the course of action. Such a position obviously begs a lot of political questions, because it takes little account of the non-academic world, which will nevertheless abruptly remind the policy-oriented social scientists of its existence.

In summary, then, the positivist interpretation of the policy sciences accepts the principle that the only way to gather objective, factual information that is capable of verification and refutation is to isolate the *process* by which knowledge is acquired from the *values* which originally inspired the desire to acquire that information. When we fail to achieve such a separation, there is a danger that the entire exercise will become self-fulfilling, because, however unconsciously, men set about to confirm what they already believe. This approach may be viewed in terms of a methodological model: we know that 'facts' have value aspects and 'values' have factual aspects, but we can disregard these for the purposes of discussion and consider only the non-factual aspects of values and the non-value aspects of facts. Once facts and values are separated, we must create means by which they can be reintegrated. Mapping, code harmonization, and feedback represent the primary means by which a policy-relevant social science can be constructed. There is, however, a growing belief that these strategies have not worked very effectively. It is widely alleged that objective research has contributed very little to the

8. John Goldthorpe's book review of T. S. Simey, *Social Science and Social Purpose*, in the *British Journal of Sociology*, vol. 2, June 1969, pp. 228–9.

development of social policies. Whether this is in fact the case is not altogether known, since research into the utilization of research findings for policy development has been so minimal.[9] And, indeed, the very absence of such research strengthens the positivist view that public policy requires an objective social science which is capable of inquiring into these questions.

Difficulties and Pitfalls in the Positivist Strategy for a Policy-Relevant Social Science

Each of the three strategies of mapping, code harmonization and feedback is vulnerable to criticism, and their weaknesses account, at least in part, for the very modest contribution that social science has made to policy.

We shall first consider a weakness that is common to all three strategies and then go on to explore the difficulties associated with each. The strategies all proceed from a shared assumption, namely, that a desired end corresponds to some known effect; we can alter these effects when we are able to isolate the stable and universal relationship that binds each to its end.

The attempt to connect 'means–ends' statements with 'cause–effect' statements requires, first, a theoretical model that can tie cause and effect relationships together, and second, sufficient factual evidence to confirm the validity of the theory. But there are some intractable difficulties in unravelling these relationships.

9. Caplan and his colleagues at the University of Michigan have broken ground with an empirical study on this question. They interviewed 204 people who held important positions in the executive branch of the United States government between October 1973 and March 1974. The study distinguishes between data-based ('hard') and non-empirical ('soft') information and concludes that 'rarely is policy formulation determined by a concrete point-by-point reliance on empirically grounded data'. Only 13 per cent of the respondents could cite five to ten instances of use with good supporting evidence. However, there were numerous examples of the use of soft information, which led the authors to conclude that 'Knowledge is used at the top levels of government decision-making and probably to a greater extent than most experts in the area of utilization would expect.' These findings make it clear that the issue remains unsettled.

See Nathan Caplan and others, *The Use of Social Science Knowledge in Policy Decisions at the National Level*, Institute for Social Research, The University of Michigan, Ann Arbor, Michigan, 1975, p. 47.

There are no general laws in social science that are consistent over time and independent of the context in which they are embedded. The search for generalizations of cause-and-effect relationships is an illusion. No particular patterning of events will remain stable for very long, and generalization about them cannot provide a firm theoretical basis for intervention. While simplified models of economic and social reality can be developed, based upon stylized facts and heroic assumptions, none of the insights derived from these exercises provides a secure basis for the design of social policies. These models can retrospectively identify a cluster of variables which help explain variations in observed events, but their margin of error is too wide for them to be satisfactory predictors.

When we try to use social science to account for much of social life, we face what Benjamin Ward calls a 'loser's combination'.[10] There are too many variables, all of which are important, and we seem to be unable to isolate a few crucial inputs. Moreover, there is an inherent paucity of reliable information about these variables. In addition, most data used to test theory or to develop public policy suffer from awkward problems of definition and quality. For example, crime statistics report petitions, not persons, welfare statistics report cases, not families, official agencies define income quite differently, and, worse still, surveys which use similar definitions report strikingly different findings. Moreover, the efforts to improve the quality of data make analysis more difficult; for example, government series reports will shift their definitions over time, and as a result later information cannot be compared fully with what was gathered before. Finally, relationships among variables which obtained in one period may change because the contexts in which they exist have altered, as the example of inflation and unemployment illustrates.

MacIntyre's review of the epistemological limitations of social science has led him to conclude that social science cannot aspire to provide genuine, law-like, predictive generalizations. As he puts it: 'Whenever an event or state of affairs of Type A occurs, then an event or state of affairs of Type B will occur, unless (1) intelligent reflection by the agents involved lead them to

10. Benjamin Ward, *What's Wrong with Economics?*, Macmillan, 1972.

change their ways or (2) unpredictable factors deriving from creative intellectual innovation intervene.' And, we might add, unless other unpredictable factors such as war, depression, or civil unrest alter the relationship that prevailed before the crisis took place. By the nature of his subject the social scientist cannot avoid these excepting riders. 'It follows that the type of rational consensus as to past achievement and future horizons that characterize the natural scientific community cannot be available to the social scientific community.'[11]

Social science fails policy formulation both because the knowledge it has to offer is incomplete and not readily subject to refutation and because the theory that organizes information is insubstantial. Correlations between events can be identified, but there are always several possible causal linkages to account for these relationships. Policies for intervention require an understanding of these processes. But even if a theory could be specified, the external conditions under which it might apply are uncertain.

The *F–V* mapping cannot be worked out in a rigorous way because there is no adequate theory about how the *F* world is organized. Moreover, much of the cause and effect theory that is available is best understood as facts with a value signature, that is, as normative theory. In addition, the problems of programme design are not only encumbered by uncertain knowledge about how the *F* world operates but also by an inability to maximize all those aspects of the *V* world that are most strongly approved and recommended. These difficulties substantially undermine the effectiveness of the strategies we have presented for making the normative leap.

The Weakness of Mapping. It is useful to elaborate on the difficulties inherent in the mapping technique of the classical positivist. We cannot simply isolate a single end, map it onto a cause–effect relationship by assuming that end and effect are similar or identical and then pick one cause as a means to that end; many other ends also have to be recognized. There is always a multiplicity of aims, and these aims are almost always in partial con-

11. Alasdair MacIntyre, 'Ideology, Social Science and Revolution', *Comparative Politics*, vol. 5, no. 3, April 1973, p. 334.

flict with each other. This is reflected in the constant need to consider the question of opportunity costs, that is, how much of one aim am I prepared to forsake in the pursuit of another aim? By what calculus do I weigh aims that I value equally? It is this aspect of the mapping problem that calls for the most systematic attention, and it is here that we come to the essence of the task of applying scientific knowledge to action. What makes the task so difficult is that valuations emerge at all points in the analysis, and hence a sharp separation of the fact and value languages cannot be achieved.

Let us take a concrete example. Consider how these difficulties emerge in the relationship between medical science and medical knowledge. Medicine, an ancient science, is not tied to the positive outlook. It does, however, represent a good example of the general problem of multiple values in 'mapping' even though it is not an example of mapping of the positivistic variety. In medicine the F language is fused with the V language. Since the scientific language itself has a value dimension, the doctor can immediately perceive 'normal', 'healthy' or 'pathological' conditions as such. A doctor's diagnostic statement on the condition of a patient conforms to the logical requirements of description in the F language. The doctor then makes a translation into the V language when he diagnoses that the syndrome examined is pathological and that the patient is mentally or physically ill, or both. Since the patient does not want to be sick, the mapping task is relatively simple and straightforward, and a graceful normative 'leap' between the factual and evaluative is made without much stress. If the patient wants to get well, he or she must follow the prescriptions laid down by the physician. The 'leap' is so graceful because, in large part, the F language implies a normative theory of health.

We cannot leave the matter here. We have assumed that the patient is guided by a single value, recovery from illness. But clearly the problem is more complex, because there are other value clusters that are in conflict with this aim. The patient may, for example, be concerned with non-financial costs of his recovery, that is to say, with the hedonistic pleasures that have to be forsaken. A heart patient will be advised not to eat food with a high cholesterol content, and will thus be asked to forsake what may be a lifetime eating pattern for the sake of his health. Health and pleasure are clearly conflicting aims in such cases. The V language of the physician is insensitive to the value conflicts faced by the patient. Mapping is made possible, or at least easy, because the fields of conflicting values are largely ignored.

Although we have in this example introduced conflicting goals into our analysis, our discussion is still at a very simple level because we have limited our concern to individual and not collective costs. At the individual level, the sick patient must decide only if health comes first, and the poor patient may not even have this choice. But what about society? The collective economic costs involve the distribution of limited energy and skilled manpower. Society must make an optimal allocation of its scarce resources to achieve the best treatment for all patients. Yet such a strategy will conflict with a more individualistic course of action which is in favour of people paying their own way. Hence, priorities have to be made. Still another difficult issue of priorities emerges. Society values the absolute prolongation of physical life more than it does the financial or psychological costs to the individual. Are these priorities erroneous? Each moral question raises yet another equally difficult question to answer. Despite this, the practice of medicine, like the practice of mapping, code harmonization and feedback, continues: it cannot wait for an intellectual clarification of the question. The weakness of the positivist position is its failure to deal explicitly with the goals themselves as a major concern of policy analysis; it falls back on the view that science can contribute only to instrumental goals.

Most problems which remain public issues over an extended period of time involve such multiple goals which are at least partially incompatible with one another. Problems persist at the level of policy formulation and cannot merely be reduced to a search for appropriate techniques, because it is not logically possible for every variable to be at its maximum value at the same time. For example, it is not possible to achieve a welfare system that at one time provides adequate income to reduce poverty, promotes strong incentives to work and keeps governmental expenditures down. When any one of these aims is at a maximum, then the others are not. 'The question of what to optimize, then, has to be decided on other than strictly scientific grounds. The decisions one makes depend on his particular definition of the over all, or social, optimum, with economic science as such being neutral as between alternative definitions.'[12]

Whether we use the techniques of science or of art, we must find a way to relate whatever is known to whatever is valued, that is, we must link together the relevant body of information to a normative problem. When the theory itself is not normative, as in our example of medical care, it is the task of the consultant or adviser, who is conversant with both the F and the V languages, to draw together knowledge and values. Optimization strategies require that certain aims are slighted so that others can be realized, at least in part. A trade-off among conflicting objectives is thereby achieved. Such strategies are nevertheless unsatisfying, because policy-makers are unwilling to forsake some goals in the pursuit of others.

Alice Rivlin has lucidly explained how conflicting goals inhibit the effective utilization of scientific information for policy purposes:

We are failing to solve social problems because we do not know how to do it – the problems are genuinely hard. The difficulties do not primarily involve conflicts among different groups of people, although these exist. Rather, current social problems are difficult because they involve conflicts among objectives that almost everyone holds. These conflicts create technical or design difficulties which override the political ones . . . No one is sure how to do it.[13]

Mapping, as we have seen, requires the integration of the normative and the descriptive. But this procedure is neither automatic nor self-evident. It requires imagination and insight. Typically it is an activity undertaken by men of action with scientific knowledge, and men of scientific knowledge who have acquired practical experience and an understanding of how to

12. Paul Kecskemeti, 'Utilization of Social Research in Shaping Policy Decisions', Rand Corporation (Social Science Department), P-2289, 24 April 1961 (mimeograph), p. 2.

13. Alice M. Rivlin, 'Obstacles to Social Progress: Why Can't We Get Things Done', *Washington Post*, 22 July 1971.

combine knowledge and action. But as we have suggested, the *F–V* mapping may not be adequate due to the lack of an *F* theory and a coherent *V* field of preference. As a result, a considerable amount of juggling will be necessary to get the best fit. Of course, we will continue to perform the mapping task, however difficult the undertaking. Clearly, some people will be more competent at it than others. Part of their skill must involve a capacity for mutual understanding, trust and respect. This kind of relationship is likely to emerge when the policy-maker and the adviser share the same culture, each is knowledgeable about the other's wants, and each is able to understand and accept the constraints imposed on the other's *F* and *V* languages. The adviser to government must possess a sympathetic receptivity to the views of established power. It is axiomatic that advice is meaningful only if it is acceptable, and this requires that the value outlook of the advice seeker is the same as that of the advice giver. 'Sharing the purposes, practical orientation, and immersion in current problems of the policy-maker, they direct scientific effort into relevant directions,' wrote de Sola Pool more than twenty years ago in describing how the social scientist might contribute to policy.[14] We can see, then, that it is crucial to the task of mapping both to share purposes and to agree on the practical constraints being faced.

The Limited Scope for Code Harmonization. Having looked at the problems with mapping, we may consider next the weaknesses of code harmonization as a means of helping to reintegrate the fact–value languages. In the case of mapping we discussed the weakness of examining a single aim in isolation, and we concluded that the main task of analysis lies not in renouncing ends we cherish but in optimizing a mix of ends to which we assign different weights. In the case of code harmonization we confront a different

14. Ithiel de Sola Pool and others, 'Social Science and National Security', a report prepared by the Research Group in Psychology and the Social Sciences, Smithsonian Institute, Washington, D.C., 5 March 1953, pp. 17–18. The report urges more social scientists inside and outside of university life to play the role of 'problem solvers rather than scientific discoverers'. What is needed, the authors declare, 'is a prouder image of the role and along with that a great increase in numbers, improvement of morale, and clarity of purpose of the cadre fulfilling it'.

and perhaps deeper problem. Harmonization as a principle can best be understood in relation to the idea that the common good is itself a unified category, and different codes (legal, moral and ethical) are all specific aspects of this conception of the social good. Ideally, then, all codes converge on the broader ideal of the public good we hold. However, the ideal of a public good appears in a different light when we approach it from the point of view of any particular code. We find we have to accept abatement from the specific requirements of other codes. Where the codes conflict, the most typical solution is not harmonization but differentiation. We want to know which code should be applied in which situations. For example, ethical codes establish veracity as an absolute duty; but veracity in all situations would disrupt a good deal of social intercourse. We want both to tell the truth and to be considerate of the feelings of other people. There is no way to harmonize the conflict between truth and courtesy. Thus code inconsistencies are frequently insurmountable and the conflict unavoidable. There is no unifying principle to harmonize the conflict – only the principle of sensibility, the sense of what fits in different circumstances, that is, under different codes. Not only is the scope for harmonization limited, but the arguments for legal harmonization are only achieved through subterfuge. Brandeis argued that the introduction of human and ethical values was consistent with constitutional law. But the case for harmonizing the moral and legal systems under the protective aegis of constitutional law was accepted only as a polite deception. The court based its willingness to temper the legal code on its judgement of political realities, and perhaps ultimately on the belief that its decisions could contribute to the avoidance of social conflict. The Supreme Court is therefore shown to be political, because its actions are sensitive to the actual distribution of power in society.

The moral and legal problems that require harmonization by court action are always either in the middle of, or, to make the case more strongly, dominated by political forces. There is always that elusive ideal of the community good which calls for harmonization, but to reach towards it the court must be political, in the sense that it must take account of the prevailing dispersion of power. It seems doubtful whether legal prescriptions or prohibitions would be very effective in regulating morality, or pathology, even if a legal system were to make the effort. Legislation would be powerless in such situations. How could the causal agents of distress be isolated? Consider, for example, a family situation, where all members are involved as contributors to the acts of the others. Even if the subtle dynamics of the situation could be appreciated, we do not understand what effective action should be taken to improve it. I do not think, therefore, that we can postulate a 'principle of code consistency' with the legal code as the coordinating agent.

These weaknesses in code harmonization do not, however, nullify the efficacy of the legal system as a decision mechanism for integrating the F and V languages. Examples such as the Brandeis brief provide a model for drawing together the normative and the descriptive. Ward offers an optimistic assessment of the contribution that legal institutions make towards this aim. He asserts that law is directly concerned with ethical judgements; its central task is to make comparisons between individuals, and its decisions bring about social change. Moreover, legal decisions have a claim to objectivity, because they work within an institutional framework that defines a set of rules and a collection of roles to be played out by its actors. Decisions are set and precedents established on a general basis, which can be defended within the set of working rules that are created at any moment in time and agreed upon by the legal fraternity. And it is this institutional arrangement that Ward finds attractive, because it permits cumulative public learning from experience, while at the same time responding to normative issues. It is not the subject-matter of law which interests him but the way in which institutional arrangements enable the law to integrate factual and normative statements within a framework that aspires both to objectivity and to a continuing capacity to learn, and therefore to change according to a set of agreed conventions and rules.[15] But law

15. Critics of this view feel that such a procedure will not promote scientific objectivity but merely 'operates to validate the generally acceptable moral standards of the time' (quoting Learned Hand). Martin Bronfenbrenner's review of Benjamin Ward's book, *What's Wrong with Economics?*, op. cit., in *Challenge*, March–April 1973.

represents only one dimension of 'collective learning' or 'integration of experience', and an extremely partial one. In addition, we need to consider that a law, any law, not only tells people what to do to comply with that law but also how they can evade it. The law as a social instrument is always ambiguous, because it always combines the statement of a rule with that of the limitations to the rule. Expert legal advice is at a premium because it can put the stated limitations of legal rules to practical use for the client's benefit.

Code harmonization cannot provide us with the consensual value framework that is essential if mapping and feedback are to take place. Since no value framework is clearly given, the analyst must find some value system to which he can attach his understanding of social processes. The most typical way to cope with this difficulty is for the social scientist to assume that he has entered into a client–professional relationship in which the client provides the values. But 'clients' can rarely provide a clear unambiguous and internally consistent statement about what they value. This is especially true of government, where competing interests are so widespread that consensus can often be purchased only at the price of ambiguity. Indeed, the aims of policy are always ambiguous, inconsistent and conflicting, and as a result there is no simple consensual criterion, such as effectiveness, against which to judge performance. This is precisely the basic problem with the 'common good'. Under these frustrating circumstances, the analyst may decide that his task is to probe and to clarify the ambiguities, contradictions and inconsistencies of collective goals. He may, on the other hand, arrogantly, or out of frustration, assume that he knows the consensus of values (where consensus is not absent by definition) and that he can act as a judge, extrapolating the value priorities of society by virtue of his knowledge and participation as a citizen. If he pursues either route he risks succumbing to his own bias, and becomes vulnerable to the charge that he has abandoned his disinterested position as scientist and imposed his own ideology. Finally, he may argue that the best way to proceed is to assume, for purposes of argument, that such and such are the relevant values under review. But this simply evades the issues and takes as given what is most unsettled in the situation. He could, of course, make alternative assumptions about values, but he still needs to decide how broad a spectrum of values he will embrace. The more faithful he is to the diversity of views that prevail on any issue, the more tentative are the conclusions or the more hypothetical and abstract the analysis.

The Frustrations Surrounding Feedback. I want now to explore the frustrations associated with efforts to make use of the technology of social experimentation, because this is often held up as the most appropriate model for learning since it provides the most trustworthy information. Mosteller and his colleagues make the point with clarity and force. They examined about thirty different social programmes that had been implemented with great care after being subjected to a rigorous experimental design. They observed that only about one programme in six or seven seemed to do what it was supposed to do (stated goals) in any substantial way. Mosteller speculates that other programmes which are carried out in a more casual way should not be expected to have even as good a rate of success as these. And he concludes from these discouraging findings that more experimentation is needed; otherwise we can never determine which approach is worth pursuing.[16]

This approach to feedback as a process of learning is based on several assumptions. First, that improving the quality of information available to policy makers will lead to better decisions. However, a strategy of cumulative social learning must depend upon a stable policy equilibrium. This, in turn, presupposes that the process of acquiring information will bring to the fore a set of dominant criteria which faithfully reflects or, at least, is broadly consistent with the action that the established power profiles of society are willing to accept. The social scientist is viewed as

16. See Richard J. Light, Frederick Mosteller and Herbert S. Winokur, jr. 'Using Controlled Field Studies to Improve Public Policy', in *The President's Commission on Federal Statistics*, Washington, D.C., U.S. Government Printing Office, vol. 2, p. 367, 1972. The study from which these observations are drawn is not yet completed. Some of the comments are based on discussions with Frederick Mosteller.

playing an essentially passive role 'as an aid in helping society decide whether its innovations have achieved desirable goals without damaging side effects. The job . . . is not to say *what is to be done*, but rather to say *what has been done*.'[17] Finally, the continuity of political commitment is assumed and not questioned.

Let us set aside for the moment whether these assumptions are reasonable and focus instead on the conditions under which experimentation is appropriate as a method of public learning. Experimentation only makes sense (a) where randomization is politically feasible, and when no major ethical issues arise if treatment is not provided for the control group; (b) where the inputs are specific and measurable (a programme, for example, is too broad a category); (c) where there is consensus about the desired outcome, which in turn can be measured; and (d) where experiments do not hurt those on whom they are performed. Obviously, given our political system of compromise and bargaining, there will not be many circumstances when the programme input is clear, measurable, reproducible and harmless, and when the output is specifiable and translatable into some performance measure on which people will agree. Therefore the opportunities for systematic experiment are limited. However, when all these requirements can in principle be met, difficulties still persist. It seems that the almost universal result of any large-scale experiment is macro-negative. That is to say, it is impossible to detect differences between the control and experimental groups and hence to infer how much of a difference the stimulus made.

The New Jersey Negative Income Tax Experiment is an unusual example because it appears to meet all the necessary criteria. It was the most carefully conducted and sophisticated large-scale social experiment ever carried out in the United States. The experiment lasted three years at a total cost of $8 million. About one third of this total cost went for cash payments to the participating families, all of which contained an able-bodied male head between eighteen and fifty-eight years of age. Each of the families

17. Donald Campbell, 'Critical Problems in the Evolution of Social Programs', a paper prepared for the annual meeting of the National Academy of Sciences, Division of Behavioral Science, May 1972 (mimeograph), p. 2.

in the experimental group was assigned to one of eight different plans. Each plan comprised a certain guarantèe level (expressed as a percentage of the poverty line) and a certain tax rate that reduced the value of the benefits as earned income increased. The major purpose of the experiment was to determine the extent to which an income support programme for intact families would lead to their withdrawal from the labour force – so that the full or true cost of a national programme could be estimated. But difficulties emerged in the design and execution of the experiment which seriously limited the interpretation of the findings, and hence its relevance for policy decisions.

I want to review the New Jersey experiment in terms of the four criteria for effective experimentation that I have already set out. Let us start with the last criterion. No one seriously believed that an experiment which augmented the income of the poor for three years and then cut off the additional income would substantially harm the well-being of the families that participated, but some families may indeed have been hurt inadvertently. The sponsoring agency (the Office of Economic Opportunity – O.E.O.) was eager to get publicity for its experiment, and after much internal disagreement over the issue several families were interviewed on television, where they were described as working for employers who paid poverty wages. The employer of one family head was offended by this, and it is alleged that he fired the employee because of his participation in the experiment. A series of mishaps then befell the worker. He could not secure another job, and eventually his family broke up as well and he took to drink. People are complicated and we cannot so glibly link these events into a causal chain; but the example makes clear the importance of confidentiality, and in this area many unresolved moral questions intrude. It became disturbingly clear that the experimenters could not legally protect families, despite their promise that the information acquired during the experiment would be held in strictest confidence. Difficulties emerged in two ways. First, Congress wanted to review individual cases when it debated welfare reform, and second, the local prosecution office subpoenaed the files, on the grounds that they contained information about welfare clients who had defrauded the government by failing to report the income that they received from the experiment. The motives that inspired both requests were political; and the experimenters successfully resisted both pressures. But the controversy engendered by the requests did make clear that in government-sponsored research the promise of confidentiality could not always be honoured, and this naturally raised questions about whether disclosure could hurt those who participated in the study. O.E.O. asked the National Academy of Sciences to study the problem, and after three years of work a committee recommended a new statute that would explicitly protect subjects who participated in government-sponsored research. Whether there will be political support for such a statute is still uncertain.

Let us turn next to the question of random assignment. This became an issue at an early stage in the design of the experiment. Two interrelated decisions had to be made: the size of the sample when stratified by the permanent (or normal) income of the families in the experimental group and, secondly, the number of cases in each normal-income stratum that would be assigned to the several plans (defined *not* by the generosity of payment but by tax rates and guarantee levels). The stratified sample of families in each income strata would, of course, then be randomly assigned to each plan and thus each family in a low-income stratum could by the laws of chance have an equal opportunity to receive a guarantee substantially higher than its normal income. The crucial question, however, was the number of such families that were to be placed in the most generous plans, since this decision would dramatically affect the amount of money left for the remainder of the research (since costs were fixed). The issue could not be resolved and an outside arbitrator was called in to settle the disagreement within the staff. The design eventually adopted favoured assigning fewer families with relatively higher customary incomes to the most generous plans, and this decision had the effect of reducing the average size of the actual payment levels received by families and restricting the number of families who would experience a substantial increase over their normal incomes.

We next consider the question of the experimental stimulus or the input to which the families were exposed. The income guaranteed for each family was on average low – about $25 per week. Moreover, many families did not receive any payments at all, since their income was above the break-even point. They could, of course, receive payments if their earnings declined. Here the stimulus was not the size of the grant, *per se*, but the potential availability of the grant should a family decide to decrease its earnings and thus make itself eligible for benefits. To draw an analogy, we need to distinguish between a well available for drinking (a plan), even if no one drinks from it because he has other sources of nourishment, and the amount of water imbibed by those who do actually drink from the well (the actual payment level). This distinction between the plan and the payments (the well and the water) was part of the study design.[18] But the nature of the input, or the stimulus, became uncertain because of the unexpected availability of welfare payments to both the experimental and control groups. One of the main reasons for selecting New Jersey as a site for the experiment had been that the state did not have an income-support programme for male-headed families in need. However, after the study began the state launched one of the most generous programmes for unemployed parents (Aid to Families with Dependent Children – Unemployed Parents – A.F.D.C.-U.P.) in the country.[19] As a result, many of the families in the experimental group were also on welfare and therefore receiving both welfare benefits and payments from the experiment (the proportions for all families varied in the different experimental groups). Then the state discovered that it could not afford this costly programme and it reduced the size of the guarantee

18. Zvi Griliches, Professor of Economics at Harvard, proposed this analogy at the Brookings Conference held in April 1974 to evaluate the New Jersey experiment. The proceedings have been published. See Pechman and Timpane, *Work Incentives and Income Guarantees*, Washington D.C., The Brookings Institution, 1975.

19. ibid., Henry Aaron, 'Cautionary Notes on the Experiment', p. 90. As a result of New Jersey's new measure two of the eight plans became completely dominated by the welfare programme and the families in these plans were excluded from the final analysis. These were the mid-range plans that were most likely to be adopted by Congress. Deleting them, therefore, limited the usefulness of the study. But we leave this question aside since we are concerned here only with the impact of welfare on the experimental inputs and not with the use of the findings.

by forty per cent and so sharply decreased the number of families served. The families, therefore, had been subjected not merely to the guarantee and tax level of the experimental plan but also to the options made available by welfare, which in turn changed dramatically over time. To make the analysis even more difficult, fifteen per cent of the control group were always on welfare throughout the time the experiment was conducted. 'What this all means is that each household is confronted by a highly complex stimulus represented by a function that may increase and then decrease and that exhibits quirks and discontinuities ... That families ... understood the experimental stimulus ... is doubtful.'[20]

In summary, then, the experimental stimulus was not obvious to the subjects in the experiments. We have to distinguish between the plan itself, the level of the payments, the alternatives available to families after the introduction of welfare and whatever knowledge the families actually had about the choice of benefits to which they were entitled.

Finally, let us consider the criterion of outcomes. Agreement was never lost over the purpose of the experiment: labour force participation of intact families remained the focus of the study; estimates of the national cost of different programmes were not systematically pursued. When such estimates do come to be made in a different political context, questions will then come up about the short-term nature of the experiment and the problems of generalizing from the special conditions in New Jersey to the nation as a whole. However, I want to focus on a somewhat different issue here. As a result of the interest in intact families the analysis was based solely on the continuous husband–wife families in the sample. But these families represented only fifty-seven per cent of the 725 experimental families who received benefits at the start of the programme. This large attrition rate meant that generalizations had to be based on a very small sample size. 'Four of the eight plans had less than fifty continuous husband–wife recipients, divided among four distinct sites and three surprisingly disparate ethnic groups.'[21]

20. ibid., p. 95.
21. ibid., p. 89.

The findings of the study support the general conclusion that income guarantees do not promote a massive withdrawal from the labour force of white males (estimates range from a five to ten per cent reduction in hours worked); but new puzzles emerged because black families responded in the opposite direction by working longer hours. Those who wish to take exception to these conclusions can readily turn to the methodological weaknesses of the experiment for support – actual benefit levels were low, the input was not clear because of the availability of welfare as an option, and there was a high attrition rate among intact families. The experiment, designed to provide unambiguous results, yielded only broad evidence which became the subject of disagreements among technicians. Support for a variety of positions could be garnered from the same evidence, depending on one's confidence in the assumptions on which the initial design was based.

For purposes of policy, these weaknesses in the study design are crucial. Leaving aside the special difficulties that arose from the unexpected creation in New Jersey of a welfare programme for male heads who were unemployed, there is the ambiguity that the experiment focused only on male heads although the policy debate was concerned about the labour force participation of female heads of households. The decision to focus on male heads was promoted by the designers of the study, who believed that what was needed was a programme to supplement the income of male-headed intact families who worked full time, and year round, but were still poor. They hoped that the experiment would show that the income of such families could be augmented without a significant decline in work effort. The ideal of the social scientist as servant to the political process is difficult to honour in practice. The director of the Office of Research, Plans, Program and Evaluation (R.P.P. & E.) within O.E.O., who was administratively responsible for the experiment, recently concluded that social experimentation may be considered 'as much a gross political process as a detailed scientific one'.[22]

22. Robert Levine, 'How and Why the Experiment Came About', ibid., p. 23.

Although feedback from social experiment may encounter stubborn technical problems, this is no argument for abandoning the approach altogether. However, the example we have reviewed reaffirms how difficult it is to realize in practice the ideal of the scientist as a passive technician carrying out the public will. And these difficulties arise in other areas of feedback as well. Let us consider next the example of a national programme evaluation. The designers of Head Start saw the purpose of the programme as the promotion of social competence, but there was an emphasis on cognitive development in the national evaluation of the programme. This came about because academic developmental psychologists imposed the narrower cognitive focus, in part because it reflected their interests, and in part because it was easier to measure than the fuzzier concept of social competence. We can see, then, that the values of the feedback technician intrude at every stage in the process of analysis, definition, design and interpretation. The hope that a value-neutral feedback can be devised is misplaced. So, too, is the ideal of feedback as a linear process in which information is fed into the political machinery and the social scientist is merely a passive observer. The process of using facts to make value decisions is a circular one: understanding how decisions are taken breeds further understanding of how research can best be used in the process. This approach does not focus solely on the knowledge needed to understand social events (the input to the policy makers), nor does it assume that good information will automatically be used by the political process. It does assume that knowledge and involvement in the policy-making process are both crucial if the latent conflicts between the process of acting and the process of knowing are to be resolved. Yet it is precisely in this area that the separation of facts and values is most difficult to achieve.

What happens when the evaluations consistently react against the normative ideals which inspired the initial programme of reform and yield negative findings? It is in these terms that a decade of failure with compensatory education and other programmes to aid the poor have been interpreted. And what happens when the coalition that supported reforms for a guaranteed income, compensatory education, etc., falls apart, and the ideals are forsaken as impractical, dangerous or too costly in political or financial terms? If the policy advisers, who aid the politician in the task of mapping, and the technicians who provide expertise in the design of feedback systems unwillingly surrender to the prevailing trend, adjusting to their understanding of the political process, there is a danger that they may become hacks whose moral integrity is damaged by their accommodation to political expediency. If they concede the importance of a normative perspective in the analysis of feedback, they abandon the view that facts and values can be treated in isolation from one another.

The several strategies I have so far reviewed proceed from the common assumption that better factual information can contribute substantially to improving the quality of moral judgements. Knowledge, to be useful to policy makers, must be developed by experts and built upon a theory that is detached from the normative issues under debate. We are concerned here with an all-purpose theory that policy makers can utilize, whatever their goals and preferences. This is 'value-free' theory in the Weberian sense. Weber believed that a system of propositions could be developed which would provide information about the prospective effects of economic policies. He assumed that there was an economic science from which such information could be derived; he was not concerned with feedback, experimentation and the like. The implicit model here is that of the natural sciences and applied technology, and the assumption is made that theoretical knowledge about underlying natural processes is first generated in isolation from normative judgements and shielded from practical policy. This knowledge is then transformed into a new technology and applied to normative problems in the form of programmes, which in turn are periodically evaluated and modified when they fail to meet specifications. The major task is to make this model work better.

I have tried to probe the weakness of this model. Briefly, my argument may be summarized as follows: first, I have attempted to show that social science cannot develop a secure understanding of causal relationships which will permit it to predict important social events. In this sense, social science cannot be a science. Policy cannot be derived from theory alone because the forces that shape human behaviour are inherently unstable; '... any pattern of relationships we can perceive and act upon, as a theoretical basis for intervention, is likely to be ephemeral ... none of these insights provides a secure basis for inference about the performance of a social design, because their predictions have so wide a margin of indeterminacy'.[23] Thus a model that calls for an orderly transition from purpose to theory, to design, to evaluation, to prototype is misplaced. There is no convergent solution to problems, and no progress in the sense of coming closer to one truth.

My second point is that there is no consensual codification of values which permits an orderly matching of knowledge and valuation. So we cannot avoid asking to whose values the acts should be referred. Since no value framework is clearly given, the analyst may take those of his client; he may construct his own interpretation or offer alternative frameworks; or he may treat frameworks as merely hypothetical. None of these approaches is altogether satisfactory.

In Search of an Alternative Position

I am critical of the positivist viewpoint not because it is wrong but because it is incomplete. It accepts as given what is most problematic.

What alternative can we present if we wish to reject the value-decisionistic view of the positivists, which holds that values must be accepted as given since they are established by the will or by passion; that we must distinguish between grounded fact statements and ungrounded value statements; and that the gulf between goals and value judgements and the universe of facts can best be bridged by an applied science model?

The competing framework of thought we may call a *value critical* approach. According to this view, pure science requires analytic procedures that cannot be applied to the study of society. Moreover, we are not even really interested in 'pure' social

23. Peter Marris, 'Experimenting in Social Reform', in David Jones and Marjorie Mayo, *Community Work One*, Routledge & Kegan Paul, 1974, p. 251.

science – a social science divorced from action – since the meaning of social events is inextricably bound up with the values we attach to them. Hence, fact, value and theory are inseparably welded together; and the applied science model is misconceived. Joan Robinson captured the essence of this approach when she observed that

... it is not possible to describe a system without moral judgements creeping in. For to look at a system from the outside implies that it is not the only possible system; in describing it we compare it (openly or tacitly) with other actual or imagined systems. Differences imply choices, and choices imply judgements. We cannot escape from making judgements and the judgements that we make arise from the ethical preconceptions that have soaked into our view of life.[24]

A primary function of analysis is to submit goals to critical review rather than merely treating them as given. I want in this section to comment briefly on the way in which goals may become the object of analysis and by what methods of analysis a value-critical approach brings together facts and values. In the last section of the chapter I shall discuss the problems that emerge when normative and descriptive statements are integrated and how these difficulties may be faced.

From the logical point of view, ultimate value statements must indeed be taken as axioms, not deducible from other statements. But it does not follow that we must treat them simply as arbitrary postulates, as the classical positivist, value-decisionist position would require. The value-critical approach takes the line that values are not simply wishes and desires but are grounded in a fundamental structure which is central to real processes; and they can therefore become a meaningful subject of debate. We need, further, to distinguish between formal value terms, which are positive or negative propositions by definition (for example, a just act cannot be a bad act), and terms of material value, where it is not self-evident whether a positive or a negative value has been asserted. (Is equality, for example, essential to or incompatible with a just society?) The formal–material distinction should not be confused with the more traditional means–ends

24. Joan Robinson, *Economic Philosophy*, Penguin Books, 1964, p. 19.

dichotomy. In the former case we ask what right we have to make value assertions on the basis of accepted standards of truth; in the latter we decide which choices should be pursued to reach a given objective. A value-critical position treats values not merely as the accepted aims of policy but as a subject for debate and analysis. When I affirm equality as a value, I want further to inquire what this means and why it is worth while, and not simply how one can reach this end or how one can catalogue the views of those who support, repudiate or are indifferent to it.

A value-critical position can, in addition, examine specific end values in relation to others by looking at the consequences of pursuing these aims and by considering the latent goal conflicts among them. This position has been cogently developed by John Dewey who, in the pragmatic tradition, discusses the standards that are used in making value judgements. He explains that by themselves ends are 'vague, cloudy and impressionistic. We do not know what we are really after until a course of action is mentally worked out.'[25] In other words, we truly know what we want only when the consequences of pursuing our ends are more fully evident. Here social science can play a prominent role. Of course, all goal-seeking activity cannot be interpreted only as a trial-and-error process, as described by Dewey, because we are not starting from a position of initial ignorance. In principle, ethical issues may be logically isolated down to a single first premise that deals with intrinsic values, and which is therefore not subject to further debate; but in practice men always pursue many ends. They are seldom, if ever, in search of a single, sole end to which all other purposes are subordinated. Of course, some special aim may at any given time be more focal than others, but typically even this aim must be viewed as instrumental to others. Even our first principles become subject to further analysis when we sub-scribe to a number of first principles that are mutually contra-dictory. And this plurality of goals raises the basic problem of goal conflict and goal priorities. As we have seen, it is precisely at this point that the classical positivists argue that values, in the end, are only a matter of decision and preference, are not

25. John Dewey, *Human Nature and Conduct: An Introduction to Social Psychology*, New York, Modern Library, 1930, p. 36.

'objectively grounded', and are therefore impervious to verification and debate. That approach sacrifices the most central aspect of the discourse about policy issues, because the main problems of the development of policy involve these contradictions in goals; and the analyst must also consider the consequences of pursuing a given goal or selecting alternative means to reach a declared purpose. We need an examination of goal concepts in their own terms but this task is difficult because there are no final solutions and no self-evident criteria against which to judge progress. Policy analysis is essentially involved with intractable problems. End values, societal goals, etc., are inherently controversial. They cannot be treated 'scientifically' along positivist lines. Policy analysis involves the use of social science tools that produce inherently uncertain and incomplete findings, and these doubtful findings are then brought forward in an attempt to understand goals which are ambiguous and conflicting and where the elusive question of priorities is always dominant. It is nevertheless possible to cope with this intractability fairly sensibly. In this sense we are all positivists in search of general principles, eager to hold our passions in suspense so that they do not interfere with our ability to understand events.

A value-critical approach tries to understand the logic, meaning and consistency of ends, and it attempts to make a critique of values at every stage of analysis. Every F statement can be regarded as demonstrating some truth within a framework of values and assumptions. Analytic procedures themselves imply values. For example, it is in the very nature of measurement that we agree to neglect factors which may be of major importance but are not susceptible to measurement.

The value-critical perspective does not make the assumption that there are discoverable causal relationships which are stable over time. The conclusions reached through this kind of inquiry, therefore, are provisional, representing as they do a best guess in the circumstances. Research within the value-critical framework does try to discern patterns; it seeks general principles that take account of the context and co-mingle facts and values. These general principles cannot be derived solely from the aggregation of known regularities in the behaviour of separate events. Rather, the analyst's advice to policy makers is based on social understanding and depends upon the use of illustrative stories, or accounts from past experience, which suggest how the future might unfold if certain actions were taken. I use the term 'story-telling' in part to make clear that the effort is less rigorous than the positivists' attempt to develop general laws, and in part because the logical structure developed in this system of analysis is much the same as that of a story. The analyst who

uses this form of reasoning is operating on the same logical plane ... as the novelist or the dramatist. He presents, like the story-teller, a sequence of events, each event leading to the next; and, like the story-teller again, he presents the story in terms of the behaviour of a few major 'characters'. The succession of events is made to appear to be caused, at each step, by the actions of the characters; and the entire story is made to unfold according to some 'inner necessity'. Moreover, the action is of such a nature that we usually 'understand' (in Max Weber's sense of the word) what 'caused' each of the constituent events.[26]

The central element in normative story-telling is the metaphor. This means that we must rely upon actions or events that appear to be analogous to situations we already know and that permit us to reason from the familiar to the unfamiliar. Familiar concepts are brought into unfamiliar situations, and in the process they transform the unfamiliar. The metaphor enables us to describe patterns and tease out lessons. There are numerous illustrations of this process. For example, we talk about a labour-market queue, which is like people waiting in line; wage contours, which look like the lines depicting hills or mountains on a map; or fragmented social programmes, which imply that interventions are fragments of something that was once united.

Analogies imply that there is a shared pattern of relationships between seemingly dissimilar events or objects. But why would anyone recognize an analogy between broken crockery and social services? Through the metaphor we produce a construction of

26. Sidney Shoeffler, *The Failure of Economics: A Diagnostic Study*, Cambridge, Mass., Harvard University Press, 1955, p. 150.

reality that permits us to recognize that an analogy exists.[27] Broken crockery and social services have a shared pattern. Each was once whole and at one time was broken into fragments, but both can be restored to their original position if we re-cement the shattered pieces of pottery and coordinate the fragmented social programmes. It is the metaphor of the fragmentation of services which suggests to us that there is an analogy between seemingly unrelated activities.

The stories we tell can be imaginative, inventive or romantic, using experience in very subtle ways – rearranging it, combining aspects of different experiences, playing out a fantasy (as in predictions about the future). 'In writing or telling stories we aim for compactness, and we choose or select and provide sufficient context, so that what is relevant and irrelevant is pointed out.'[28] The metaphor in our story is crucial because it supplies the normative leap that provides the direction for action. Fragments should be reintegrated; the economically disadvantaged who are at the end of the labour-market queue should be brought to the middle or to the front. In these examples the metaphor relates to values (programmes should be organized as wholes) and to strategies for reducing poverty (how the positions of workers in a queue can be altered). Some metaphors, such as the wage contours, are in this context descriptive rather than normative, although the same metaphor applied to a different process may also imply values and strategies for policy.

It is possible to assess 'objectively' the relevance of the analogy, that is, the fit between the story and the circumstances to which it is now being applied. In so doing we inquire whether the story is true. Is it true, for example, that social services were once united into a coherent whole, or were they always organized as pro-

27. My views about the role of metaphors in making the normative leap in policy analysis were developed with my colleague Donald A. Schon in a joint seminar at M.I.T. An extensive literature exists on this subject. See, for example, M. Black, *Models and Metaphors*, Ithaca, Cornell University Press, 1962; and Robert A. Nisbet, *Social Change and History*, New York, Oxford University Press, 1969, especially Chapter 8, 'Reflections on a Metaphor'.

28. Martin Kreiger, 'Advice', Center for Advanced Study in Behavioral Sciences, Stanford, California, 1973 (mimeograph).

grammes isolated from each other? Is the analogy truly descriptive or merely normative or both? That is to say, it is a normative statement that programmes should, for many reasons, be organized as wholes; it is a factual statement when we affirm that they were indeed once integrated and that some special circumstances caused them to be split apart; and it is again normative when we say that they can and should be reunited.

Criticism of the truthfulness of a story (of what happened) is in principle fairly straightforward. The validity of the explanation of what happened – interpreting why the sequences of events occurred – is much harder to assess. The validity of explanations is elusive. The rules seem to be partly aesthetic and partly logical: the story should be the simplest, most comprehensive, internally consistent explanation we can offer, and it should also be consistent with possible explanations of similar events. We should ask too if the explanation that the story provides can be generalized, for we tend to reject explanations in terms of the personal qualities of particular actors – not so much because they contain no truth but because they are unique. (Of course, unique configurations do call for unique explanations, and we cannot dismiss the role of the individual as necessarily irrelevant.) The interpretation given to the story determines its relevance as an analogy for the possible future course of events.

An impartial interpretation of evidence is central to the relevance of social science for social policy and by 'objective' social understanding we mean an understanding that can best answer these criteria. This may prove difficult for the analyst because in seeking policy-relevant stories that analyse facts to reach normative conclusions he is necessarily immersed in the events he is trying to explain.

The analyst must take his own aspirations into account when he examines social phenomena and probes the ambiguities, contradictions and inconsistencies of collective goals. Since he cannot altogether do this, he risks ideological bias. Those who accept a value-critical approach, while recognizing that analysis necessarily has a subjective aspect, nevertheless claim to be able to achieve a 'controlled' subjectivity in that their subjective preferences are guided by rational and intelligible criteria. Since, in the end, we must deal with a reality which transcends the here and now, this objective reality will provide at some future time a criterion against which to judge our subjective reactions. However, we cannot resolve any disagreement by looking at present evidence, because the evidence we need is not yet available. Nevertheless, reality is transcendent: at some later time the evidence will be available, and we may at some future date be able to resolve the question that is now at issue. By then, of course, time has already taken care of the problem. In this sense, reality is an open system. In the course of time, the truth or falseness of a proposition can be revealed. However, and this is crucial for policy analysis, at any one moment in time we do not fully understand reality and we must therefore accept our beliefs as a matter of faith.

The *value-critical* approach, as we have briefly sketched it, assigns to a policy-relevant social science only a modest role in generating a plausible understanding of social processes. This is largely, I think, because we cannot be dogmatic about values or self-assured about the analytic techniques of inquiry. The value-critical approach is itself a middle position, because it is not as detached, or *value neutral*, as the empirical positivists, nor as partisan as the radical activists – who assume that we can only be in support of, or against, a social group or a social force.

In examining alternatives to positivism, it may be useful to comment on an overtly ideological social science, which assumes a morally right approach and in which the techniques of analysis are informed by the whole ideology. Marxism is an approach to policy analysis which is *value committed*; it provides an explicit moral position with a historical analysis of the development of political economy. This approach takes for granted certain causal relationships and general laws; it believes, for example, in the instability of capitalism and asserts that capitalism generates class polarization. Moreover, the Marxist dialectic provides an analytic method for investigating issues. The dialectic process (in which class and power or, more strictly, the means of production and the social relationship of production, are the critical factors) is assimilated within a value-committed framework and provides a basis for predicting the future of capitalist society. The scientific method is pursued within this paradigm or framework of thought.

New information reinforces and reinterprets this world view. Anomalies that are inconsistent with the original premises must, of course, be attended to. Why, for example, has class polarization not taken place? One way to deal with such an anomaly is to shift the time perspective within which the prediction is expected to occur. We can always find ad hoc auxiliary hypotheses which immunize the theory against criticism. These difficulties are inherent in all scientific work.

Contained within its own assumptions, this approach can be very powerful in explaining social processes. There are, of course, drawbacks. The analysis is constrained within the initial framework and limits the analyst's capacity for self-criticism; and the policy conclusions are acceptable, by and large, only to those who share the framework.

The *value-critical* approach provides a relatively doubtful and uncertain position because it accepts neither the advantages of a claim to pure science (the *value-neutral* approach) nor the moral embrace of pure ideology (the *value-committed* approach). It tries to submit each issue to impartial analysis, mindful that it can never altogether be successful in what it attempts. The analyst who works within this framework may yearn for the self-assurance that the rigours of science or the faith of ideology can provide. But he cannot be tempted by these false idols, nor can he possibly undertake his work without method and belief. This tension provides the basis for creative work and informs the value-critical posture towards questions of policy.

Integrating Facts and Values

In the rest of this essay I want to discuss a number of issues that arise when one assumes that facts and values are always integrated and cannot be isolated from one another. I shall first elaborate on the ideological perspectives that are typically encountered in the analysis of policy. I call them value screens because they serve to screen in and out certain evidence and to provide, as well, a framework for interpretation. I shall then discuss the problems of bias, ethics and legitimation which arise when the positivist view of the world is challenged.

Value Screens

If knowledge about society is inevitably interwoven with the beliefs and ideology that we hold, then we must know what these frameworks of belief and ideology are and how they influence analysis. A key demand in the positivist outlook is to keep one's own ideological bias out of the analysis of social events; although values may legitimately influence the selection of problems, they should not influence any other aspect of the inquiry. Anti-positivists tend to distinguish between their own 'truth' and others' 'ideology', exposing themselves to the charge of tacit ideological bias. MacIntyre is sharply critical of this tendency, which he caustically labels 'epistemological self-righteousness', and he notes that the 'claim to a privileged exemption from such distortions seems to be presupposed when such distortion is identified in others'.[29] Succumbing to this self-righteous bias, the anti-positivist does not present his position as an 'ideology' to be accepted and rejected as a mere reflection of will; he speaks about values as objectively subsisting entities.

Although I believe that values can be analysed rationally, they must also be recognized as unashamed biases, that is, as presuppositions not readily amenable to inspection and criticism. This must not be interpreted as an over-relativistic position. Of course, when two people debate their irreconcilable biases, no fruitful resolution is possible. But it does not follow that one bias is just as good or bad as any other. In the course of time the truth or falsity of conflicting views may be revealed.

Myrdal, one of the few social scientists who have written extensively on this subject, has advised that social scientists should simply announce their biases and values so that the reader can then take them into account when he examines the data presented and the arguments based upon them. But this presupposes that researchers know what they believe, that ideology is given. I doubt if this is always the case. Indeed, often the most

29. MacIntyre, *Comparative Politics*, vol. 5, no. 3, April 1973, p. 322.

difficult problem is to explain the framework of thought by which the researcher has organized his data and which also shapes his interpretation. So, the first question must be, what do we value, what is our ideology?

It is useful to distinguish between matters of style and questions of substance. Style affects the content of analysis and its mode of presentation. Two policy analysts who share a very similar value perspective may nevertheless interpret events quite differently because their styles diverge. The matter of style is personal and idiosyncratic. There are, of course, many dimensions of style; only a few are listed here. Some analysts are optimists; they enjoy calling attention to what is possible. They seek to identify the constraints which can be modified and the areas where accord about ethical disagreements can be reached. By contrast, others are attracted to the kind of analysis which exposes weakness in institutions. They enjoy documenting the failure to achieve shared goals and displaying the underlying contradictions and conflicting interests that inhibit agreement. It is through style that perversity or disagreeableness, graciousness or consideration, cynicism, scepticism, optimism, and other dimensions of personality, temperament and belief find expression.

It is the substantive value screens, however, that are critical to an understanding of the way in which values and analysis subtly, but decisively, affect each other. I want, therefore, very briefly to identify three value screens that serve both as a system of beliefs and as a framework within which to understand events. Each person's perception of reality is influenced by a normative theory that helps to explain why things are as they are. By its nature, all knowledge is selective: it focuses on some items and neglects others. Facts, after all, only have meaning when they are placed in some broader framework of thought and belief.

The first value screen I want to identify sees in *the malfunctioning of institutions and organizations* the causes of most contemporary problems and also the means to their resolution. This ideology is broad enough to include national institutional arrangements at the level of the economy and the policy, but it is also concrete enough to consider dysfunctions of specific bureaucracies at every level. Criticism can be launched, for example, at the operating assumptions on which the legal system itself is based, or at the performance of a specific court located in a specific jurisdiction and manned by particular judges. Ideally, the analyst who works within this framework will try to select specific examples that help to make vivid and concrete the general pattern of dysfunction prevailing in the larger institutional framework. This need not be a radical approach, one that goes to the root of the situation. Institutions are continuously in disequilibrium, and the task may be defined in more limited terms as correction through manipulable policies. In this more limited sense, the economic planner is prototypical of the approach that emphasizes manipulation of macro- and micro-institutional arrangements in order to achieve desired goals.

The second perspective calls attention to *the failure of people to cope*. This approach is associated with social work, but it has more general applicability. In its pure form, mismanagement is associated primarily with personal inadequacies. We might assume, for example, that there is a normal distribution of competence in living and that there will always be a bottom five to ten per cent who are unable to cope because of their intellectual limitations (low I.Q.) or emotional difficulties. More typically, however, the institutional-oriented approach I have just mentioned meshes with this people-oriented approach. When one asks why people cannot cope, the answer may be given, for example, in terms of institutions' failure to teach them to do so; and this can easily become translated into a criticism of institutional performance. This line of reasoning may lead, as well, to a cultural interpretation of individual incapacities. An example is Moynihan's controversial thesis that two hundred years of slavery have produced a tangle of pathology in the Negro family.[30] But whatever the broader theory, central to this second approach is the assumption that it is necessary to change *people* before they can take adequate advantage of the institutional opportunities available to them in society. Of course, I believe it is arrogant to assume that it is possible to change someone else: in the end, a

30. For an analysis of this thesis see Lee Rainwater and William Yancey, *The Moynihan Report and the Politics of Controversy*, Cambridge, Mass., M.I.T. Press, 1967.

person must alter his own attitudes, values and behaviour. An agent of change can hope only to create incentives and resources that will enable people to change themselves. One direction implied by these assumptions is that of self-help, a solution that has a long intellectual tradition in liberal democratic societies. What distinguishes this approach from the institutional perspective is the belief that intervention must take place at the level of the individual.

The third value screen emphasizes the importance of *power*. It is expressed in its purest form in the Marxist argument about social class: the nature of the society is determined by the structure of power. The privileged class will always seek to maintain its power and advantage. It may, indeed, make concessions in order to retain its position when threatened, but these concessions will be limited to areas that are not crucial. This can of course, in principle, become an irrefutable or meaningless argument, because all changes can be interpreted as evidence of the cleverness of the privileged classes in maintaining their position. It is only when a class loses power altogether that the shrewdness argument collapses, although it may prove difficult to maintain the original view when an upper stratum is losing some power and retreating. Belief in the central importance of class power can adapt to an alternative view, that the sources of power in society are more diffuse and fragmented; there is not one class struggle but many struggles among many classes. When power is widely diffused, it is more likely that the distribution of power in society can be changed by an evolutionary process. The pluralist position holds that new political coalitions are possible and that therefore people can alter their own situations through their own social actions. Political action, short of revolution, can produce real social change. Traditional Marxists reject this position. Both perspectives have in common, however, the view that power is crucial.

This approach also overlaps with the other two value screens. The distribution of power, after all, affects people and institutions. Thus it can be argued, for example, that the maintenance of class power destroys people's sense of identity, it infantilizes them and makes them part of a dependent social class. In this and other ways access to power and the psychology of individuals are linked together. The distribution of power also affects the performance of institutions: it is a major function of institutions, after all, to reinforce established power arrangements; they serve as agents of control, inculcating within individuals the accepted, established social arrangements, even though they may be interpreted as benign forces making possible the very existence of society itself. The argument about power can be very subtle as well. Even when institutions serve to limit a dominant group's power position, this apparent restriction of established power may be seen as a way to prevent the system from collapsing under the strain of non-compliance by its members.

All these ideologies direct our attention to specific facts, and they also help to organize them. In this sense all research is biased: it works within an interpretive framework enabling the analyst to make policy-relevant sense of the facts that he observes.

Not all ideologies emphasize specifically one of the themes of institutions, people and power. The study of social policy is complicated by the analyst's recognition that there may be some merit in each view, so that some synthesis of the three approaches is required. Suppose we associate each position with the *liberal* political tradition (institutions need to be reformed), the *conservative* (people are accountable for their own failures and achievements) and the *radical* (fundamental change is inhibited by the distribution of established power, so that important reform is possible only through revolution), then we may find that many people simultaneously hold liberal, conservative and radical views. But even such eclecticism, the reluctance to make a choice because competing explanations are so obviously complementary, is not value-neutral; it is itself only a middle-of-the-road ideology. And even here, because resources are scarce and tough decisions must be made, one is forced however reluctantly to make choices. Those who select an eclectic–synthetic approach have to make yet another choice, because a synthesis can be organized from two perspectives at least – from power to institutions to people, or the reverse. Taking the first perspective, we might, for example, argue that there is a complex distribution of power in society and that this influences the performance of institutions and specific bureaucracies. An individual's sense of worth, identity and well-being is wrapped up in his relationship to these institutional bureaucratic arrangements. But the synthesis can also be made from the second perspective, starting at the other end. We live, Freud believed, in a neurotic society that suffers from the inhibiting, repressive nature of institutions. These oppressive and neurotic features of human behaviour come to be reflected in the institutions we create. Our institutional structures and purposes faithfully reflect the kinds of people we are; and they encourage the concentration of power in the hands of certain personality types who are best able to exploit the primitive nature of man's neurotic personality. I am describing very crudely here the ways in which these differing ideologies can mesh together; but theories can be developed which are sophisticated, complex and subtle. The interplay between people, power and institutions can be ingeniously drawn; but however imaginative these arguments may become, their elegance should not obscure the basic point, that each offers a competing framework of thought. The research and analysis we undertake and the policies we recommend are best understood as variants and combinations of these frameworks. Evidence is largely assimilated within a framework and is seldom, if ever, sufficiently powerful to let us make an objective choice among these competing interpretations of the way things are and of what has to be done. This theme is more fully explored in chapters 4 and 6.

The Problem of Objectivity

Once we understand what we believe and how beliefs influence the analysis of policy, we face three different problems: how to avoid distortion of the evidence; the ethical issues involved in gathering and using information; and the question of legitimacy.

First, then, we have to discover how we can prevent our ideology from distorting our understanding of the reality that we seek to explain and alter. No one can claim privileged exemption from distortion; the problem is how to guard against it. There is no wholly satisfactory answer. But there are suggestions as to how this distortion might be minimized. Myrdal argues that there are four logical means by which we can protect ourselves from bias:

To raise the valuations actually determining our theoretical as well as our practical research to full awareness, to scrutinize them from the point of view of relevance, significance, and feasibility in the society under study, to transform them into specific value premises for research, and to determine approach and define concepts in terms of a set of value premises which have been explicitly stated.[31]

MacIntyre joins Myrdal in calling for self-consciousness as a strategy to reduce bias, but adds a sceptical note: 'We have to discover the distortions of ideology first of all in ourselves and learn to live with them, at the same time that we learn, through self-conscious awareness, to avoid being their victims.'[32] In turn Ithiel de Sola Pool and Stevenson urge the postponement of judgement in the struggle between evidence and belief.[33]

In addition to becoming self-aware and delaying judgement, we can fight distortion by submitting to outside criticism, not only from those who share the same framework of analysis but from those who are hostile to it. Yet another approach has been suggested by S. M. Miller, who argues that social responsibility towards an organized movement can serve as a corrective to ideological distortion. When one makes a deep commitment to a social movement that one hopes will, in the end, be successful, and when success is rooted at least partly in the movement's ability to adapt to changing reality, then the individual is prevented from surrendering completely to ideology and neglecting new factual information that may conflict with his beliefs. Objectivity or truthfulness are important when a person is committed: that is, when the consequences of action matter. Hence, if a person is rational (in the sense of wishing to accomplish purposes in the real world), the more committed, the stronger the attachment to certain values, then the greater will be his concern with the objectivity and the actual existence of the evidence on

31. Gunnar Myrdal, *Objectivity in Social Science Research*, Duckworth, 1970, p. 5.

32. MacIntyre, op. cit., p. 337.

33. Ithiel de Sola Pool, 'Some Facts About Values', *PS* (Newsletter of the American Political Science Association), vol. III, no. 2, spring 1970.

which that person acts. This interpretation would be very comforting indeed if convincing evidence could be developed to support it. In fact, a passionate commitment to beliefs seems to inhibit the search for true knowledge.

It is also possible to guard against distortion by drawing on the same external criteria – coherence and accuracy – that the positivists employ. In an age of science we are all positivists to some extent. I suggested earlier that a possibly important alternative to the search for general predictive laws, in the positivist tradition, is the narrative method of linking together isolated events, empirical studies and policy intentions which I call 'story-telling'.

In order to tell a good story it is often necessary to become immersed in the events, so that one can really understand how the facts fit together in some coherent whole. However, this very involvement exposes us to the risk that we may sacrifice objectivity in the effort to achieve understanding and relevancy. We do not want objectivity alone without deep insight into the phenomena that we are observing, because then we run the risk of developing a 'science of nothing',[34] which is rigorous but not capable of explaining anything truly important. But equally we should avoid a creative insight that is no more than the bias and distortion of the story-teller. On this issue Mannheim was an optimist; he believed that 'participation in the social process, which renders one's perspective partial and biased, also enables one to discover truth of deep human import. The productivity of social participation as a source of knowledge, plays a more important role than the limitations which participation in the social process puts upon knowledge.'[35] But how can we guard against distortion? Ward has suggested that objectivity in story-telling by those who participate in the events can be tested, at least partially, in two ways. First, the evidence for particular statements can be subject to verification, and second, the interaction between the parts of the

34. Daniel Lerner and Harold D. Lasswell, eds., *The Policy Science: Recent Developments in Scope and Method*, Stanford University Press, 1951, p. 28.
35. Karl Mannheim, *Essays on the Sociology of Knowledge*, ed. Paul Kecskemeti, Routledge & Kegan Paul, 1952, p. 1.

story and its whole provide an internal source of corroboration. 'A good story makes the facts support the theory and the theory the facts.'[36] Of course, the problems of interpretation discussed on p. 77 cannot altogether be avoided.

The Problems of Ethics

The second problem is that of ethics. We need to consider the ethical difficulties that arise when descriptive and normative analysis are brought together, and when the roles of the active person (policy maker) and the knowing person (social scientist) are blurred. A policy-relevant social science must proceed from the premise that thought and action cannot be separated. This position is vividly expressed by Kecskemeti:

A fruitful application of scientific knowledge to policy is not possible if the separation between the 'expert' and the 'practical man' remains complete ... When science is to be applied to 'policy' the practical man must 'know' something, and the expert must 'desire' and 'value' something. The gap between the unenlightened 'wish' and the goal-neutral 'information' must be filled.[37]

Unfortunately, when the gap between the unenlightened wish and the goal-neutral information is narrowed, moral and ethical problems enter; and these can also undermine the effective use of social science for policy. A specific example may help illustrate the point. A number of innovators in educational policy have been attracted to the idea of permitting parents to use public funds to send their children to schools of their own choice; they believe that the free exercise of choice could promote competition among schools for pupils and for money. Those schools that fail in this competitive bidding will be forced to close, and the process will in the long run increase the quality of education. The concept of educational vouchers also has appeal as an end in itself, because it serves to expand parental choice.

The idea of introducing choice and competition into public

36. Ward, op. cit.
37. Paul Kecskemeti, 'The Policy Sciences: Aspirations and Outlook', op. cit , p. 535.

education is so novel that it seems reasonable to experiment before adopting such a policy. It becomes immediately evident, however, in the design stage of the study that fact and values cannot be isolated. What form should the voucher take? Should private and parochial schools be included in the competition? Should parents be free to supplement the basic amount of the voucher with their own resources? Conservative economists, such as Milton Friedman, contend that the validity of the voucher principle can be tested only in an unrestricted experiment. Liberals, such as Christopher Jencks, fear that an unregulated system will promote class and racial segregation: under the guise of competition it will multiply the privileges of the advantaged classes by providing a direct public subsidy to private and sectarian education.[38]

The Nixon administration decided to experiment with two approaches. A restricted voucher scheme was initiated in the Alum Rock School District of California and there were plans for an unrestricted experiment in New Hampshire. The Rand Corporation received a contract from the federal government to carry out an evaluation of the Alum Rock experiment. It was one of the conditions of the grant that Rand would test the educational achievement of the children with nationally standardized tests. Obviously the results of the test scores, judged against national norms, should provide parents with information that will help them in making educational decisions for their children. But many experts believe that the standardized tests are not responsive to educational innovation; and the researchers at Rand do not have any confidence in their scientific validity. They doubt that

38. Evan Jenkins, 'A School Voucher Experiment Rates an "A" in Coast District', *New York Times*, 29 May 1973. The five-year-voucher experiment was begun in September 1972 at a projected cost of seven million dollars, or a little over a million dollars per year on average. The 1975–6 school year is the fourth year of the demonstration. At present fourteen schools and about 9,000 pupils are enrolled in the programme. Only one public report has been prepared to date by the Rand Corporation, although a number of informal reports have been circulated. The published report is titled *Public School Voucher Demonstration: The First Year at Alum Rock*, Rand Report no. 1495 prepared for the National Institute of Education (N.I.E.), June 1974.

the tests are truly important in judging school performance, especially if there is only a weak relationship between school achievement as measured by these tests and later success in the job market. They have, however, been committed to administering them and to publishing the results. In its deliberations Rand had to weigh two alternatives. If it publicly condemned the tests as irrelevant and misleading it would have to explain why it agreed to administer them in the first place. If it released the tests, or only casually called attention to their weaknesses, then Rand might be helping to support a false criterion for judging school effectiveness. Moreover, there has been a haunting fear among the evaluators that they have had to 'sell out' morally as a condition for 'buying-in' the goodwill of the funding agency whose support is crucial to the survival and health of the organization. Rand has been caught in a moral bind. If it does not fully disclose the limitations of the test scores as it sees them, it is being dishonest; but if it reveals the defects of the test, it is being inconsistent – how can you justify, except on the grounds of expediency, administering a test you do not believe in? The ethical conflict between integrity and consistency is difficult to resolve. The initial agreement by Rand to publish the test scores of the voucher experiment fully implicated the researchers in the findings of the study.

The handling of the test scores raises further moral questions, because there are conflicting public interests to be served. Leaving aside the question of the validity of the test, it seems clear that the principals and teachers in the experiment have a stake in avoiding publication of the findings. Early reports will hurt the morale of those responsible for the innovating programme. As one principal explained, 'When you plant something you don't tear up the roots to see if it's growing.' But the parents, as consumers and as tax payers, have a stake in early disclosure of the findings. The conflict between accountability and commitment surfaces with all new programmes because innovators are reluctant to expose their efforts to review lest this hurt their cause. The shortage of time is only one example of the kind of argument advanced to protect commitment.

I hasten to point out that equally difficult moral questions arise when the researchers are not so directly implicated as partners in the experiment. For example, researchers responsible for the negative income tax experiment in New Jersey discovered, to their dismay, that they could not in honesty tell the subjects of the experiment that all the information they provided would be held in confidence, as is customary in such studies. Congress, after all, has a legal right to review studies commissioned by the federal government, and it was prepared to exercise that right when it believed that the findings of the study could contribute to impending legislation on welfare reform. It was dissuaded from taking this course of action on the grounds that a review of individual cases in the absence of aggregate figures could be misleading. If, however, the researchers responded to the Congressional right to review and truthfully told their respondents that information acquired during interviews could be disclosed, they could also have forewarned them with what is technically known as a Miranda writ. And as a result of this warning, information acquired in the interview could be brought forward as evidence in a court trial. If the researcher was truthful to the interviewee he placed the latter in legal jeopardy; if he wanted to protect him legally from self-incrimination, the researcher could not be truthful about the conditions under which he worked.

Moral problems may plague the researcher; they also haunt the consumer of social scientific findings. Professions such as social work and planning cannot really claim that their interventions are built upon a tested body of knowledge. Intervention is justified more in terms of the values sought than the technology applied.

Few people today would wish to persuade the world that casework can be regarded as a technology pure and simple, and that casework policies can be developed on the basis of the facts, and the facts alone, about social organization. There is relatively little resistance against the idea that judgement has to be exercised on the facts . . . and that one of the most important ways in which judgement must be exercised is in regard to whether the facts of social life are good or bad, and whether it is possible to improve them. There is, of course, a great deal to be done to teach moral philosophy really adequately to social workers, but that is all the more an objective to be striven for, rather than to be neglected, in the future.[39]

39. T. S. Simey, *Social Science and Social Purpose*, Constable, 1968, p. 18.

Of course, the problem becomes even more difficult when the facts on which policy recommendations are based are themselves in doubt. Because there are no dependable laws to apply to important policy issues, because the information necessary to a decision is always incomplete, legislators, administrators and professionals must act on partial and unsatisfactory knowledge. What ethics or principles can serve the expert when the knowledge on which his advice is based is, by its nature, indeterminate and inconclusive? It is of little use to tell him that the knowledge he needs for a decision may eventually be available to decision takers of the future.

The Problem of Legitimation

This brings us to the third problem in integrating facts and values. How do we legitimate the role of analysis in policy making if we unashamedly announce that social scientists cannot separate factual and normative statements? After all, the social scientist's claim to participate in the process of decision taking is justified on the ground that he is concerned with means, not ends – a technician computing the best solution to a given problem.[40] His authority is technical and not moral. How can this problem be resolved? So long as his task is defined for him by some democratic process, he usurps no political prerogative. But in practice the best solution rarely looks the same from every legitimate point of view, and the advantages and disadvantages of alternative choices can hardly ever be estimated objectively in comparable terms. Let us take, for instance, the relatively limited question of highway layout. If the analyst's only problem were to maximize the flow of traffic, the technical choices might be manageable. But roads also destroy amenities, divert customers, and influence the development of housing, so that the decisions have different consequences for different people, and their gains and losses cannot be measured on a single yardstick. How does one weigh

40. For a more extended discussion of legitimacy, see Martin Rein and Peter Marris, 'Poverty and the Community Planners' Mandate', in Bernard Frieden and Robert Morris, eds., *Urban Planning and Social Policy*, New York, Basic Books, 1968, pp. 428–31.

unspoiled countryside against so much faster traffic? How does the noise and danger to a neighbourhood weigh against the convenience of the commuters? The choice lies between various kinds of benefits which are distributed unequally among different interests. But it is just such complex problems that most need rational assessment.

Because of the intrinsic difficulty of submitting social decisions to impartial cost–benefit analysis, it may be decided to abandon the attempt altogether, in favour of a more anarchic resolution of competing interests: if everyone campaigns for his own choice, a tolerable compromise should work itself out. Lindblom argues that 'one of the merits of partisan mutual adjustment is that it is adapted to situations in which there are no criteria adequate for resolution of a policy problem by a central decision maker'[41]. He believes that the mutual adjustment resulting from this process yields a rational assessment of alternatives. But although each individual decision maker may be calculating rationally, it does not follow that the collective outcome will also be rational. In practice, the outcome is characteristically much less constructive. Either the conflict ends in stalemate, or the compromise is scarcely rational from any point of view.

To avoid this situation, we need to put planning beyond the reach of short-sighted political considerations. An exploration of alternative choices can be convincingly analysed only in the absence of short-term political pressure. Therefore, at some stage, and to some degree, decisions must be taken out of the political context and handed over to the social scientist for analysis. The more complex the problem, and the longer the perspective within which it needs to be examined, the more decisive is the social scientist's influence likely to become. But such a review cannot be shielded from value considerations. So the crucial dilemma of planning cannot be avoided: the problems can best be solved by dispassionate analysts, but the costs and the benefits to be analysed do not lend themselves to objective assessment; they cannot be isolated from normative judgements that shape the analysis and constrain the alternatives assessed.

41. Charles E. Lindblom, *The Intelligence of Democracy: Decision Making Through Mutual Adjustment*, New York, Free Press of Glencoe, 1965, p. 296.

One can hope to avoid the difficulty by treating the planner as an advocate for one particular point of view. Since the complexity of social problems calls for expert analysis, why should not every interest promote its own plan? Even though they are not measurable, the costs and benefits of alternative decisions could then be evaluated in terms of the client's interest; the political conflict would be engaged between policies which were rational solutions at least from some standpoint. But since the outcome of political conflict is usually compromise, the fundamental difficulty merely reappears at another level. If the compromise between the plans of interested parties is itself to be rational, it too must be planned. Advocacy requires adjudication. Thus the social scientist as advocate implies another actor as judge who can interpret the arguments to the jury. And we are still left with the question: By what rational procedure does the arbitrator of social plans justify his recommendations? There is no satisfactory answer.

In practice, the consensus of values which seems to inform society frequently offers the analyst a frame of reference for his arguments. However, when the lack of consensus is itself the problem, this formulation cannot apply. Cleavages of interest cannot be settled by 'consensus'. They call for some decision mechanism such as arbitration. But we should exploit whatever consensus does prevail before we call for arbitration. Of course, a consensus is not a massive rock-like datum existing in a self-contained manner. It is eminently sensitive to 'feedback' of all kinds. Nevertheless there will be some common initial principles even if they are formulated at a very general level and easily pursued into mutual contradiction. There will also be conflicting interpretation of the consensus, but it does provide a context against which an analysis of problems and policies can be disinterestedly presented. And this suggests how research can relate to politics in a democratic society.

According to this perspective, political leadership is less concerned with deciding policy issues than with providing a language in which the issues can be argued. Its principal function in planning is not so much to endorse a specific outcome as to establish the assumptions on which an objective analysis of problems can be based. But this formulation of the political role is not altogether satisfactory. The daunting questions remain: Who will do the planning? Who will be helped? And who will be hurt? In this context, questions about power are inescapable. Still, even power cannot be exercised effectively without some measure of consensus. Those who are subordinate to power are willing to comply only so long as they believe the system is legitimate. And so we are, however reluctantly, driven back to a consideration of that elusive consensus on which the functioning of society depends.

If it is once accepted that the interaction of immediate interests need not result in a sensible policy from any point of view, the rest seems to follow. Some form of planning based on the analysis of evidence, and authoritative enough to override these interests, must intervene. But in a democratic society, governments at every level remain highly sensitive to the wishes of their electorate and every group is capable of applying political sanctions with the resources they command. The analysis of issues, therefore, has to be withdrawn from political control. The social scientist's only independent authority lies in the rationality of his analysis, and he cannot function without a generally accepted basis of normative argument in which fact and values are integrated. And since policy analysis deals in costs and benefits that can be assessed only subjectively, it must appeal to a common system of values, something only political leadership can provide. This in turn is supported by the electoral process, which is both crude and illogical as a means of deciding issues but works much more ably to define a consensus.

An argument of this kind can, in theory, confirm the social scientist's intellectual authority, because it can clarify the logical connection between his specific proposals and the shared values on which they ultimately rest; however, it helps him only where these values and their interpretation are indeed both shared and honoured. The political process is the primary means by which shared values are created. It is within the context of shared values that social scientists contribute to policy, and it is only in these circumstances that cumulative learning is possible.

Chapter 3
Values, Social Science and Social Policy

The Relationship between Reason and Purpose

It is almost universally acknowledged that rational thought should inform the development of public policies. The term 'rational thought' may not actually be used, but the view that policy should be the consequence of rational review is so thoroughly accepted that it is not seen to deserve notice. Yet, implicitly, the assumption remains.

Often this assumption is associated with the set of beliefs we might identify as the 'science and technology' dogma. According to these beliefs, the study of reality, science, produces fundamental understandings, and then another field concerned with practical applications, technology, solves problems of immediate human concern by applying the appropriate elements of our fundamental understanding. In the area of social policy, according to this view, we must develop an understanding of social reality so that we can subsequently apply that understanding to the development of policy. Research should be directed towards increasing our fundamental understanding of social conditions and the processes that create them. To seek understanding is not controversial. Although the proper interpretation and application of that understanding may call for unusual experience, insight and powers of invention, the research findings will contain the materials on which the practical application can be based. Administrative and political problems may inhibit the process but, in principle, it should be possible to complete the sequence of research leading to understanding and of understanding leading to recommendation. Or, in a more sophisticated form of this science and technology view, we may think of the process as iterative, believing that we can move from research to initial understanding to application, to more research, to further understanding and new application, to recognition of new problems, to still more research, etc. In short, a procedure can be established which allows for feedback.

These assumptions are not so much false as overstated. They are plausible, and so they contribute to inevitable frustration when an increase in scientific knowledge is not, after all, accompanied by an increase in our ability to design and change policy. Alice Rivlin, after attempting to evaluate the usefulness of the P.P.B.S. (Programming, Planning, Budgeting System) introduced in the Federal Government, concluded 'So far analysts have probably done more to reveal how difficult the problems and choices are than to make the decisions easier.'[1] Efforts to make use of systematically gathered and scientifically based information in policy decision making have revealed only how difficult it is to make choices when policy requires the synthesis of multiple, equally valued but conflicting objectives. A recent statement by Ida Merriam, Assistant Commissioner of Research for the Social Security Administration, expresses the frustration even more pointedly. She writes: 'There is a growing recognition that much of the federally supported extramural research, particularly in the social sciences, has added little or nothing either to basic knowledge or to practical decision-making.'[2] This view is widely held. Whether it is in fact valid must itself be the subject of further study.[3]

1. Alice M. Rivlin, *Systematic Thinking for Social Action*, Washington, D.C., The Brookings Institution, 1971.

2. Ida Merriam, 'Social Security Research: The Relation of Research and Policy Planning in a Government Agency', *Journal of Social Policy*, vol. 1, part 4, October 1972, p. 290.

3. I discussed five neglected paths between research and policy (research as containment, research as power, research as legitimation, research as policing and research as social reform) in 'Policy Research: Belief and Doubt' (with S. White), a paper presented at an international round-table on The Market for Policy Research conducted by the Committee on Political Sociology, I.P.S.A./I.S.A., and the Institut für Empirische Sozialforschung (EES Vienna) at Vienna, 29 September–3 October 1975.

Three obstacles appear to frustrate the potential contribution of empirical research and, more broadly defined, social science theory and knowledge to policy formulation. First, there is the inherent conflict in the political decision-making process: different people want different things and make use of the political process to satisfy their respective interests or 'disinterested' aspirations; second, reality is so complex it defeats our ability to locate the sphere of understanding which we should apply; third, knowledge presupposes a framework to interpret it, but in a pluralistic system there are only competing frameworks, and social science findings are seldom so conclusive that they permit a firm choice from among them. I want briefly to call attention to the first two types of obstacles and then to elaborate on the third.

Democracy and Rational Decision-Making

The conflict between rationality and democracy derives from the view, widely held among American political scientists, that there is no public interest which can be distinguished from sectional and group interests. 'The grounds advanced by the . . . group theorists for denying the existence of the public interest are that as any proposal which becomes practical politics is opposed by some group, there cannot therefore be a single public interest.'[4] Those who consider only private or sectional values real argue that their optima are adjusted in the democratic process, and that 'rationality equals the societal optimum' cannot be achieved in any other way. In democratic societies there are only conflicting interests, each seeking to maximize its influence through the political process. Even the desire by social scientists to make use of rational analysis in influencing public policy must also be interpreted as a form of partisanship, one rooted in the desire to win more influence for academics and, correspondingly, to weaken the influence of other groups who now shape policy. So the global, societal optimum is achieved through the interaction of many groups.

To make this general discussion about interest groups and

4. L. J. Sharpe, 'American Democracy Reconsidered', 1972, p. 48 (mimeograph).

information more concrete, we may consider the following situation. Policy concerned with the building of atomic-generating plants, so long as this remains only an economic issue, can be decided by reference to projections of future energy needs and by consideration of economies and diseconomies. There will, of course, be interest groups whose own economic stake is dependent on the use of one sort of fuel or another, or on continued expansion of energy resources, and so forth. But the bargaining points will be fairly clear to begin with, or will become so after a while, and compromise may be reached. If not, then the conflict will, at least, be between clearly identified adversaries over clearly defined issues. There is a procedure for resolving conflicts of efficiency which is generally accepted. But when construction of the atomic-generating plant takes on social implications, when it is recognized that the plant will contribute new danger to its environs or raise issues about the social consequences of various waste disposal programmes, the matter becomes more complex. Threats to environment, safety and so on, complicate the planning problem, but it is not simply a matter of 'social' v. 'non-social' values. If the danger to the environment is great, society must renounce a major source of energy, i.e., sacrifice abundance of energy, a crucial value, for the sake of the even more important one of safety, survival, etc. But those who argue on the other side are not necessarily unethical and anti-social. Energy requirements are also a 'social' need. Now there are sharply conflicting values and many more parties than can easily be dealt with; they include all those who were previously engaged and, in addition, defenders of the neighbourhood or community and environmentalists. Compromises become extraordinarily difficult to work out, partly because so much of the cost, to all of the parties at least, is in their anticipated quality of life. It helps, of course, to have as much understanding as possible of the reality under debate; but the debate cannot be ended by this additional understanding; and as the debate becomes more complex, and the competing values and interest groups become more visible, the issue may appear insoluble. Nor could it have been entirely anticipated that the pollution potential of the enterprise would become a salient public issue. Economic gain and loss is a persistent concern, but beliefs about what determines the quality of our lives are constantly changed and redefined. There is no consensus about how costs and benefits to different groups should be assessed or how much weight should be assigned to economic gains and social externalities.

There is an intractable conflict of purposes between political decision-making, which is about the power of competing interest groups, and analytic research, which is about rational problem solving. Rationality does not, in this context, imply that some definable logical procedure has been followed which has exhaustively scrutinized all possible options or considered all relevant information. Rather, it suggests that, at the least, the process of making a decision made use of whatever resources of knowledge, judgement, imagination and analysis were available in the circumstances. The question is not whether we should utilize *all* the scientific information we can get, but what are the relevant scientific facts. To disregard real, scientifically discoverable risks is irrational. The worrying questions are whether the political system is capable of acting intelligently in some non-partisan sense. And is the whole notion of impartial intelligence inapplicable because there is no common good or established means of determining it?

One suggestion for the resolution of these problems is to distinguish between questions of implementation and questions of policy. Questions of implementation assume that the objective is given and ask only how to reach it, or what other unintended consequences might follow from its pursuit or achievement. Questions of policy, by contrast, ask for an ordering of goals or objectives and are by nature less amenable to dispassionate understanding.

But efforts to distinguish between ends and means are often superficial. The consideration of one requires elimination of the other. But although policy and research may be distinct from one another conceptually, there is a natural interplay between them when they operate in the real world, and little is to be gained from trying to delineate their separate terrains.

Other efforts to integrate research and the political process argue that research must accommodate itself to the political process. The analyst should first understand how decisions are taken in government, and then, based on this understanding, determine where and how in the process research can best be introduced. Research it is argued must be more flexible and resilient if it is to be of use to political leaders and administrative heads.

Still others take the view that 'There can be no agreement either on goals or on societal relationships that link programme inputs to sought-after outputs . . . American society is inherently incapable of being goal-oriented for deep-seated ideological reasons; accordingly, applied cybernetic rationality cannot be the basis of social accounting.'[5] Setting aside ideological issues, the extraordinary difficulty of reconciling and weighting multiple and conflicting interests limits the potential for rational policy making. We must accept, therefore, as the best solution whatever the political process produces. But sometimes those who hold this view go farther by *identifying the political process itself with rational decision-making*. The disjointed–incremental school holds that when certain conditions are met, such as representation of all interested parties in the political process, the outcome must yield a rational decision. This is what Mannheim termed 'procedural rationality'. But this view is also vulnerable. Though the process may be just, its product may still be both unjust and unrelated to the knowledge base.

The Complexity of Social Phenomena

Even where there are no immediate clashes of interest, implementation of research findings may still be problematic because of the complexity of the situation for which the policy is proposed. Head Start offers an example. It is not at all clear where the roots of academic competence are to be found, or how strong is the link between academic achievement and future earnings; and so the underlying theory of the programme is uncertain. But if we assume that academic competence does begin with very early

5. Brian J. L. Berry, 'Social Accounting Systems: Problems in Conceptualization and Realization', (a paper presented at the annual meeting of the National Academy of Sciences, May 1972).

exposure to academic tools, and accept such competence as a good in its own right, we would still have to know how schools, teachers, families and peers impinged on Head Start students in order to discover precisely how the scheme worked. I do not claim that the programme does not work or should not have been tried. But I do suggest that in social areas the success of an application depends on the impact of diverse factors in addition to the one we regard as fundamental.

In this context, it may be useful to distinguish between the laws which emerge from physical laboratories and, in turn, guide applied research in the industrial laboratories, as opposed to the kind of understanding which comes out of the sociological study of real situations, but which rarely leads to the formulation of strict causal laws. In the 'laboratory' sciences, there are strict (causal) and probabilistic regularities; in the human setting, there are many 'regularities' – regularly experienced needs, 'habits', conduct regularized by norms[6] – but there is also 'spontaneous' non-habitual behaviour – play, imagination, etc. These tend to describe the functioning of what Lawrence Frank has called 'organized complexities'. These complexities are affected by external events, and so long as the externalities are unknown, there will be uncertainties about the future even though we may have full knowledge about the past.

Inferences based on past research can never be applied to a situation that has 'significantly' changed. And the likelihood of significant change in social areas seems unusually great. For this reason, knowledge in the policy arena is not entirely self-correcting. Scientific research requires that one continues to experiment until the experimental results and the theory correspond, with the data serving as a correction to the theory and the theory as a guide to the experiment. But in policy-oriented research, there is no way of anticipating dramatic changes in the social context which will have serious consequences for the implementation of

6. Other regularities also exist; for example, some have been identified in relation to the dependence of young children on attachment figures for healthy development. This example has important applications that are not immediate – for instance for personality in later life, and for the problems early deprivation can create.

whatever policies are selected. A reasoned argument based on past situations must surrender to the uncertainty of future events, thus weakening the knowledge base from which policy proceeds.

Ideology and Research

These problems of competing interests and the complexities involved in predicting social events lead to the suggestion that we replace our former model of rational thought with a new one. In this modified model we would not expect research to lead from understanding to policy, but would see each policy as a probe enabling us to acquire new insights into the current nature of reality.

But this more modest model is also faulty. The difficulty arises from our own processes of learning and organizing understanding. New information is assimilated into a paradigm that is remarkably persistent and resistant to change. Policy paradigms are a curious admixture of psychological assumptions, scientific concepts, value commitments, social aspirations, personal beliefs and administrative constraint. They are not able to organize disparate evidence and predict future patterns. They are more like personal belief systems, not entirely manifest, encompassing various contradictions rather than seeking to eliminate them. We clearly need to distinguish between personal and collective paradigms, but we do not understand much about the development of either.

The term paradigm is used here to suggest a working model of why things are as they are, a problem-solving framework, which implies values and benefits but also procedures, habits of thought, and a view of how society functions. It often provides a guiding metaphor of how the world works which implies a general direction for intervention: it is more specific than an ideology or a system of beliefs but broader than a principle of intervention. The concept of the poverty cycle is an example of a policy paradigm. The image of a vicious cycle provides a working model of the causal interactions that are believed to result in poverty, a moral interpretation of the responsibility for intervening in this causal chain and a guide to the interventions that are therefore relevant and right.

Typically we incorporate new sources of knowledge and information so that they are compatible with the policy paradigm we hold. And while it does appear that new paradigms will under certain circumstances achieve hegemony, the process by which this occurs is not well understood. Some will argue that it is not so much that people change their paradigms as that the people who hold unsatisfactory ones die out or are repudiated. Yet to suggest that individuals never change their paradigms is to over-state the case. Some individuals change their minds when there is strong invalidating information or when somebody proposes a 'better' paradigm; or they revise their sense of reality in response to depressions and wars. But whether the often ambiguous and incomplete information derived from social science research can also serve to modify our belief systems seems in general unlikely, unless we have only loose attachment to these beliefs.

Let us consider a specific example to illustrate how a paradigm can resist change. In cities throughout the United States there has been a substantial increase in educational expenditure for ghetto schools through the introduction of compensatory programmes. But studies of these efforts indicate that they have contributed little to changing the level of educational achievement as measured by standardized tests. A Rand study which reviewed educational reforms such as the augmentation of resources, improvements in the processes and methods of education, and variations in the organizational environment of the school, came to the conclusion that 'Research has found nothing that consistently and unam-biguously makes a difference in student outcomes . . . Research has not discovered any educational practice that offers a high probability of success.'[7] What can be said about these findings? After the methodological arguments have been aired, the implica-tions remain stubbornly inconclusive, largely because the same evidence can be used to support sharply different views. Those who were initially committed to the reduction of educational

7. Harvey A. Averech and others, *How Effective is Schooling? A Critical Review and Synthesis of Research Findings*, Rand Corporation, December 1971, p. iv.

inequality can argue that the findings demonstrate only that not enough has been done. Those who were initially sceptical that academic potential can be modified will say that the findings confirm their presumptions.

Some people believe that even when programmes fail, commitment to them must be sustained by the Government because when we jettison programmes we also abandon commitment to the ideals they represent. Moreover the programmes may be rejected prematurely as failures: 'Let us suppose that a man is drowning thirty feet from shore. A rescuer throws him ten feet of rope. He drowns. It would scarcely be logical to conclude: "Rope is no use in the prevention of drowning." '[8] Failure, according to this framework, usually demonstrates that the programme had not tried hard enough, long enough, consistently enough, and with sufficient resources to accomplish its task. In his message to Congress in support of the Equal Educational Opportunities Act of 1972, President Nixon partly adopted this view:

While there is a great deal yet to be learned about the design of successful compensatory programmes, the experience so far does point in one crucial direction: to the importance of providing sufficiently concentrated funding to establish the educational equivalent of a 'critical mass', or threshold level. Where funds have been spread too thinly, they have been wasted or dissipated with little to show for their expenditure. Where they have been concentrated, the results have been frequently encouraging and sometimes dramatic.

Others, however, begin with the belief that Government intervention is ineffective in most areas of social policy, or worse still, that it generates more problems than it solves. They interpret information that reports the limited success of educational inter-

8. *New York Times*, 27 February 1973, 'The Short Rope'. This editorial rejects a statement in President Nixon's radio talk on 'Human Resources' where the President asserts that money for social programmes to aid the poor had flowed from Washington 'in a seemingly inexhaustible flood'. The *Times* argued that there was no flood and that 'Every Great Society social program was seriously underfunded – at levels below Congressional authorization – because of spending on the Vietnam War between 1966 and 1969 ... Some of the ... programs' need more money, others need more time.

vention, for example, only in such a way that it corroborates what they already knew; and so they recommend that the programmes be ended or assigned a low fiscal priority. Government should do as little as it can politically get away with. If the data had shown that there was improvement, they might have raised the issue of the cost required to produce a benefit, or they might have explained that the success was due to 'creaming'. Positive findings are perhaps a bit *more difficult to explain away* than negative findings, but the difficulties are not insuperable – just as negative findings can be discounted as the result of measurement errors, or the diffuseness of goals, or of an insufficient input. In the very frequent instance of inconclusive findings, different parties can choose which findings they will pay attention to. In these and other ways paradigms can be defended against new data. Research findings may be used to support the view you already hold, but if they do not support it, they need not be interpreted as invalidating it.

These conclusions are not limited to one field of social policy, nor are they fresh insights unnoticed by other observers. In his reflections on the vigorous academic debate over the bussing of children to racially integrated schools and whether it affects their school performance, James Q. Wilson has formulated two general laws to cover all cases where social scientific evaluation judges public policy programmes. He argues that either all or no interventions produce their intended effect, depending on the prior beliefs held by those who conduct the inquiry. This anomaly arises largely because different standards of evidence and methods are applied, but also because the same evidence is subjected to different interpretation and weighting.

Studies that conform to the First Law will accept an agency's own data about what it is doing and with what effect; adopt a time frame (long or short) that maximizes the probability of observing the desired effect; and minimize the search for other variables that might account for the effect observed. Studies that conform to the Second Law will gather data independently of the agency; adopt a short time frame that either minimizes the chance for the desired effect to appear or, if it does appear, permits one to argue that the results are 'temporary' and probably due to ... the reaction of the subjects to the fact that they are part of an experiment; and maximize the search for other variables that might explain the effects observed.[9]

Social Policy Framework and Utilization of Research

I have briefly reviewed three obstacles that inhibit the influence of research on policy development. The first two difficulties, namely that of reconciling the ideals of democracy with those of impartial rationality, and the complexity of the social events which research needs to understand and predict, have received attention in the literature of the subject. Neglected, but perhaps of greater importance, is the third problem: that all knowledge must relate to a framework of interpretation, because only thus does any information make sense. If knowledge is to be useful in a collective way, politics aside, a widely shared viewpoint of interpretation is required. There are, however, only competing perspectives, and research, which makes sense only in terms of them, is unable to help in choosing among them. This conclusion offends our cherished belief that learning from experience is not only necessary but possible. If policy commitments are only with difficulty informed by evidence, what can we count on? What can we do?

The work of Kuhn, especially his concept that paradigms are replaced in response to crisis, may be relevant for understanding the contribution of social-science research to established policy paradigms. Kuhn argues that science does not develop only by the gradual accumulation of new knowledge, the correction of previous error, and the addition of new discoveries, but by a series of crises in adaptation. Normal science begins with puzzle solving within the context of an accepted paradigm that organizes disciplinary realities. Anomalies are discovered from the usual puzzle-solving activities, and these become increasingly hard to assimilate into the dominant paradigm. A scientific crisis emerges when scientists become aware that the paradigm's organizing capacity has collapsed and a substitute is at hand. Because there is a substitute available, abandonment of the earlier paradigm

9. James Q. Wilson, 'On Pettigrew and Armor: An After Thought', *Public Interest*, no. 30, winter 1973, p. 133.

becomes possible. Otherwise, people will still cling to the earlier formulations. The crisis is followed by a scientific revolution in which a new integrative paradigm is constructed, usually by the powerful insight of a single man of genius – although fundamental discoveries are seldom unique. What follows then is a struggle for acceptance, because the new paradigm offers a reformulation of the problem and a redefinition of the kinds of data that bear on it. In times of crisis, the scientific criteria of interpretation are themselves in doubt. The acceptance of the new paradigm is a strategic decision based on the judgement that it will contribute to a more complete understanding. As such, it is very much like a radical policy decision. Over time the new paradigm is itself subject to a broadly similar process of challenge and assault. Galileo's new physics was revolutionary; it toppled one academic élite structure and eventually brought a new one into being. But relativistic physics left the establishment essentially unchanged. Science, then, develops as an alternation of crises and sustained exploration of an established line of thought.[10]

Turning to social science, one can see a parallel with Kuhn's interpretation of the development of science. Knowledge about social issues, to be useful in a collective way, presupposes a widely accepted framework to interpret it. By analogy with Kuhn's analysis, we would expect:

(1) That research is not generally designed to challenge the paradigm but to develop understanding within the framework of its assumptions. That is, if a policy does not work, the evaluation is not taken to discredit it but to refine and convert the particular application of the theory. The negative evaluation is itself challenged and fault found with the method by which the research conclusions were reached. This procedure should lead to continual improvements in the power and sophistication of the theory and to more successful applications.

(2) That this process will lead in time to a crisis of confidence

10. Thomas Kuhn, *The Spreading of Scientific Revolutions*, 2nd ed., University of Chicago Press, 1970, pp. 10–25. For criticisms of Kuhn, see I. Latakos and A. Musgrave, eds., *Criticism and the Growth of Knowledge*, Cambridge University Press, 1970.

in the theory, when it begins to show more and more unaccountable inconsistencies with the evidence. A new theory, with different implications, a different sense of moral responsibility, a re-conception of the problem, will then take its place and run the same course.

But does the relationship between research and social policy follow this pattern? Are there really social policy paradigms? Is there ever such a consensus of approach? And if these paradigms direct research, does research reciprocally undermine the paradigm? Science is a more or less enclosed system, with research its whole life. But research is only one influence (perhaps a very small influence) on the determination of social policy. There are two possible approaches to these questions. The *sceptical* position leaves little scope for research to contribute to policy; the cautiously *optimistic* view suggests a potential role for research and is preoccupied with ways by which this role could be made more effective. Both perspectives warrant further analysis and debate. As with most competing paradigms, evidence can be marshalled in support of either interpretation. I shall discuss both here and then develop at further length the more optimistic one. Choice between them is a matter of faith, not truth. 'Faith' and 'truth' are not mutually exclusive, truth implying faith, but not vice versa. If we consider a proposition true, we *cannot* refuse to believe in it. If we believe in a proposition, we can still grant the possibility that we may be mistaken. Even so, the pragmatic interested in policy research may assume, as an act of faith, that if the quality of his work is good, it will be worth while and useful in the long run, even if he cannot know whom it will influence or when. There is no more sense in his worrying about the ultimate validity of his enterprise than in a scientist worrying about the philosophical foundations of induction. It is much easier in practice to recognize good research – its moral sensitivity, the coherence and power of its interpretation, the carefulness of its method, the quality of its evidence, and the imaginativeness of its insight – than it is to explain why or for what purpose it is good.

A Sceptical View

There is seldom, if ever, a consensus over policy: there are always competing paradigms. So research on social policy never acquires the relative consistency of interpretations found in scientific work. For example, much of the writing on poverty has taken place within a conceptual framework that sees poverty as a function of inadequate opportunities or resources to establish a reasonable quality of life. As this framework is developed, it absorbs data about the lesser opportunities of the poor for advancement, their inadequate living conditions, their greater incidence of disease and their lower life expectancy. All these observations extend and enrich the fundamental idea that poverty is injustice and that much of this injustice has to do with in-equitable distribution. But these same data, perhaps given different emphases, and organized with different observations, could contribute to the enrichment and development of other frameworks or paradigms. For example, poverty may be seen as another culture, a way of life in which, perhaps, having uncommitted time is more important than the amassing of human capital through education or job experience. Virtually the same data, given different weighting and organized differently, can serve both paradigms. Clearly the interpretation of research findings is always controversial, because they are related to different paradigms held by different people, and there is no rational method of arbitrating between these interpretations.

Besides, policy is determined by a complex perception of social, economic and political issues on which social science theory and empirical research findings are only one, rather obscure, influence. Policy paradigms change in response to social, economic and political changes – that is, they change because they have to rationalize a different reality, not because research has revealed that the interpretation of earlier circumstances was wrong. Nevertheless, when socio-political and economic realities change, there is a scramble for new ideas, and a new perspective is sought to serve as an organizing framework for the development of specific programmes. This new policy framework is, of course, determined by ideological preferences as well as by social and political realities, for the emergence of new concepts and basic presuppositions, or their becoming suddenly 'respectable', seems to be an essential component of 'social change'. But the older frameworks are not altogether forsaken: administrative pragmatism and eclecticism provide continuity with the past. So policy influences new theoretical formulations, inspires research, and fashions the relevance of the findings but the reverse relationship does not hold.

An Optimistic View

The main planks in the sceptics' platform are, first, that evidence does not help in the social choice between competing frameworks of thought and, second, that research follows policy developments and the framework of values which contains them, but the process is never reversed. The optimistic view holds that public policy typically evolves from what is initially a common framework of thought, without which there would be no action at all. Research in the short run contributes to policy when findings are consistent with the accepted framework. In the long run, research and theory contribute also to alterations in the framework. As a policy-relevant social science develops in sophistication and experience, it will increasingly serve policy objectives. Studies of the utilization of commissioned and non-commissioned research in the decision-making process would, if an adequate time frame were adopted, reveal that there is more scope for high-quality social scientific investigation than the sceptics allege.

We may consider the optimistic position in more detail. It does seem clear that no consensual social theory is as well worked out as the major theories in the natural sciences. Nevertheless, some paradigms and interpretive frameworks are dominant in political action. They are translated into legislative programmes that reflect, at least for the moment, views held by large segments of the population. Policy does represent a consensual framework for action. T. H. Marshall argues that 'Without a foundation of near consensus no general social welfare policy would be possible.'[11]

11. T. H. Marshall, 'Value Problems of Welfare Capitalism', *Journal of Social Policy*, vol. 1, January 1972, p. 20.

Such a consensus is an intrinsic part of most stable contemporary societies, although it is not possible to say with precision where the consensus comes from. Marshall believes that it is part of an autonomous ethical system that is neither the summation of individual preferences, as revealed in the market, nor the outcome of interest-group policies mediated by the democratic process. By its nature, this system of values is intrinsically authoritarian and paternalistic.

While multiple and complex social policies exist among the sub-units of government at all levels, the conflicts between them are nevertheless subordinated to the more general social policy that contains them. Policy flourishes when the consensus is strongest (e.g., after wars and economic reversals).

If policy is largely framed within a consensual framework, then the sceptics' position is overstated. Social science knowledge does contribute to the improvement of social programmes when that knowledge is based upon widely shared values and when the political competition among vested interest groups is at a minimum. We would expect research findings to be particularly useful when social science inquiry does not attempt to demonstrate that values should be changed. This occurs in a field of settled policy, where the crucial tasks are administration and implementation. In addition research agendas defined by policy makers will also be informed by the consensus.

The usefulness of research for policy varies with the type of research undertaken, its source of financing and its administrative relationship to the policy maker. The urgent question is how to reorganize and re-finance research so that it can better serve policy objectives. One approach takes the view that politicians and administrators should just specify the knowledge they require and then purchase it from universities and other sources, paying a reasonable fee for a product called 'information'. Commissioned studies such as these create little tension between research and action, since the researchers have a contractual obligation to provide a product specified in advance. As a result their research is likely to be used. Indeed when research is undertaken at a high degree of particularity it is most likely to meet the requirements of administration and fit within an acceptable framework.

Research is most likely to be accepted and applied successfully when the primary task of the study is technical – to devise ways to alter the known poor fit between available resources and accepted aims. For example, how can a city's fire service be reorganized so that it is more efficient and effective in its own terms? Here research will provide better ways of getting things done within the existing bureaucratic terms of reference.

Research can also be useful to policy when it sets out to discover negative side effects that can threaten the political acceptability of a programme. Sometimes a government commissions *ex ante* studies which check the effects of a programme. For example, in 1971 the British Parliament decided to discontinue the provision of free school milk to children over seven years of age. To quell political opposition, the bill called for a dietary and clinical survey of children in selected areas to monitor the impact of the policy on the physical well-being of the children exposed to it.[12]

This type of research may be called 'applied research' in contrast with 'basic research' proceeding from the social scientist's discipline rather than from immediate policy considerations. Here the research questions, methods and time requirements are not framed to take account of the political constraints of power and the bureaucratic constraints of mandate, and this accounts for their limited usefulness in the short run. The Rothschild report[13] on research policies for Britain makes this distinction between 'basic research' and 'applied research and development', and argues that apart from a small fixed proportion of research funds to be allocated for freewheeling or basic research, most research funds available to scholars outside the Government should be allocated by Government Departments acting as 'customers' to academics acting as 'research contractors'. The customer will both specify the problem to be studied and review the methods of inquiry. The more immediate, as well as the long-range, require-

12. The example is drawn from a stimulating memorandum prepared by Antony King, University of Essex, entitled 'On Studying the Impacts of Public Policies', January 1972, p. 2 (mimeograph).

13. 'The Organization and Management of Government R & D', *A Framework for Government Research and Development* (Cmnd 4814), H.M.S.O., 1971.

ments of government departments will shape the research agenda. This policy accepts as a self-evident truth the proposition that research studies requested by administrators and politicians, and paid for by the government department that commissions them, will be useful to policy makers because they are based upon an intellectual perspective shared by both researchers and government. It follows from this viewpoint that if the research interests derive from a perspective which is not shared by the government, the immediate usefulness of the findings will be in question. Only if the findings are so compelling or so graphic as to convince those who do not share the same framework of thought will this not be true. And for the reasons reviewed earlier, this seldom occurs. When the dominant paradigm is stable, the less the framework is shared, the less immediate will be the impact of research on policy in the short run. However, when paradigms are in transition, research that challenges earlier frameworks may become more, rather than less, influential. (This will be reviewed later.)

But the approach suggested by the Rothschild report worries those responsible for inaugurating research. It robs them of the autonomy they deem essential for independent and creative analysis; it substitutes short-term experimental gains for lasting and more fundamental insights, and it thus threatens what is most essential to science – open, independent inquiry informed by the researchers' curiosity, with minimum external constraints. Moreover, the policy itself is untested, for it is not based upon any prior analysis of the relationship between research use and the nature of the contractual relationship with researchers.

An alternative approach to increasing research's usefulness to government has been expounded by David Donnison. It calls attention to the weakness of the process by which knowledge is diffused and relevant information assimilated. The knowledge needed by the policy maker may be available but he does not have access to it, either because he fails to recognize that it exists, or because the information is so technical that he does not appreciate its practical usefulness. What are needed are intermediaries who can effectively relate the four autonomous segments of a highly interrelated system – those of politics where policy is made, technology where hard and soft innovations are born, professional and administrative practice where established policies are implemented, and research. 'We must develop social networks of creative, well-trained scholars with a policy oriented turn of mind, capable of moving in and between the worlds of practice, politics and technology. They must be firmly rooted in the academic world – whether they work in universities or not – so that they keep in touch, intellectually speaking, with students and colleagues there.'[14]

There are numerous variations on the general theme that policy makers and researchers must find ways to interact with each other. Some researchers view the policy maker as part of the research process and insist that both meet periodically to discuss their tentative findings, so that users of the research product are involved in the process of study. They assume that participation enhances the policy makers' commitment to use the study results and encourages them to see research as a process and not simply a conclusion.

On the other hand research may be viewed not as a cooperative venture in which it serves as an ally to established policies (whether by formal contractual relationship or by an informal process of communication and learning), but as part of a political process which involves disagreement and contention. It can represent either the natural function of a machine which works well, or a factor contributing to the breakdown of the machine, so that a different type of operating mechanism may become necessary.

Research may serve as moral witness or social critic. When it does so, it accepts, in common with those studies commissioned by government, a shared set of goals and a shared conception of the instruments and processes for achieving them. And in good Weberian tradition, the researcher maintains that the social scientist has no authority to challenge these statements of purpose. He is not trying to persuade those who hold different values or are committed to alternative means of achieving them. He is merely making internal criticisms of the means–ends chain to show how those involved in a given policy have failed to understand the

14. David Donnison, 'Research for Policy', *Minerva*, vol. X, no. 4, October 1972.

consequences of their own actions. This kind of research also assumes that once negative facts are known, everyone must accept their moral implications. It proceeds from the premise that there is a consensus of opinion about purposes, so that if the facts are valid, and the implications are judged undesirable, government will act to rectify the conditions or account for its failure to do so. Research is thus used as a strategy of shame, to embarrass government into doing what it accepts as morally right. Of course, when government's declaration of intent turns out to be only symbolic exposure will not lead to effective action but to a scramble for new symbolic programmes.

This strategy sometimes requires modification. Research can monitor whether policy is achieving what it has set out to do only if government has a policy to implement, that is, if it has established a definite, unambiguous course of action directed to a specific and definable aim. But this is seldom the case. Government typically lacks coherent policies. For example, it may spend money on in-patient health services, community care and hospital construction; and these expenditures will lead to a very definite pattern of resource allocation within the field of medical care. But this pattern is brought about by the independent decisions of a wide variety of bodies, each made disjointedly, incrementally, and unrelated to each other. Government as a whole has no overall resource allocation policy; hence research cannot demonstrate a mismatch between aims, underlying processes and outcomes. In these circumstances, research may act as social critic calling attention to the failure of government to 'consciously choose a particular course of action or a particular allocation of resources'.[15] It cannot act as moral witness demonstrating how government has failed to honour its commitments, because there were no commitments; government had surrendered to a non-policy. Research as social criticism may, in addition, set out to show that the picture of reality implied by existing intervention is false, muddled or inconsistent. The outcomes cannot be as intended, either because there was no initial intent or because the world works in a different way from that imagined by the policy makers.

Research as moral witness and as social criticism is much harder

15. King, op. cit.

for governments to assimilate, to accept, and to act upon in the short run than are consensual studies. This is partly because it challenges the conventional interpretation of reality and because it does not accept the constraints of resources and purposes under which governments act. But even here research does not question the values themselves, except indirectly, by implying that something has gone wrong in the weighting and ordering of multiple and conflicting aims. Nevertheless the governments do, over time, come to incorporate the views of their critics. Thus, research that is either consensual (contract research and intermediaries who make the supply and demand system for information work effectively) or contentious (moral witness and social critic) can influence the direction of policy.

The optimistic argument reviewed so far establishes only a limited terrain within the framework of a dominant paradigm in which research can contribute to shaping policy. But can more detached analysis that challenges the very assumptions on which policy operates also exert influence?[16]

Dominant policy paradigms are by no means static and un-resilient. They may resist falsification, but they are also open to development. They evolve over time. And social science ideas, together with social, political, and economic changes, play a role in the development of these policy paradigms. The influence of research is often diffuse, oblique, and always embedded in the changes it reflects. The process is a complicated one and it is difficult, if not impossible, to isolate the unique role of research and to disentangle whether research is a cause of policy or a consequence of it. For the interplay of knowledge and ideals, political manoeuvre and intelligent problem-solving is bound to be very subtle, ambiguous and complicated – a subject which is itself an important theme for empirical research.

Schematically, it may be possible to represent one possible

16. When it attempts to examine the values that underpin policy, research may take the form of a philosophical reappraisal of ethical and ideological perspectives rather than an inquiry into facts and realities. Polemical essays such as Michael Young's *The Rise of the Meritocracy* can be as perceptive and revealing as more empirically based studies, because they spell out the logical consequences of pursuing a particular perspective.

context in which research contributes to basic policy changes. First, there is a broad consensual framework, which represents what Parsons calls common values. These common values have an integrative effect upon society. Social processes are, by definition, a mode of integration of social action: the very fact that we have a society means that basic value differences among men will be worked out. Society is a collection of potentially mutually beneficial interacting units. This consensus, in turn, helps to create a political context that shapes research priorities and helps to define what is regarded as useful inquiry and acceptable social science theory. Values, politics, and research form a closely interwoven fabric. Over time there are discernible changes in the character of the fabric. These are brought about by technological changes, which, in turn, influence events as well as following them. Thus research is not simply a passive servant to its economic and political masters. It moulds, as well as is moulded by, the consensual framework of values that prevail in society at any time. In this process, social science research and theory help to evolve an ideology of thought; and this in turn influences the values that subtly alter the economic, social, and political context as well as being influenced by them. Social science may take the form of social criticism during one era, and its ideas may be repudiated for the moment because they threaten the *status quo*. But in other periods, especially during times of economic change and political unrest, there is a search for new ideas to help legitimate, make understandable, and direct these broader societal forces.

It seems that the optimistic view must assume an integrative concept of society defined in terms of common values, and it must reject the competing view that the mode of any society is a predominantly conflicting one. If it is possible to show at any moment in time that a consensus of opinion has been achieved this might lend support to the argument that society is best viewed in an integrative mode. But supporters of the conflicting model of society assume that a common value framework and stability are achieved through the imposition of one group's standards on another: integration can thus be interpreted as the dominance of one group. Power in society allows only the realization of the goals of the dominant group, and it frustrates the goals of the subservient ones.

Two examples set within different time perspectives may illustrate how research can help to change policy paradigms. The first example, taken from the field of mental health, explores how the subtleties of the processes are worked out in the short run, over a period of a decade or so. The second, tracing the development of policy in regard to those who are economically destitute, looks at the same process over a much longer period spanning two centuries. Robert Rapaport has suggested that the diffusion of social science knowledge may follow a biological analogy: new ideas, like new organs, may first be rejected by the body, but then may gradually experience semi-acceptance, until finally the new organ is incorporated. A theory to account for this process of repudiation and final embrace of social science knowledge has not yet been developed. Some who have observed the phenomenon feel that intermediaries and an informed network of colleagues play important roles. To understand the contribution of research to organizational policy, it is necessary to take into account the time-lag between initiation and acceptance, and the subtle process of rejection and partial or eventual acceptance, since this may take place over a period of several generations.[17]

A study undertaken at the Chestnut Lodge Sanitorium and eventually published by Stanton and Schwartz in their classic book *The Mental Hospital* illustrates how the diffusion of research findings can operate in practice. The study, by a sociologist and a psychiatrist, attempted to show the potential scope of 'milieu therapy' for patients in a mental hospital. The analysis provided a critique of psycho-analytically oriented psychotherapy, that emphasizes one-to-one relationships between a patient and his physician in isolation from the administrative and organizational milieu in which the therapy takes place. The researchers tried, in their inquiry, to document the ways in which the context undermines the therapeutic process. They isolated specific social processes, such as covert disagreement among the staff, and were able to illustrate the effects on patient behaviour. So this research

17. Robert N. Rapaport, 'The Therapeutic Community Revisited: Some Aspects of Social Science Diffusion' (mimeograph, n.d.).

revealed an important flaw. It weakened the belief (the paradigm) that recovery from mental illness can be achieved solely through interaction between the patient and his therapist. This critique of the hospital's operating assumptions was so fundamental that the hospital as a whole could not accept its implications for the running of the institution, nor its implicit and explicit recommendations, without witnessing a major upheaval. And although the research study, which received wide acclaim, was accepted as an important analysis by members of the staff of the host hospital, its findings were ignored. The study was widely read by professionals in other institutions and by the next generation of sociologists and clinicians. There is little doubt that at least some people had already come to believe in the desirability of reaching a different balance between individual and milieu therapy. The introduction of new drugs around 1956 provided a new technology, and this could now make a different approach feasible. But in order to present a cogent argument for their views, its exponents had needed empirical research that provided persuasive documentation. The Stanton and Schwartz book, published in 1954,[18] provided a useful ally. Together with subsequent research that tried to link social form and patient behaviour, it helped influence the general climate of opinion by making available for the first time empirical evidence that offered intellectual justification for a new approach. Although this point of view had always been in the intellectual climate, no evidence had been marshalled to demonstrate or articulate it. It was only after the study became known that the framework was accepted as a serious therapeutic approach. Findings of the study came, in time, to play an important role in the education of clinically oriented personnel. Thus teachers served as intermediaries linking research to its potential users, and young people going to work in state hospitals were influenced by the general notions underpinning the research, and further developed its implications for the structuring of wards. Some of the younger psychiatrists who worked at Chestnut Lodge at the time the study was conducted, and were influenced by it, also carried the concepts to other

18. Alfred H. Stanton and Morris S. Schwartz, *The Mental Hospital*, New York, Basic Books, 1954.

hospitals and saw them implemented. They too played the role of intermediaries, spreading the approach to new settings. There is unfortunately no firm evidence that the hospital which initially rejected the findings came later to be influenced by them. But institutions are not monolithic. They do not react as a whole to innovative ideas. Apparently some members or units of the hospital came, in time, to accept certain aspects of the study; and several other milieu projects did follow the Stanton and Schwartz study. But it is difficult to establish whether these reflected the interests only of specific staff members or acceptance of the findings and the general approach by the hospital as a whole.

As a second example of how studies contribute to changing policies, we can review the treatment of the poor. In Britain early-nineteenth-century political economy developed the view that those who accepted poor relief should be 'less eligible' or more uncomfortable than the lowest paid independent labourer. This guiding metaphor was translated into legislation and embodied in the Poor Law Amendment Act of 1834. Implementing this principle required a major policy innovation. A central authority and a small paid inspectorate set out to abolish the local practice of aiding the destitute in their own homes (outdoor relief). Relief was to be offered only to those who agreed to enter a workhouse. These were then to be classified as able-bodied and non-able-bodied, and the able-bodied were to be subjected to the principle of 'less eligibility'. The aim of the legislation was to drive the able-bodied poor back into the labour market where they could win personal dignity through work. The New Poor Law was interpreted as a final solution to the problem of pauperism, for it would reshape the moral character of the able-bodied poor.

These administrative reforms, and the critical ideas on which they depended, owed their origin to the social theories developed by Bentham and his followers. The poor law reform of 1834 offers an example of the influence of a normative theory of political economy upon legislation at a time when the development of the factory system required a more mobile labour force to serve it. Theory helped to explain and to guide the public response to an industrial order organized around market principles of supply and demand.

But the New Poor Law of 1834 did not result in the promised efficiency. Research throughout the nineteenth century in England attempted to discover the anomalies in the New Poor Law paradigm, and it served as the nucleus upon which modern social policy grew. 'The distant future lay with those whose empirical observations enabled them to repudiate the paralysing fatalities of the principles of 1834 and the theory on which they rested.'[19]

Policy-oriented social science in the mid-nineteenth century was narrowly empirical in focus, aimed at describing social conditions and measuring 'the economic costs of the social wastage inherent in unregulated industrialism'.[20] Its purpose was to discredit and to expose the inadequacies of the New Poor Law doctrine which established a rigid distinction between poverty and pauperism. Official statistics showed a steady decline in pauperism. The number of paupers on relief fell from 8·8 per cent of the population in 1834 to 2·5 per cent by 1900. These statistics suggested that improved poor law administration and a rigid standard of living had together combined gracefully to eliminate poverty as an urgent social problem.[21] Yet, the studies of Booth in East London (1887) and Rowntree in York (1899), based on what in their day were massive statistical surveys, showed that about 30 per cent of the population had incomes inadequate to maintain themselves. These facts lent support to a new theory of collective responsibility, which was further developed in the writings of the Webbs. The Webbs believed that citizenship should provide each individual with the right to a nationally imposed minimum standard for education and training, employment and income retirement, medical care, etc. Once the principle of universal entitlement was accepted, there were still competing options as to how these goals could best be satisfied. But the new guiding policy metaphor influenced the course of legislation in the early twentieth century and helped produce the Beveridge Report

19. O. R. McGregor, 'Social Research and Social Policy in the Nineteenth Century', *British Journal of Sociology*, vol. 8, no. 1, March 1957, p. 148.

20. Quoted in McGregor, ibid., p. 146.

21. Michael E. Rose, *The Relief of Poverty 1834–1914*, Macmillan, 1972, p. 15.

and the reforms of 1948, which ushered in the welfare state.

Once these reforms had been implemented, they too were subjected to new empirical investigation and criticism: Beveridge's approach failed to produce the guaranteed minimum it promised. New theory came to replace earlier conceptions of the minimum. Poverty is seen by at least some social scientists, such as the late Richard Titmuss in Britain and Lee Rainwater in the United States, as inequalities in the command of resources, and especially those inequalities that derive from the exclusion of specific groups from the dynamic and evolving life-style, rights and opportunities available to the average members of society. If the earlier principles were forged from studies that sought to document the wastage of unregulated industrialism, the new principles are evolving around issues of equity in the distribution of public resources: who pays and who benefits and who is excluded from established policies? Does the distribution of public largess multiply privileges or redistribute advantages? Empirical studies have provided preliminary documentation for the generalization that in the context of a democratic liberal political system it is the middle class that benefits most from the high-cost sectors of governmental intervention; and the broader the definition of social policy, the more nearly does this apply. The social policies that emerge from this perspective reject minimum subsistence as a relevant goal of public intervention and also the concept of poverty as a failure to achieve subsistence standards, defined in absolute terms. When poverty is viewed as exclusion from membership in society, public policies become necessary which will attempt to alter the distribution of resources. The impact that these new ideas may have on future policy remains uncertain, but a debate along these lines has been launched.

This brief review of the development of policy paradigms is broadly consistent with Kuhn's ideas about the way in which paradigms can be modified. The examples suggest that research evidence does help to make an assault on older, widely held paradigms and that these new findings make it harder to interpret knowledge in the accepted way and also contribute to the development of new paradigms. In this view, social science theory and empirical research play a definite part in the complex process by which society constructs its perceptions of reality, defines what its problems are and determines what principles of intervention should guide its action and inaction. Research influences the climate of opinion in which research develops, perhaps more than it influences specific decisions.

Who is Right, the Sceptics or the Optimists?

It is a mistake to assume that the matter is settled. Which is more valid, the sceptical or the optimistic view, depends on an act of faith rather than on evidence. More systematic research on research may suggest that research's contribution to policy is limited, either because analysts have failed to provide useful answers to the questions about which government is concerned (most studies dispel myths rather than propose solutions), or because government cannot assimilate or use the knowledge, when it is available, for a variety of administrative and political reasons. However, those who have faith that research and social science can be used by government will continue to seek ways in which our understanding of social processes can be improved and the obstacles to utilization overcome.

But the responsibility is not all on the policy maker's side. The researcher must also come to terms with those who have power to make policy. He can follow one of three broad strategies. He may work out his analysis in the abstract, unrelated to the political process, and without asking where the policy backing for his conclusions will come from. He can assume that there is and ought to be a division of responsibility between those who set out to describe reality and those responsible for action. Or, if there are no takers, because the research findings are ignored by those in power, the researcher may then proceed in a different way. He may, for example, conduct his work so that he directly influences those in power, or, alternatively, interest groups in opposition to established power. But he may have to barter some autonomy for this influence. Alternatively the researcher himself may enjoy a position of power (usually because he has achieved scientific prestige from other contributions), and thus be able to meet established power on equal ground. If he enjoys a position of status, then what he says may not be ignored altogether. The researcher has only three choices with respect to power: he may ignore it, leaving it outside his considerations; he may subordinate some of his autonomy to power; or he may have an independent base of power won by his own prestige.

A Modern Research Strategy in the Optimistic Tradition

We have reviewed three research strategies in which empirical findings contribute to the development of policy: a *consensual approach*, whereby government contracts for the information it wants or intermediaries bring together knowledge producers and knowledge users; a *contentious approach*, whereby research acts as *moral witness* for the failure of society to honour its commitments or as a *social critic* when government has established no commitments to be honoured; and a *paradigm-challenging approach*, whereby the researcher acts independently of the established framework, tries to expose its fundamental weaknesses and proposes alternative principles of intervention, assuming that political support for the assault will follow at a later time. While research is typically undertaken within one or another of these frames of reference, it is not uncommon for a single study to shift from one strategic level to another to accommodate the varied motives of the researcher. But the kind of evidence needed to advance each strategic position is different. If researchers want to be influential and to avoid personal frustrations they must be clear about the interpretive context in which their studies are framed, and also about the different levels of evaluation. This means that those who conduct empirical research in the hope of being useful in the development of policy must guard against two dangers. The first is the subtle transition from one style of analysis to another, so that the conclusions drawn will not follow from the original premise. For example, a researcher may attack a paradigm but nevertheless want to be of immediate use, which in most cases is not possible; thus he may be led to make a set of recommendations which are altogether irrelevant to his starting assumptions; or he may refrain from using his radical perspective in fashioning his research design, but nevertheless impose it in his final appraisal of directions for action. The second danger that threatens the credibility of the analyst is the confusion of levels of analysis. For example, he may have evidence to show that a programme does not work, from which he may inappropriately infer that the theory of intervention is misconceived or that the goals it espouses cannot be implemented. These two dangers often overlap because the style and level of analysis intercept. A *consensual* approach proceeds from agreed-upon aims; it asks whether policies, and the specific programmes that implement them, work as intended. Programme evaluation provides, of course, one of the basic ways of making such an assessment. A *contentious* approach proceeds in a more disputatious manner, searching for the very areas in society where our social ideals are not honoured, not because we try and fail but because we do not make an effort in the first instance. A *paradigm challenge* occurs when the validity of a theory of intervention is scrutinized.

How then do we move ahead to develop a viable social policy paradigm? Little systematic work has been done on the study of policy paradigms, but three main questions seem to be relevant: (1) What are the main goals or purposes to be pursued? (2) What theories or principles of intervention might be pursued to achieve these purposes? (3) How can we determine whether programmes are in fact consonant with these theories, and whether, in fact, they work as intended? If we integrate the answer to these three questions we should be able to build up a policy paradigm.

As we have suggested, the study of paradigms must consider not only the paradigms themselves, and their relationship to other frameworks, but also their dynamic interplay within social, political and economic contexts. The following section, however, is a more limited and circumscribed presentation. It examines the purposes, strategies, and programmes of social policy *per se*, without considering their relationship to the broader social setting in which they are located.

The Disparity between Ideals and Realities

Since a social scientist has no claim to moral authority, what contribution can he hope to make to the question of social goals? As an analyst he can document the disparity between existing ideals and established realities by empirical study; and as a member of society he has an intuitive sense of which disparities may be most acceptable politically. Whatever process he employs to select a problem for study, he proceeds on the assumption that policy should attempt to narrow the disparities which are revealed. And of course this works best for those ideals in society on which there is substantial accord. But is there agreement about our social ideals? While there is some measure of consensus about social aims within any specific sector of social policy, it seldom obtains for all sectors. Decisions are typically made by autonomous departments who pay little attention to one another and who are not subordinated to a single unambiguous policy objective. Governments seem uncommitted to a single embracing purpose but tend to seek multiple aims that are contradictory and conflicting. And yet despite this conflict of intentions and apparent absence of an explicit consensus and social purpose, those who hold an integrative view of society may after all be correct in believing that there is an elusive consensus on a deeper level. Superficially we see a discordance of belief systems and ideals; the underlying agreement and integration in society are hidden, and it may require some effort to identify them. So the social ideals and belief systems that underpin them need to be discovered. This is the first task of the researcher as critic.

I suspect that there is no rigorous way by which the analyst can tap the crucial issues of the day. But an examination of the issues brought to public attention suggests that there are obvious shifts in interest. In Britain, for example, in the mid-1950s, researchers and politicians were apparently preoccupied with the problems of the aged. This slowly gave way to a concern for poverty among children, then to the problem of low wages and most recently public attention has been riveted on the circumstances of the disabled. Perhaps one process by which the researcher may uncover issues and illuminate their importance can be explained in the following way. When the treatment of special groups seems inconsistent with an implicit ethical standard, a diffuse dissonance is established which announces that the state of affairs is morally wrong. The researcher understands this dissonance from his role as citizen and from his moral sense of what offends him, and is thereby guided in developing his research questions.

The researcher then attempts to document the size of the group affected by the disparity between shared ideals[22] and actual performance – on the grounds that the case for change is more compelling if many people are affected. So quantitative studies of the incidence of hunger, poverty, ill health and chronic unemployment provide evidence about the seriousness of the gap between ideals and realities, and can then be used to argue that the disparity needs to be redressed. Pressures for reform are substantially strengthened if they present the idea not only that something is morally wrong but also that this state of affairs is socially dangerous. Pragmatism thus reinforces morality. While need and demand studies may support a variety of paradigms, they tend to reinforce those that arise from impatience with the *status quo*. 'Need'-oriented research typically uncovers unmet needs, for needs are rarely fully satisfied and social ideals are almost never in accord with social reality. Indeed no one actually expects the real and ideal ever to be identical. On the other hand, the evaluation of real programmes presents the obverse problem. To start with *ideals* suggests that we may need to do more. To start with *programmes* suggests that whatever we do fails, because research reveals the failure to achieve goals.

Democratic political systems are responsive to strong political constituencies. Many public policies are initiated by interest groups that are articulate and powerful. Sometimes indeed the interest group involved is mainly concerned to keep quiet the gains it has made, as in the case of business interests that have won generous oil depletion allowances. It sometimes seems to be a

22. Some research tries to develop new social ideals; for example, some studies have tried to demonstrate that technological developments have made work redundant, so that we should prepare for a society that allocates work rather than leisure as a scarce resource.

peculiarity of welfare policy that the case for its reform is expected to be substantive as well as political. Interest groups are therefore anxious to marshal whatever empirical evidence or persuasive argument they can to support their case. However, the kinds of arguments which the spokesmen for welfare programmes develop to identify the state of dissonance will tend to influence mainly those with whom they share the same culture and values – in short, the same paradigms. To widen political support, spokesmen for welfare programmes tend to broaden their argument so that it will appeal to different groups. However morally compelling an argument may be in terms of equity and decency – that the poor should have decent housing, for example, because it is dehumanizing in an affluent society to subject individuals to a lower standard of well-being than that enjoyed by most members of society – it is seldom politically persuasive on such grounds. To win support, the case for decent housing is therefore stretched: good housing will reduce juvenile delinquency and enhance the capacity of children to make use of their schooling, because, among other things, it will provide them with a place to study. Those interested in reducing crime and expanding education are advised to support the case for better housing. But the validity of the argument becomes weaker as the search for political support is broadened. And in the end, the persuasiveness of reformers lies more in their ability to apply pressure than in the substance and moral justification of their arguments.

Another way to broaden support is to present appealing or dramatic imagery to those who hold different paradigms but who are not strongly committed to them, or those who hold conflicting paradigms simultaneously. New imagery may even affect those who are already committed to an opposing paradigm by shaking their conviction in the essential rightness of what they believe. Qualitative studies play an important role in this process. Scientific researchers rarely make effective use of such studies because they are limited by their own turgid prose and are seldom able to evoke a sense of affront and outrage. This sense of injustice is more effectively achieved by journalists and fiction writers. Their reporting can develop new imagery about reality and may influence people to examine or modify their paradigms. These vivid accounts can also evoke empathy for the poor, the sick and the disenfranchised, and call attention to the negative social consequences of poverty, illness and alienation.

Theories of Intervention

Having noted the difficulty of achieving ideals, those who wish to influence public policy must consider what kind of theory of intervention can help reduce the disparity between ideals and reality. A policy paradigm is incomplete if it fails to specify how goals might be achieved, although, oddly, they often contain only an implicit political theory as to how these means can be implemented. Research can confront existing theories of policy intervention, and it can also contribute to the development of new theories. But in either event, it will not be definitive in invalidating or in producing theory. Social theories reflect world views of how society functions, but policy paradigms are broader than scientific theories, because they contain normative as well as descriptive dimensions. Whatever theory is developed, it must be at once ideological and empirically linked to real social processes. If it is to be politically possible, that is to say practical, it must be phrased in such a way that it is socially acceptable within whatever seems to be the arena of decision making.

Consider the paradigm which holds that an individualistic society should provide its members with the opportunity to step up the social ladder. The paradigm embodies the ideal of equalizing opportunities, and that of assuring that a permanent underclass does not develop whereby disadvantages are perpetuated from one generation to another. Most studies of social, occupational and income mobility have not in fact been organized within a policy or action framework. They merely describe and analyse the pattern of social stratification and social mobility within society, and are therefore of little immediate use in the formulation of specific policies. Policy does not necessarily flow logically from a review of patterns and trends. However, such descriptions do contain an implicit normative framework. Those interested in policy will search these studies for clues as to the factors that frustrate opportunity, so that action can be based on an interpretation of these processes.

The initial values of the paradigm, however, do not determine the final form of intervention. Are institutional barriers the crucial factor in inhibiting the equalization of opportunity, or is individual incapacity a more urgent obstacle? 'Equalization of opportunity', after all, may function to eliminate the 'incapable'. Yet theories of intervention to encourage individual social mobility tend to favour either an individualist or a structuralist perspective, if for no other reason than that limited resources force a reluctant choice. It seems that a theory of intervention must follow one of two directions for policy. Each view 'presumes a different conceptual framework, steers attention to different variables, poses problems of a different order, and suggests different methods of approach to solve these problems'.[23]

The dominant theory of intervention with regard to equalizing opportunity holds that increased educational achievement by individuals is crucial to the alteration of opportunity, although the precise process by which this occurs is subject to different interpretations. The failure to acquire cognitive skills is most often assumed to be the critical factor. But recent research has attempted to challenge these accepted theories of intervention. A study by Christopher Jencks convincingly shows that there is only a weak relationship between educational achievement, I.Q. and future income.[24] Jencks's study, by calling attention to dispersions within a given level of occupational achievement, questions the belief that educational institutions contribute greatly to inequalities in eventual class, position not to mention the assumption that

23. Roland R. Warren, 'The Sociology of Knowledge and the Problem of the Inner Cities', *Social Science Quarterly*, December 1971, p. 473. Logically, Warren observes, we may not need to make a choice: 'Isn't it perfectly possible to consider poverty as an integral property of the social structure, while at the same time acknowledging ... [that] individual people may experience serious social handicaps because of their poverty, and may need individual help to overcome these deficiencies?'

24. Christopher Jencks and others, *Inequality: A Reassessment of the Effect of Family and Schooling in America*, New York, Basic Books, 1973; Penguin Books, 1975.

there is a compelling relationship between I.Q. and economic success in later years. To trample so unrelentingly on cherished ideas without proposing alternative theories of intervention must create ideological confusion. It is not surprising that Jencks and his colleagues have been accused of being both too radical and too conservative; yet what seems most certain in the absence of a politically viable alternative theory of intervention is that their findings will very likely be assimilated by all paradigms without causing dramatic change, unless the ideals of equalizing opportunity are totally repudiated or a different theory of intervention posited.

A different ideal is the proposition that the promotion of individual mobility is less essential than the promotion of collective mobility. This approach does not attempt to eliminate stratification, but it does seek to change the degree of inequality by shifting the position of the groups at the bottom relative to those at the middle or top. It would accomplish this by raising their prestige levels, working conditions, salary levels, fringe benefits or some combination of these approaches. This view directs attention not to the failure of the poor but rather to the failure of the mechanisms for allocating resources and prestige among different occupational and social groupings.

Yet another theory has been developed which calls attention to the existence of a dual labour market. It is argued that the low- and high-wage sectors are discrete and discontinuous. Low-wage employment is characterized by dead-end jobs in which there is little opportunity for on-the-job training and economic advances. As long as these jobs exist, certain types of workers – the less well-educated, youth, women, ethnic minorities – will be attracted to them. Policies directed to changing the characteristics of the individual, such as their skill, educational achievement and motivation for work, must in the end fail if no effort is made simultaneously to alter the structure of job slots in the labour market. After all, if native workers refuse to accept these dead-end, low-paying jobs that are subject to high levels of unemployment, industry will recruit migrant labour for whom these new jobs will represent an improvement in their relative economic position. The crucial task, then, is to alter the structure of employment by redefining tasks within a job, and a job within an occupation (an institutional theory of intervention) rather than the structure of individual opportunity (an individual theory of intervention).[25]

Programme Evaluation

Specific programmes translate the broadly defined theory of intervention into concrete actions, and it is these programmes that are subject to evaluation. The case for evaluative studies is compelling. What, after all, could be more rational than to evaluate the outcomes of public policy? There is no sense in enthusiastically supporting policies or reform if we never find out whether they work. Yet, although the case for evaluation may be self-evident, here, too, we observe that prior paradigms tend to invade the methods of analysis and the interpretation of the findings.

One strongly held argument maintains that if we are to produce better information about which government interventions work and which do not, it is necessary to design social programmes deliberately as experiments. Reliable and valid information about social processes and social programmes can only be gathered through the experimental approach, where random selection is the crucial strategy. Social scientists must 'prepare themselves so as to be methodologically ready for a future "experimenting society" '.[26]

An alternative framework proceeds from the assumption that experimental evaluations on their own miss certain processes and outcomes crucial to an understanding of any programme intervention. This approach implies that the study design must be supplemented with a prepared and sensitive observer to the process.[27] The emphasis on observation as well as research

25. See, for example, Peter B. Doeringer, 'Low Pay, Labor Market Dualism, and Industrial Relations Systems', Discussion Paper No. 271, Harvard Institute of Economic Research, January 1973.

26. Donald T. Campbell, 'Critical Problems in the Evaluation of Social Programs', a paper prepared for the annual meeting of the Division of Behavioral Sciences, National Academy of Sciences, 19–20 May 1970, p. 1.

27. Robert S. Weiss and Martin Rein, 'The Evaluation of Broad Aim Programs: Experimental Design, Its Difficulties, and an Alternative', *Administrative Science Quarterly*, March 1970.

design responds to three problems encountered in traditional, experimentally oriented studies:

(1) There is a tendency to concentrate evaluations on immediate, discrete, quantitative measures of change, even if outcomes cannot be measured in that way and even if they are not altogether related to the purposes of the intervention.

(2) Evaluative studies have a tendency to eschew the long-term, slow-maturing, qualitative changes that are hard to measure, in favour of short-term changes, even when such a procedure imposes alien goals on a programme.

(3) There is a tendency to evaluate programmes in isolation from the context in which they must operate. For example, compensatory educational programmes may be evaluated within the context of a particular school but ignore the external forces that impinge on it. A school may go through a yearly financial crisis because it must balance its budget by April although state reimbursement funds are not decided until June. Teachers must be notified six months in advance of dismissal – so they may be dismissed in April only to be rehired in June. Such a procedure could have a demoralizing effect on their morale. The negative aspect of such policies and procedures may far outweigh any positive contribution that the compensatory programme could have on the children's educational achievements.

In brief, then, traditional evaluations yield uncertain findings because they are too crude and narrow and too short-term in their scope. Moreover, the attention to outcome alone neglects the broader institutional context in which the programme operates, and this can nullify whatever positive results may be achieved.

The problem involves not only competing methods of evaluation, but also conflicting ideas about which purposes and findings should be emphasized. Peter Marris, commenting on the experiments with community action and model cities in the United States, and community programmes in Britain, argues that 'The distinctive quality of these experiments in social planning is their attempt to explore the adaptability of the process of government to demands: first that they should bring the people they serve into their counsel, as party to the discussion, negotiation and choice of policies, and secondly that they should integrate the functions of government intelligently around problems as a whole.'[28] If the experiments are seen to be concerned with the malleability of government to innovation rather than with the development of strategies for reducing poverty, then, clearly, they must be judged by different standards. Measures of the performance of government rather than short-run achievements of the individual are required. Again the unresolved question as to the purpose of experiments with broad social aims is exposed.

But even when there is general agreement about aims, and objective evaluations are undertaken to determine whether they have been met, at the crucial moment decisions about the continuation of a programme may be judged by altogether new criteria. Thus, programmes which actually succeed in meeting their purposes may nevertheless become unacceptable. For example, it is widely assumed that the experiments with community-controlled schools were rejected because they failed, but in fact 'The decision to abolish the experimental districts was made in the absence of data on the effects of this experiment on schools and children.'[29] Marcia Guttentag argues that community control, which has been widely acknowledged as a failure, was in fact, according to the findings of later research, a success. One of the aims (and, many have argued, the prime aim) was to change the behaviour, aspirations and attitudes of ghetto residents through a strategy of participation. People change as they try to change their world. The Harlem experiment with community-controlled schools created deep conflict between professionals and consumers, but it also changed the aspirations of the adults and increased the educational achievement of the children who participated in it.

28. Peter Marris, 'Experimenting in Social Reform', in David Jones and Marjorie Mayo, *Community Work One*, Routledge & Kegan Paul, 1974, p. 250.

29. Marcia Guttentag, 'Children in Harlem's Community Controlled Schools', *Journal of Social Issues*, vol. 28, no. 4, 1972, p. 18.

Conclusion

Since every type of study yields different information and is responsive to different questions, there is a danger that we may shift
our levels of analysis and draw conclusions from inappropriate
sources of data. It is, after all, difficult to determine when the
theory of intervention is right but the programme implementation
is faulty, or when the theory is wrong because the ideals which led
to the theory are miscast. At least three options are possible:
(1) The ideals were right but the implementation was inappropriate, perhaps because the design of the programme was faulty,
or the level of commitment was insufficient, or the critical
threshold was not reached (the medicine didn't work because the
dose was too weak). (2) The ideals were right, but the theory of
intervention was wrong. Education, for example, is not a key to
the equalization of opportunity and income because the link
between education and income is very elusive and indeterminate
in a society whose occupational structure is changing. (3) The
ideals themselves are impractical: no theory of intervention could
achieve them and new ideals are needed. Banfield has argued, for
example, that the effort to alter the time preferences of ghetto
adults, that is, their ability to plan for the future, is a self-defeating
task and that new and more realistic goals are required.[30]

In evaluating a policy paradigm it is important to be able to
assess whether the ideal, or the theory of intervention, or the
programme which translates that theory into a specific course of
action is defective.

Programme evaluations can only say something about programme implementation. Many evaluative studies of the poverty
programmes were of limited use because they only inquired
whether the programmes worked or not – these 'go/no-go' studies
could not suggest how to make the programmes work better.
When the ideal remains firm and the theory of intervention is
unaltered, research seems useless if it is unable to suggest areas

30. Edward C. Banfield, *The Unheavenly City*, Boston, Little, Brown,
1970.

for specific programme improvement. For example, so long as there has been a continuing commitment to the legitimate goal of helping youngsters to compete on equal terms in school, and it has been assumed that early education is important in shaping academic achievement and that ability is related to future income, negative findings about the Head Start programme have simply produced a diffuse sense of dissatisfaction and frustration, discrediting both the value of research and the programme.

Somehow evaluative studies seem, in the end, almost always to react against the reform itself, to support the preconceptions of those who believed to begin with that nothing works. But we cannot conclude from this that we should be satisfied with the reform without evaluation. Few would argue that reform is an act of faith and that what matters is the faith and not the outcome. If we are concerned about outcomes, then we must see that programmes do what they are intended to do. But because evaluations seem so consistently to assault the reform itself, there is the danger that negative findings may give premature and unwise support to the cynical and the reactionary and may discourage and demoralize the idealistic.

As we suggested earlier, if one is interested in criticizing the theory of intervention, rather than the specific programme, it is necessary to look at processes and try to examine how events occurred. That is to say, were the inputs to be evaluated those called for by the theory? For example, if community action theory holds that all interested parties should collectively define the problems and priorities of ghetto residents, and create new programmes out of this assessment, then the test of the theory requires a study of these processes. We would want to know whether things worked out according to programme intention. Such a review might show that the programme did not arise from the processes implied in the theory but was imposed ad hoc. And so the validity of the theory cannot be in question because the theory was never implemented, and hence its effectiveness cannot be judged. The customary support for outcome studies while process studies are rejected shows yet again how the study of the effectiveness of policy is itself subject to undetected paradigms.

If one wants to question ideals rather than the theory or the programmes, then research needs to re-examine the assumptions on which the ideals are based. For example, if structural unemployment persists, so that a substantial portion of the population is always unemployed, the ideal of equalizing opportunity can only mean equalizing the risk of being unemployed.

We conclude, then, that we should not draw conclusions from the results of one kind of research when those results actually relate to another type of research. Social policy research is at great risk of being totally inconclusive because it moves too quickly from ideals to theories of intervention and programme specifics when no such progression can be justified. To use research productively, it is important to be clear at what level of analysis the research is relevant. When the data relate only to the implementation of programmes, conclusions about ideals and theories are inappropriate.

I have tried in this chapter to illustrate the resistance of personal paradigms to change and the stubbornness of categories of thought, despite alternatives suggested by research. Sceptics take this as evidence that only a weak link is possible between research and policy. Optimists argue that such a conclusion is premature. Research undertaken within a common framework of thought can both by contention and consensus influence the development of policy; moreover research and theory can help reshape policy paradigms as well, but their contribution cannot be isolated from the many other forces that impinge on decisions. I have set out the arguments in support of each position as impartially as I can. In the final section I have tried to illustrate how prior-held frameworks shape the ideals sought, the theories of action proposed, and the evaluations undertaken (the sceptic's view). The optimists, of course, reject this and point to the many examples where research does appear to contribute to policy at least in the long run, and sometimes in the short run as well. But the process by which this occurs is a complex one. More importantly, I have tried to show that policy-oriented research is in danger of falling into disrepute when researchers inappropriately shift among the three levels of analysis discussed. I am a sceptical optimist, for I optimistically believe that an awareness of the limitation of each view permits one to avoid being the victim of either.

Chapter 4
Policy Analysis as the Interpretation of Beliefs

If we intend to analyse an issue of social policy, we must first find the proper perspective for setting a problem. This search for a perspective raises the question as to whether the study of policy is only a field of interest or a discipline. Those who say that policy studies are merely a field of interest argue that there is no single meaningful framework which includes such varied subjects as: programme objectives – narrowing wage differentials or income redistribution; programme design – means tests v. universal provision; and programme administration – of fields such as medical care, housing, education, etc. The nature of social policy,

its characteristic methods or principles, its differences from public administration and business administration, are not clearly defined. Is it a science or an art? Is it social science or social work? Is it really an intellectual discipline with distinguishing characteristics?[1]

If one takes this approach, one is likely to conclude that the only way to analyse policy impartially is to proceed from the theory and method of particular academic disciplines or professions. Thus, individual policies will be analysed only from their legal, historical, sociological, political, or economic perspectives. To proceed from this assumption is to abandon altogether the hope of developing the study of policy in its own terms. Perhaps this is the only sensible approach, yet it does seem worth the effort to search out a broader framework that proceeds from the nature of policy itself. But even this will prove insufficient because 'policy' is not a self-contained framework either. The study of

1. Arthur Seldon, 'Commitment to Welfare: A Review Article', *Social and Economic Administration*, 2 July 1968, p. 198.

'policy' leads us to more fundamental questions, not only about intent but actual performance.

The Terrain of Social Policy

What then is the study of social policy all about? I believe that social policy is, above all, concerned with choice among competing values, and hence questions of what is morally or culturally desirable can never be excluded from the discussion. But what then shall we use as a standard for judgement? I regard the primary subject matter of social policy as egalitarianism – that is, concern with the problem of the more equitable distribution of social goods. 'No other value serves so efficiently in the work of distinguishing among the varied ideologies of the present, and, for that matter, of the past couple of centuries. What one's attitude is toward equality in the whole complex of social, cultural, and economic goods tells us almost perfectly whether one is radical, liberal, or conservative.'[2] In this chapter I want to explore how opinions about equality intrude in the process of analysis.

My starting point is that it is not only sterile to pursue techniques of analysis divorced from issues of purpose, but it is also misleading because techniques arise to serve purposes and therefore imply value assumptions. But, if it is no good simply to pursue techniques, neither is it good to just debate issues of social values, for the discussion can easily drift into an abstract argument about social ideals. The outcomes of such an analysis must be unconvincing, for the analyst is not, and does not claim to be, a moral authority – so he has no particular role in this debate. The worthwhile course is one which relates the actual working of social policy to questions of value. And this, it seems to me, has two aspects. The first is analogous to jurisprudence in the teaching of a law – the analysis of the principles underlying different conceptions of policy. These principles are not the same as the fundamental value choices which direct the goals of policy, but rather they are operating principles. They represent an attempt to

2. Robert Nisbet, 'The Pursuit of Equality', *Public Interest*, 35, spring 1974, p. 104.

integrate various social ideals with a practicable rule of application. Examples are the principles of universal coverage, or selection by need, or citizen participation, or the principles for allocation of educational, housing and welfare subsidies, or the institutional forms for distributing benefits. Still, however ingenious
these general rules of design for transforming purpose into
programme, by themselves they are insufficient. We must also
look at the outcomes of action – how purposes and results relate
to each other, what dilemmas and consequences arise from trying
to implement a conception of social justice or a theory of intervention. Following on from our discussion in Chapter 3, on
theories of intervention, we conclude that the study of social
policy requires an analysis of the interaction between values,
operating principles, and outcomes. If any of these is lost sight
of, the analysis tends to be non-productive. Simply comparing
values and outcomes (as radical idealists often do) leads to frustration – since there is no examination of strategy. Simply comparing values and operating principles of policy is to surrender to
doctrine and to an abstract debate about good practice based on
what is presumed to be consistent with our ideals. Simply comparing operating principles and outcomes alienates idealists, who
reject the view that choice must be contained by the framework
of present legislative possibilities – and it easily becomes parochial for it indicts the system without reference to the values that
should motivate it. When the match between purpose, principles
and outcomes is found to be weak, the analyst must be prepared
to suggest politically acceptable changes either in ideals or in
policy or both. Proposals for change will be influenced by judgements about what is politically feasible, to the extent that policy
analysis is inspired by the desire to help implement social ideals.

Clearly, these aspects of policy are inseparable. Ideology and
beliefs attach to means as much as to ends; beliefs about what is
right are tied up with acceptable, feasible operating principles;
and what is rational depends on what is judged to be feasible –
for a policy can hardly be termed rational if it has no possibility
of winning political acceptance. Policies are in fact interdependent systems of: (1) the abstract values we cherish; (2) the operating principles which give these values form in specific pro-

grammes and institutional arrangements; (3) the outcomes of these programmes which enable us to contrast ideals and reality; (4) the often weak linkages among aims, means and outcomes; and (5) the feasible strategies of change this pattern suggests.

Few studies of policy attempt to draw these themes together. I have accepted this state of affairs and have resisted the temptation to present a grand synthesis. Instead, a more limited alternative is to seek to understand and illustrate how values and ideology inform the analysis of policy by research scientists as well as by agency officials at every level of policy making. To approach the analysis of policy through a study of the beliefs of policy analysts is to reaffirm the position that the discipline, or field, of social policy is essentially about moral and ethical values.

How do values come into the analysis of policy? The first, and most obvious, intrusion is the way analysts interpret the purposes of policy. Here they assert what for them is both technically feasible and morally right. Second, systems of beliefs are seldom mutually reinforcing or internally consistent. More typically, the various aspects of these values are in practice in partial conflict with one another. So the analyst must sort out priorities for action and take account of adjustments and compromises. Third, people attach as much ideological importance to form as they do to purpose. There is an ideology of means as well as of ends. Fourth, analysts of policy are specifically concerned with being useful, and this preoccupation with political feasibility may affect their interpretation of values. On the one hand, values can be subordinated to the pragmatic sense of what is possible, accepting a preferred solution within the limits of feasibility; on the other hand, it can lead to a commitment to alter the political climate, thus extending the range of acceptable policies. Finally, values influence the ways in which outcomes are interpreted, partly in the measures used to assess change, but also in the implications drawn from the outcomes.

The Purposes of Policy

That belief systems and values play a special role in defining research questions is now widely accepted in social science. But despite the importance of understanding the professional–political creed that guides the choice of research areas, the content of the belief systems has been difficult to disentangle, and consequently their concrete effects on the interpretation of research findings have not been systematically examined. We have been content to assert that values are important and to substitute this assertion for an analysis of either the nature of the value complexes which inform research questions or the consequences of holding one or another set of beliefs.

Characteristically analysts seek to marshal evidence to demonstrate that what they believe is essentially correct. This is not to deny that objective data may also threaten, rather than confirm, cherished beliefs, but seldom are the findings of empirical studies so compelling and unambiguous as to overthrow them. This can be illustrated with an example.

Here in brief are the salient features of a belief system concerning social policy and the 'welfare state'. Central in the system is the view held about *equality*, where at least two extreme positions can be identified. The liberal tradition holds that equality helps civilize society and, by promoting fraternal bonds and decreasing the structural sources of discontent, also assures its stability. The conservative tradition regards equality that is produced by public policy as a constraint on personal freedom and a threat to economic growth because it weakens those economic incentives that are needed to encourage work, risk-taking and the assumption of managerial responsibility or undesirable jobs.

It is not monetary differentiation – much as egalitarians like to dwell upon it – that galls and occasionally humiliates; it is rather the type of differentiation that comes from unequal intellectual and moral strengths, unequal applications of resolve and aspiration and unequal benefactions of luck.[3]

3. ibid., p. 104.

The conservative position rejects egalitarianism, accepting the view that man is by nature unequal and all moves towards equality must be justified. They therefore embrace that form of humanitarianism which seeks to assure a minimum protection for all citizens, that is, the elimination of subsistence poverty is held as an ideal.

The instruments of intervention to reduce poverty or inequality are as sacrosanct as the ideals they service, for the ideology of means is as formidable as that of ends. Some view the market and economic growth as the most efficient means to improve well-being, and when these fail, cash transfers are preferable because they also preserve personal liberty. Others, while recognizing the beneficial effects of growth, seem more preoccupied with its cost. Market imperfections are troublesome, and while cash transfers are still accepted, social services seem to be more important elements in the strategy of redistribution. Proponents of both belief systems acknowledge that the more broadly social policy is defined the less redistributive is its effect. Some think situational and environmental forces calcify within the aid system to inhibit life chances, while others believe the political system sufficiently open for individual initiative to overcome these constraints and make policy an ally in this.

Priorities of Beliefs: Efficiency, Choice, Equality

There is as much possibility of choice in the ordering of priorities within a belief system as there is among conflicting belief systems. Establishing priorities is one of the central concerns in social policy, reconciling the goals of economic efficiency, freedom of choice and equality. Here then is a fertile field in which the preferences of the analyst intrude, whether subtly or overtly.

One commonly accepted practical strategy for resolving conflicts between efficiency, choice and equality usually translates into a preference for cash transfers as contrasted with benefits in kind. The argument runs as follows: concerns about choice and equality should be expressed in general legislation for taxation of income and wealth and by direct cash transfers, which allow the recipient to spend his additional income as he pleases. Efficiency is best achieved by action designed to make the market operate more competitively. Tobin explains the economists' preference for general egalitarianism as follows:

> While concerned laymen who observe people with shabby housing or too little to eat instinctively want to provide them with decent housing and adequate food, economists instinctively want to provide them with more cash income. Then they can buy the housing and food if they want to, and if they choose not to, the presumption is that they have a better use for the money. To those who complain about the unequal distribution of shelter or food, our first response . . . is that they should look at the distribution of wealth and income. If the social critics approve that distribution, then they should accept its implications, including the unequal distribution of specific commodities.[4]

Of course, not all economists are willing to accept the heroic assumption that taxation and cash transfers are neutral in allocative efficiency or, more controversially, that inefficiencies in the distribution of subsidized commodities present a very large problem, even when the subsidies are substantial. In addition to these criticisms, Aaron and von Furstenberg have tried to show that the argument in support of cash transfers is built on an inappropriate model, for the rationale for *social* action is based on a *one* person model in which it is assumed that 'the donor cares only how the recipient perceives his own welfare'.[5] But the more the presumed preferences of the donors of public largess are taken into account, the more the rationale of public policy tends to restrict the consumer's freedom of choice.

James Buchanan carries this feeling to its logical extreme when he asserts 'one must search diligently to find much social concern expressed for the prudent poor whose lives are well ordered and stable'. He states that the primary justification for redistributive policies is to prevent the well-off from suffering when they see how the poor live: therefore, they are willing to pay only for those services which supervise and control the consumption and

4. James Tobin, 'On Limiting the Domain of Inequality', *The Journal of Law and Economics*, 13, October 1970, pp. 264–5.

5. Henry J. Aaron and George von Furstenberg, 'How Inefficient Are Transfers in Kind: The Case of Housing Assistance', n.d. (mimeograph).

behaviour of the poor. Buchanan believes that the general public is unwilling to finance transfers of general purchasing power, 'but they are probably willing to finance specific transfers, either directly as income-in-kind or indirectly in purchasing power that is earmarked for some specific item of spending (vouchers)'.[6]

But even acknowledging the extensive use that governments do make of in-kind programmes (for example the distribution of free food commodities; food stamps which reduce the cost of food items; Medicare for the aged and then Medicaid for other groups in need; public housing; and, in recent years, a series of differentiated housing subsidies such as rent supplements), we need not assume that the only motive for such action is to control the behaviour of the poor by restricting their consumption. Many might agree that the real problem is not how to render the lower classes more tractable, but how to give them a meaningful life. The unresolved question is to what extent this aim must be tied to the equalization. Tobin argues that interest in specific egalitarianism arises because

the social conscience is more offended by severe inequality in nutrition and basic shelter, or in access to medical care or legal assistance, than by inequality in automobiles, books, clothes, furniture, boats, etc. Can we somehow remove the necessities of life and health from the prizes that serve as incentives for economic activity . . .?[7]

So equitable distribution of specific resources may often be justified on grounds not of expanding personal freedom, but rather that to contain them reduces the embarrassment of the well-to-do and conforms to the ideals of the donors. Socialist theoreticians have also generated similar arguments. For example, Crosland explains: 'the first argument for greater equality is that it will increase social contentment and diminish social resentment'.[8] To what extent does greater equality produce political stability and discourage deviation? Some analysts with a more conservative bent, such as Glazer, have tried to show that

6. James Buchanan, 'What Kind of Redistribution Do We Want?', *Economica*, 35, May 1968, p. 1990.

7. Tobin, op. cit., p. 265.

8. Anthony Crosland, *The Future of Socialism*, Jonathan Cape, 1965.

although the relative economic position of Negroes has improved, narrowing inequalities, neither stability nor conformity has followed. 'As the Negro's situation improves his political attitudes are becoming more extreme.'[9] Donnison has noted, as if in direct response to Glazer's observations, that 'societies that grow more equal may prove to be not more, but much less, fraternal . . . Liberals who lose their nerve at this discovery are apt to turn against equality, and liberty too.'[10] If equality does not necessarily promote conformity and stability, and if these are valued, then more direct, coercive programmes may be considered necessary. Administrative discretion in the allocation of those social services which are needed and wanted by the poor can be employed to promote conformity to standards of 'acceptable' behaviour.

I have divided societal values as if there were two mutually exclusive classes: on the one side, the 'moral' values concerned exclusively with the 'equal', or at any rate 'more equal', or 'equitable' distribution of social goods (mainly income, health, education); and on the other, issues concerning institutional stability, the socio-economic *status quo*, public order, etc.

This dichotomy is overdrawn and over-simplified. Equalization has its practical–pragmatic aspects; institutional stability (public order) has its moral dimensions. In fact the pragmatic side of 'equalization' often comes out in the course of a liberal analysis; moral and other societal values linked to continuity of institutions do not. The latter is always considered to be geared to the privileges and comfort of the upper class, which is, of course, a distortion, making simple what is complex.

In welfare policy the moral value of equality, i.e., fairness of distribution, is an essential (in some sense even the ultimate) value consideration. Nevertheless, we must put it in a wider context where it cannot be treated as the single value or even the single moral value to be taken into account. For, as we saw earlier, although in practice a single value tends to be isolated, there is in fact a whole multiplicity of value perspectives. And

9. Nathan Glazer, 'The Negro's Stake in America's Future', *The New York Times Magazine*, 22 September 1968.

10 David Donnison, 'Liberty, Equality and Fraternity', *The Three Banks Review*, Edinburgh, 1970.

the ideological positions that policy analysts take on this ancient question of equality and social control, with the reduction of personal choice it must imply, provide the frameworks for proposing new programmes and for evaluating established ones. The position we take leads to the selective attention to data. For example, Steiner's thoughtful analysis of the 1967 Amendments to the Social Security Act is organized to show that training to reduce welfare rolls depends on the availability of facilities and day care.[11] These, he argues, are costly and difficult to implement on a large scale. By exposing the weakness of the service approach, he lays the groundwork for his conclusion that a cash strategy which expands personal choice is preferable. Different values, such as a concern that the poor are not adequately protected against coercion, or the opposite view, that we should attend to socially necessary, that is legitimate, coercion, could lead to a different selection of evidence and to different interpretations of the same facts. 'The normative leap' we take is only partially influenced by the data.

The effort to make the operation of the market more efficient may lead to increased inequality. For example, some people believe it wrong to give everyone the same education – thereby depriving the gifted of an education that will enable them to develop their special gifts – on the grounds that this would be unfair to the less gifted. But those who reject the call for 'no élitism' may, for example, propose that personal choice should be expanded by the use of educational vouchers, which permit parents to send their children to any school of a certain standard, and not simply to state schools. They argue that by exploiting market efficiency the quality of services can be increased. But the extended voucher proposals would increase the inequality of education, for high-income parents who send their children to private schools now pay 'not only the extra costs but also part of the expenses of educating the children of the less affluent'.[12] So those who assign a high priority to promoting equality suspect that arguments in favour of expanding personal choice and

11. Gilbert Steiner, *The State of Welfare*, Washington, D.C., Brookings, 1971.
12. Tobin, op. cit.

relying more on efficient market mechanisms rather than on government intervention mask an interest in containing and reduced the extent of redistribution. Moreover, a basic flaw of the concept is that the rationale of competition, weeding out the weak and strengthening the efficient, is not applicable to any system of general education.

The value perspectives we have reviewed cluster together and serve as core ideas for both conservative and liberal interpretations of social policy. The research in social policy inspired by politically conservative groups, such as the Institute of Economic Affairs in Britain, has emphasized the importance of freedom of choice, of the market as a mechanism of intervention, and of the importance of income as it contributes to extending the quality of life. In a democratic society these strategies, when combined, appear to restrict the redistribution of resources and, thus, preserve inequalities. Traditionally, liberal and more radical groups have tended to distrust the market as a mechanism of distribution and to emphasize the redistribution of non-economic and economic resources by social policy outside the market, thereby promoting equality as a social aim. However, conservative thought has influenced the liberal–radical position. Increasingly, attention is being given to the problems and issues of choice, freedom and the role of the market.

In this context, it is interesting to note that the criticisms of the political right and the political left in the United States are in agreement that one of the major defects of America's welfare state is that it has created a bureaucracy that has robbed clients of their rights and freedoms. The left is especially critical of the emerging new forms of the welfare state, for it views them as a new system of social control which seeks conformity as the price of security. As the liberal and the radical have come to accept the conservative emphasis on freedom of choice, some have increasingly turned to the role of the market as a mechanism for expanding freedoms, and to a scheme to promote local control through the decentralization of service systems.

But the link between ideology and policy is not that simple and tidy. For example, local community control has been the hallmark of political conservatives, while the liberals favoured increasing centralization of public services, on the assumption that equity was more likely to be achieved by centralized adminis-tration. But as issues of freedom, dignity, control and choice emerged as priorities in welfare policy, liberal doctrine has been challenged. The net effect has been a fusing of the positions of the political right and left, leaving many analysts feeling that ideology is no longer an important factor either in politics or in the analysis of policy issues. As these traditional lines are redefined, many settled value priorities have been subjected to vigorous reassess-ment. Policy analysis is no longer ideologically based on an integrated belief system about efficiency, choice and equality, and how they relate to each other. Nevertheless analysts continue to assign priorities to these competing aims, and these priorities do serve as a loose basis for the analysis and interpretation of specific policy issues.

Attachment to Institutions

In this section I intend to focus on the institutional means by which broad values and specific priorities are translated into policies. The dichotomy between means and ends is often artificial. It is a mistake to assume that an assessment of means is neutral and that the ideological debate centres on social objectives only. Reality is more elusive. Institutional arrangements themselves imply ideological meaning. For example, there are those who support the market on ideological grounds, as an institution for intervention, and those who distrust it, placing their faith in government institutions. In the debate about the role of the market, reformers have in turn denied it any major role in social policy and then claimed several decades later that it is a valuable counter to organizational rigidities in the social services. I shall concentrate here on those studies which ask, in effect, what a given institution can do best or, conversely, why it fails. In the first case the questioner assumes that the institution is valuable in its own right, so we must discover a useful function for it. This problem is most likely to arise when an institution is attacked, or when its functions atrophy or are transferred to other sectors.

The recent commission on public education in England offers an illuminating illustration of this general thesis. The English public school system was heavily attacked when the Labour Government came to power in 1964. A commission was established to examine its role. Yet, the underlying value that informed the commission as it proceeded to answer its charge was, how can the institutions' strengths best be preserved? One solution proposed that the public schools could be made more democratic if they were required to recruit half their pupils among groups of state-supported students. Similarly in the United States health and welfare councils are concerned with the question of how their institutions can best preserve voluntary social welfare agencies. This broad question serves as an organizing theme for a substantial amount of research sponsored by councils.

Of course, a researcher may inquire what is wrong with an institution, rather than how it might be set right. For example, Titmuss distrusts the role of the market as an instrument of social policy. Accordingly, he wishes to separate social and economic policies. A comparative empirical analysis of the procurement, supply, distribution, processing, transfusion and financing of whole human blood in the United States, in Britain and in other countries provides Titmuss with concrete, specific evidence to expose the limitations of the market as an instrument of provision. In the United States, blood is treated as a commodity and sold in an open market, while in England the giving of blood is voluntary. In England, only two per cent of all blood collected is 'wasted' as a result of administrative inefficiencies, as compared with thirty per cent in the United States. Even more disturbing is the fact that donors inspired by profit are generally the social outcasts of American society, who pass on some 75,000 cases of hepatitis yearly, which account by some estimates for almost 10,000 deaths. Titmuss concludes that 'the private market operating in this area of social policy tends to promote dishonesty and increases diswelfares; it is economically inefficient, and it is destructive of voluntary gift relationships and a sense of community'.[13] By contrast, the gift of blood to strangers encourages the integration

13. Richard Titmuss, *The Gift Relationship in Social Policy: From Human Blood to Social Policy*, Allen and Unwin, 1971.

of the individual with his society, for altruisms reinforces social integration.

The desire to preserve or challenge institutions underlies much analysis of policy, which then becomes essentially an attempt to present a persuasive case in support of beliefs held on other grounds. It is always hazardous to impute intent but it does seem to me that the writings of Glazer may be best appreciated as an attempt to restore traditional institutions which are threatened by the emergence of the 'welfare state'. Fortunately, Glazer has attempted to make the framework of his analysis explicit:

in the attempt to contain the sea of human misery, government created new institutions to serve as a dyke, to protect workers against the evils and inefficiencies of an unbridled early industrialism. Paradoxically, government intervention to deal with the breakdown of the traditional ways of coping with distress – family, ethnic groups, the neighbourhood, and the like – encouraged the further erosion of these institutions. Efforts to deal with distress perversely increased it. Policy expanded, changed, and created new problems as serious as the ones it hoped to displace. The sea of misery is not drained, but is refilled by the revolution of rising expectations, the revolution of equality, and the inherent limitations of financial resources, professional skills, and knowledge. No easy rescue from these contradictions is at hand, but some part of the solution of our social problems lies in traditional practices and traditional restraints.[14]

The logic of the argument provides a criterion for the evaluation of policy – does it preserve or erode traditional institutions or aid in the creation of new ones?

While some analysts, in examining new proposals for welfare policy, are concerned with the extent to which they serve to redistribute resources (usually defined in more individualistic terms as benefit adequacy), to reduce stigma and to increase the rate of utilization by those in need, Glazer is concerned with the impact of reform on the preservation of the family and of initiative. Not that Glazer is indifferent to other aims, but he seems more preoccupied with safeguarding traditional forms and

14. Nathan Glazer, 'The Limits of Social Policy', *Commentary*, vol. 52, no. 3, 1971.

values. As he has come to recognize this bias in his analysis, he has reluctantly concluded that he has drifted to conservatism, and the lucidity of his self-analysis lays bare its critical assumptions. As Myrdal has claimed, the policy analyst should not deny his values but make them explicit.[15]

The Outcomes of Intervention

Some people believe that equalization can best be achieved indirectly through economic growth rather than directly through specific policies. However, it can also be shown that economic growth increases inequalities for some groups. This value assumption leads the analyst to inquire: Who tends to be left behind during periods of growth and development? Research on housing in London, for example, tried to document who gets hurt when there is a general improvement of housing quality. The study, which focused on those who are left out, discovered that the outcomes were complex, since it was not only the poor who were left out, but also those with large families, migrants, students and other transient groups. Many of these groups are not poor at all. The analyst requires new questions by which to identify new needs during different stages of economic and social development.

According to the values of the analyst, the same facts can lead to different interpretations as to how the circumstances of disadvantaged groups have been improved and the extent to which there has been a vertical redistribution of social welfare resources. Behind the meaning of social facts lie hidden values. Consider the case of the relative improvement of black and white incomes.

In October 1967, the White House released the report *Social and Economic Conditions of the Negroes in the United States*, which provided evidence that an upper-middle-income class had

15. Gunnar Myrdal, *Objectivity in Social Research*, Gerald Duckworth, 1969. He writes: 'Value premises in social science research must satisfy a number of conditions. They must be explicitly stated and not concealed as implied assumption' (p. 64).

already been created in black America. In 1966, twenty-eight per cent of all black families had incomes of over $7,000 a year. This figure was double the proportion in 1960 and four times greater than the proportion receiving such incomes in 1947. But this account of social progress can be reinterpreted and a grimmer analysis can be drawn from the same data. When the position of blacks is compared to whites in the $7,000 per annum income grouping, the portrait of improvement seems less substantial. In 1947, there were fifteen per cent more whites than blacks at this income cut-off point used to designate the middle-income group-ings. But in 1960, there were twenty-four per cent more whites than blacks. In absolute terms a black middle class seems to have failed to keep pace with the increase of white families in the same income bracket. It has also been pointed out that to reach the median income, $7,000, it takes three times as much effort on the part of black families as it does on the part of white families, when effort is defined as the number of workers in each family unit.

Six years later the debate continued unabated. In a provocative article in *Commentary* Richard Scammon and Ben Wattenberg argued that the blacks were marching 'across the invisible line into the lower-middle and middle class'. As evidence they cited statistics which show that black families headed by a male under thirty-eight years of age and living outside the South had achieved income parity with comparable white families. Indeed, when wives worked the economic position of blacks was better than that of whites. These gains are so impressive that they are best described as 'nothing short of revolutionary'. Herrington Bryce, reading much the same evidence, draws different conclusions. He points out first that those families who had achieved income parity comprise only ten per cent of all black families. Moreover, black median income remained stubbornly at fifty-nine per cent of white; the actual number of blacks in poverty increased by 300,000, leaving one third of all blacks in poverty as compared to nine per cent of whites; and virtually all of the one million families who had left poverty were white. By focusing on poverty rather than the emergence of a black middle class, and on the relative position of blacks as a whole rather than selected élite sub-groups,

Bryce concludes that the economic progress for blacks has been disappointing.[16]

If the same facts are set in a different time perspective the interpretation may alter because the context in which the facts are viewed is changed. For example, in an illuminating discussion of health expenditures in England, Titmuss compared the central government's level of expenditure for working-class groups at the turn of the century with expenditure after the introduction of the National Health Service Act in 1946.[17] He was able to demonstrate that the amount of public resources going to the working-class had actually declined rather than improved. Similar attempts have been made to demonstrate lack of progress in education and housing.

In the United States, Banfield has developed the opposite position. He has tried to demonstrate, for example, that there has been substantial improvement in the urban housing stock since the Second World War, and yet we continue to be dissatisfied with the quality of housing available in inner cities. To explain this discrepancy between real achievements and the sense of crisis, we must recognize that standards have risen faster than our material improvements. To achieve a sense of progress we must expect less, rather than try harder. The villain of the piece is expectation rather than performance.[18]

The emphasis on outcome presupposes that means and ends can be analytically separated, as opposed to the more pragmatic orientation which accepts their fusion. Those responsible for developing and implementing policies often accept the latter position. The conflict between the analyst and the practitioner frequently resides in this philosophical difference. I have argued that, when the aims of policy are broadly and vaguely defined,

16. For a review of the debate see Tom Wicker, 'Up the Ladder, but how Fast?', *The New York Times*, 22 July 1973. A comprehensive review of this issue can be found in Sara Levitan and others, *Still a Dream: the Changing Status of Blacks since 1960*, Cambridge, Mass., Harvard University Press, 1975.

17. Richard Titmuss, 'Health', in Morris Ginsberg, ed., *Law and Opinion in England in the Twentieth Century*, Stevens, 1959, pp. 299–318.

18. Edward Banfield, *The Unheavenly City*, Boston, Little, Brown, 1970.

more attention should be given to understanding the nature of the *inputs* and the *processes* that link these inputs to desired outcomes. It is especially important in social policy to guard against evaluating what I call 'non-events'; that is, we must make sure that no substitution of resources has occurred, that there is in fact a programme to evaluate, and that resources as allocated are also resources as received, from the consumer's point of view. The study of processes is important for other reasons: even if we establish how inputs and outputs are related to each other, we cannot modify their relationships unless we understand the processes by which they are joined.[19]

Obviously the analyst's values are not the only factor in evaluation. Independent criteria also play their part, but these explicit criteria are not always self-evident. For instance, what are the relevant criteria for evaluating a legal programme which initiated class actions or citizen participation in community action programmes, or for weighing the outcomes of programmes which contain multiple aims – if we could agree on what these aims were?

A distinction can be drawn between substantive and procedural outcomes. The former is concerned with specific choice and the latter with the process by which decisions are made, or the logic of problem-solving.

One approach to the *substance* of policy is offered by Eveline Burns, who explains that 'intelligent policy formation, i.e., the attainment of the best possible compromise between conflicting objectives, can be expected only if people know what they are choosing between. And the choice is not of an "either-or" character but between relatively more and relatively less. There are no absolutes.'[20] Knowledge about the consequences of policy, she asserts, does not provide sufficient grounds for policy choice. Even when social measures may lower the general level of output, we may decide to pursue them because 'men attach value not only to economic considerations but to other ends as well'. These

19. Robert Weiss and Martin Rein, 'The Evaluation of Broad-Aim Programs: Experimental Design, Its Difficulties and an Alternative', *Administrative Science Quarterly*, 15 March 1970, pp. 97–109.

20. Eveline Burns, *Social Security and Public Policy*, New York, McGraw-Hill, 1956.

trade-offs produce a system which lacks consistency and coherence. Knowledge of the system enables one to highlight these contradictions, but does not provide a strategy for avoiding them. So the clarification of choices and their consequences does not offer, by itself, rules for choosing. The essential substantive issue in policy analysis is the reconciliation of aims – each desirable, but most also conflicting.

The approach to analysis which focuses on outcomes through rational *procedures* calls for information, analysis, decision, implementation, feedback, and re-analysis. The validity of the model does not require that information ever be complete, because the process is self-correcting as feedback leads to re-analysis, that is, the reassessment of policy in the light of experience. Progress in making rational policy choices will be hastened with the development of better tools for securing information. Whether the emphasis on systems of information can be applied independently, without substantive knowledge of a problem (such as poverty or delinquency), or an understanding of the needs of special populations (like the aged or children), or insight into the structure and history of specific programmes (like housing or social work), remains a pragmatic question to be judged by experience.

One specific form of this procedural approach, the American Programming, Planning, Budgeting System (P.P.B.S.), has been formalized at the federal level. But to apply the model requires some articulation of social objectives: it is most relevant where the goals are clear. Unfortunately, P.P.B.S. cannot produce the kind of information that is needed to clarify political choices in many crucial areas. Some of the limits are suggested by William Goram, former Health, Education and Welfare Assistant Secretary for Programming–Budgeting Systems, in remarks made in the 1967 Hearings Before the Subcommittee on Economy in Government of the Joint Economic Committee. (Emphasis has been added.)

Would the total benefits from an additional million dollars spent on health programs be higher or lower than that from an additional million spent on education or welfare? *If I was ever naïve enough to think this sort of analysis possible, I no longer am.* The benefits of health, education, and welfare programs are diverse and often inangible. They affect different age groups and different regions of the population over different periods of time. No amount of analysis is going to tell us whether the Nation benefits more from sending a slum child to pre-school, providing medical care to an old man or enabling a disabled housewife to assume her normal activities. The 'grand decisions' – how much health, how much education, how much welfare, and which groups in the population shall benefit – are questions of value judgements and politics. The analyst cannot make much contribution to their resolution.

At its best, rational analysis tries to develop a calculus for summing up the costs and gains of public policies for different societal groups over time; but it cannot provide a decision rule that determines which groups should gain or lose. Rational analysis must 'buck-up' to the political process the ultimate decision. It places its faith on the assumption that information facilitates 'good' decisions, but it offers no criteria for judging what is a 'good' decision except the circular argument that it is one informed by information.

Attempts to make the benefits of different social action programmes which reach different clientele comparable, have floundered on the stubborn and, perhaps in the end, intractable problem of identifying a common base for comparison (commensurability). Moreover, to rely chiefly on measures of the increase in future income not only raises difficult technical questions of how to assess the present value of future income (the problem of the size of the discount rate), but creates an illusion of a spurious consensus, for many are becoming disillusioned with the concept of increasing the material income as the single overarching goal to which all public policies must be subordinated. Shadow prices for non-income benefits are as arbitrary as they may be ingenious. But even more disturbing than the inability to contribute to the problem of the allocation of resources among programmes such as health, housing, education and welfare, is Alice Rivlin's conclusion that little is known about how to increase the effectiveness within a single programme area. She observes that 'there is scant analytical basis for predicting the behaviour of individuals in response to changes in incentives or availability of new kinds of services'.[21]

Rivlin seems confident that if better information is generated by the programme, analysts will have more to contribute. Perhaps so, but social science analysis seems to be better at dispelling beliefs than at inventing effective programmes. Major policy studies in recent years confirm this judgement at many levels. The Westinghouse experiment showed little change in performance in the first and second grades as a result of the Head Start programmes. The Coleman report concluded that despite wide differences in the measure of educational achievement at elementary and secondary levels, they cannot be accounted for by differences among the schools.[22] Probing more deeply into the basic norms of a liberal democracy and an industrial economy are empirical studies which confirm beliefs held at opposite ends of the political spectrum – that races are unequal and that the will to work is not threatened by income guarantees.

How can these shattered illusions about education, race and work be used politically? Moynihan suggests that to tell the truth as a basis for presidential initiative is a great political mistake. Politicians and administrators who use these social science findings will be in trouble. There is much to commend his position. Perhaps the critical question when observation offends beliefs and common sense is: when should we abandon or modify beliefs and have the political courage to act on these findings, and when should we repudiate the studies for their methodological weakness, holding firm to our beliefs?[23] This conflict between dogmatism and openness is found in science as well as policy analysis.

21. Alice M. Rivlin, *Systematic Thinking and Social Action*, Berkeley, H. Rowan Gaither Lectures, 1970.

22. James S. Coleman and others, *Equality of Educational Opportunity*, Washington, D.C., HEW-GPO, 1966.

23. For a review and analysis of the general ineffectiveness of evaluative studies in federal social policies, see Joseph Wholly and others, *Federal Evaluation Policy*, Washington, D.C., Urban Institute, 1970.

Political Feasibility

Analysis of policy issues is also shaped by the analyst's search for solutions that are politically feasible. The commitment to feasibility is based on a desire to influence the development of policies. Since political considerations play a prominent, if not the dominant, part in shaping policy, the analyst will shape his analysis so that it takes account of these political factors. In saying this I do not wish to suggest that there is a crass sell-out of beliefs or a gross distortion of evidence in order to produce politically usable reports and recommendations. Nevertheless, in subtle but important ways the wish to be relevant influences policy analysis. The most obvious way that this occurs is in failure to press the analysis to those root causes that, at present, are politically unresponsive to change. 'Welfare colonialism' or white racism may be unacceptable interpretations as causes of poverty and social unrest at one time, yet received ideas at another.

Subordination of policy analysis to politics is usually taken as the foundation on which the political process operates. But in reality 'many of the pleas for more research, a more technically trained higher Civil Service, and a reorganization of the process of government are really pleas for a different political system which will hand over the management of public affairs to experts in particular skills or professions'.[24]

I am not challenging the relationship between policy and politics, but rather examining different approaches to it. The first approach attempts to document how politics affect policy choice. One practical purpose of such inquiries is to present a spectrum of policy options that might be relevant under different political environments. In practice, criticism of new policies is often based on an inaccurate assessment of political possibilities. The second approach uses research as a political strategy to win

24. Lord Plowden and Sir Robert Hall, 'The Supremacy of Politics', *The Political Quarterly*, 39, October–December 1968, p. 368.

acceptance for changes to protect vulnerable programmes when they are under attack.

Before turning to these approaches, it is useful to reaffirm the central thesis of this chapter that behind the analysis of political feasibility rests the analyst's belief system about the process by which policies change, which influences the kind of analysis pursued. The dominant mode of thought on this subject in American political science is that of incrementalism. 'Democracies change their policies almost entirely through incremental adjustments. Policy does not move in leaps and bounds.'[25] Within this setting the political processes of bargaining, logrolling, and coalition-building are, of course, the major factors that produce a situation where past decisions are the best predictors of future ones.

Much of the tradition of policy analysis is based on procedural values that emphasize pragmatism and progress, although there are some variations of this basic theme. If muddling and incrementalism are the processes by which change takes place, in what sense is it ever legitimate to assume that there is any policy, if we take policy to mean agreed objectives implemented by some consistent and mutually reinforcing course of action? Policy, which implies a consensus and a course of action, is itself a misnomer, for it masks the ambiguity of aims and obscures the contradictions in legislative action. For example, our economic policy, anxious about inflation, acts to slow down the economy, thus decreasing the volume of employment available to those very groups a manpower retraining programme is supposed to place in the market. Typically, we have programmes without policies, and many programmes are themselves internally contradictory, since they avoid choice among conflicting objectives. The same processes also stress a close relationship between growth and change. To improve the position of the poor, programmes are needed which encourage more for all, that is, an overall growth in volume. This strategy assures political acceptability. At the margin of growth, a fair share, or perhaps a greater share, can be

25. Charles E. Lindblom, 'The Science of Muddling Through', p. 344 in Nelson W. Polsby, Robert A. Dentler and Paul A. Smith, eds., *Politics and Social Life*, Boston, Houghton Mifflin, 1963.

allocated for the poor. While growth is not a sufficient condition for redistribution, it is a necessary one. Finally, most professional activity, especially in planning, is rooted in a theory of reform based on a similar theory of incremental pragmatism. The hallmark of planning is a stubborn optimistic pragmatism which has 'the confidence that problem-solving man could reduce any of his difficulties by adapting appropriate processes of management or experimentation'.[26]

The concept of political feasibility is often closely associated with the idea of incremental change. The theory of disjointed incrementalism holds that, in the end, muddling and compromise are the only rational approaches to the management of conflicting multiple and ambiguous goals. This school of thought has had an enormous impact on planning and policy analysis. The incrementalists see resistance to change not as stupidity but as the muffled rationality which is the outcome of political bargaining. But this form of trade-off can take place only when all groups with a stake in the outcome of a given issue have access to the political process. Inequalities in the distribution of influence and power destroy the rationality of the process by failing to make available to weak groups the resources they need to enter into the bargaining arena. But what happens when groups with incompatible ends have 'equal' influence? Is the result deadlock? The dilemma of democracy is how to redistribute resources to politically weak and inarticulate groups in the interests of justice, without producing paralysis and reducing the capacity of government to act. Every policy analyst must come to terms with the philosophy of incrementalism. His assessment of the ability of specific policies to cope with the problems for which they are designed will rest upon whether he repudiates, embraces, or compromises with the doctrine of incrementalism.

There are some alternative radical, but not revolutionary, approaches to providing changes on behalf of marginal and disadvantaged groups. One of these rests on the belief that concessions can be won by strategies of disruption. Cloward and Fox

26. John W. Dyckman, 'Introduction to Reading in the Theory of Planning: The State of Planning Theory in America' (mimeograph, n.d.).

Piven have recently argued that improvement for the poor is best created by exploiting the natural rage of those who are aggrieved, who spontaneously seek redress by politics of confrontation rather than cooperation.[27] Organizers who try to channel these efforts into more formal organizational structures for barter undermine their viability, because the poor lack the sophistication to convert the process to gain.

The idea of counter-structures as strategies of change has been proposed by reformers at the Cambridge Institute, to provide a more permanent pressure for significant reform. While the problem of co-opting the successful efforts remains unresolved, proponents still believe that much can be achieved. Towards this aim they have supported legislation such as the Community Development Corporation and are encouraging the creation of new towns built as counter-institutions.[28] Yet even these more radical approaches to change accept that a gradual and evolutionary process, contained by professionalism and cooperation is at work. Nevertheless the distrust of incrementalism encourages at least an openness to competing views of what is politically feasible.

The Prediction of Feasibility

How do beliefs about incrementalism influence studies of feasibility which try to relate more systematically the political environment with policy choices that can be translated into legislation? What is politically capable of being implemented will, of course, vary under different political circumstances. Yet, to study prevailing public or legislative opinion and to map out a strategy based on this analysis has a built-in conservative bias. Since political leadership can create new environments of acceptability, there are

27. Richard A. Cloward and Frances Fox Piven, 'Poor People's Movements and How They Die' (mimeograph), 1970.
28. For a description, see Matthew Edel, *Community Development Corporations*, Cambridge, Mass., Center for Economic Development, 1970. For a critique, see Martin Rein, *Social Policy: Issues of Choice and Change*, New York, Random House, 1970.

different ways of looking at feasibility depending on one's objectives and power to exert influence.

In his study of the development of policy in medical care Marmor offers a detailed account of the decision-making process in the debate about Medicare and Medicaid under the Johnson Administration.[29] He points out that the strategy of hospital insurance for the aged sought by the Administration was largely based on an assessment of the hostile political environment that existed in the 1930s. Under this strategy the greater risks of the most vulnerable groups were selected – hence the decision to limit legislation to hospital insurance for the aged. Since the Second World War, Democratic administrations have continued to support this political strategy. But after Johnson's resounding defeat of Goldwater, a consensus Congress emerged, breaking what McGregor Burns called the 'deadlock of democracy'. In this altered political environment there was receptivity for a bold expansion of the strategy – insurance to cover the costs of physician care as well. An unprepared administration thus found itself accepting a programme of physician services without an adequate analysis of how to manage the complex problems associated with its implementation. One result was skyrocketing physician costs. Marmor accepts the importance of political factors, but criticizes the political cost-benefit analysis, which failed to recognize when the political climate had changed.

The failure to recognize when non-incremental policies are acceptable is also central to Manly's criticism of Cavala and Wildavsky's prediction that 'Income by right is not politically feasible in the near future. The President will not support it and Congress would not support it if he did.'[30] The prediction was partially wrong, as the Family Assistance Plan of 1970 did pass the House, although it never managed to get out of the Senate Finance Committee. Manly argues the analysts should have

29. Theodore Marmor, *Politics of Medicare*, New York, Humanities Press, 1970.

30. John F. Manly, 'The Family Assistance Plan: An Essay on Incremental Policy-Making', a paper delivered at the Annual Meeting of the American Political Science Association, September 1970 (mimeograph). William Cavala and Aaron Wildavsky, 'The Political Feasibility of Income by Right', *Public Policy*, 38, Spring 1970, p. 349.

considered 'the question of how a guaranteed income plan (or something close to it) might become feasible, instead of operating on the assumption that it was unfeasible . . .' Manly explains that when fundamental change in welfare became admissible, tolerance for the existing system was undermined. Presidential initiative for reform, especially from a Republican president, helped to alter public and congressional opinion, and a strategy was sought for making an innovation acceptable by creating a Bill which stressed work requirements and provided wage supplementation for the working poor (who were largely white). A straight poll of congressional opinion to determine support is misleading. More useful, Manly argues, is a micro-analysis of the internal coalition structure of Congress. In the specific committee through which the Bill had to pass the conservative coalition was weakening, and leadership in the House Republican party had shifted to younger, more issue-oriented members who were responsive to change. Rather than assuming that innovative changes in policy are a rarity, analysts need to turn their attention to the conditions under which these changes are feasible.

Strategies to Promote Feasibility

Research is used both as a means to understand an issue and as a strategy for broadening a programme's acceptability. Studies are often generated to save a politically threatened programme or to enhance the acceptability of a new one. The move to adopt a policy of combining public assistance payments and social services provides one example of the effort to combine policy analysis and political feasibility. For example, a research strategy published under the title, *Public Welfare: Time for a Change*,[31] called for a series of interviews with knowledgeable individuals to discuss problems of welfare and to encourage proposals for constructive alternatives. In addition, the evidence from ten demonstration programmes at state and local levels was drawn together to illustrate the practical value of increased professional social services. The opinion of experts and the findings from social

31. Elizabeth Wickenden and Winifred Bell, *Public Welfare: Time for a Change*, New York, N.Y. School of Social Work, 1961.

experimentation were assembled to make the case that professional social services 'resulted in improved family relationships, better housing, employment, or sometimes self-support'. Although this conclusion is cautious, the major strategy of the analysis was to try to give public welfare a positive image by emphasizing the contribution of social services to the reduction of economic dependency.

Such studies as *Time for a Change* and the more experimental demonstration studies designed to determine the effectiveness of social services in reducing dependency may be interpreted as a political strategy to rescue a programme from assault by national and local newspapers. The research provides a rationale that helps to protect the programme against attack at a time when open confrontation of crucial policy issues would hurt it.

As the political climate has changed, as open confrontation to redress injustice to blacks becomes more accepted, and as the welfare rolls dramatically rise, the avoidance of issues and the creation of myths such as 'services reduce dependency', are no longer acceptable. In this new political climate a shift from a service to an income strategy emerged. But how can the use of cash transfers be made more politically acceptable?

One of the greatest impediments to ideas about assured income is the fear that it might substantially reduce work incentives, thus multiplying costs. If labour force participation rates were greatly reduced, the economic viability of the system would be threatened. But, theoretically, increased income can produce two different effects – it can increase the desire to work as higher income augments the desire for still more income, or it can lead to the substitution of leisure for work. Policy is inhibited by uncertainty. Social experiments, designed to test the impact of levels of income guarantee and different marginal tax rates on labour force participation, could contribute much to dispel the fears of policymakers. (For a fuller discussion of this issue see Chapter 2, 'The Fact–Value Dilemma', pp. 64–6.)

A competing strategy for enhancing the feasibility of an income guarantee programme by research emerged within the Office of Economic Opportunity. O.E.O. had two policy research initiatives – one in the Community Action Program, which had the responsibility for launching and evaluating community demonstration projects as a strategy to promote innovation, and the second in Research, Program, Planning and Evaluation (R.P.P.&E.) which was responsible for long-range planning and evaluation of ongoing efforts. Conflict between these two groups inside O.E.O. took the form of a disagreement as to whether the Negative Income Tax experiment should be a social experiment or a demonstration project. A demonstration attempts to show that an innovative idea can be done – that it is administratively feasible, politically acceptable, and programmatically effective. By contrast an experiment is an attempt to estimate the order of magnitude of a response to a particular question. Its main focus is on using planned variations (rather than those which happen to exist already in the world) to get a specific answer to a specific question. In the case of N.I.T., the experiment was concerned with estimating the cost and the labour force response of families to a series of income guarantees and their accompanying rules for benefit. To a significant extent the disagreement between the O.E.O. offices was not just technical but reflected the different position held by activists and researchers. The activists viewed social science as taking an energetic role in proposing substantive solutions to policy questions, subtly blending science and belief but masking the contribution of ideology. Researchers, and especially those favouring a purely scientific approach, took the view that science should play a more passive role in the political process, with the scientist as a technician designing and reporting on the findings of social experimentation, whatever the result might be. A compromise between the demonstration and the experimental approaches was agreed.

One other way in which policy analysis can contribute to political feasibility is by systematically assessing public preferences and attitudes. On the assumption that governments cannot be more ambitious than those they govern and still survive politically, liberal democracy is still profoundly committed to the utilitarian argument that people should be enabled to ascertain their own ends and that each person is the best judge of his own well-being. J. S. Mill wrote: 'The most ordinary man or woman has means of knowledge immeasurably surpassing those that can be possessed by anyone else.'[32] But this position has its difficulties. People can be deluded about what's good for them. However, improvement of my way of life should not be imposed from above, not because 'I know better', but because I cannot enjoy my gain if I must give up my freedom to get it. So it is the task of policy analysis to provide policy-makers with some understanding of the consumer's will and how it changes over time.

Within this framework of thought, Etzioni has argued that we must develop a programme of insurance as protection against subsistence poverty.[33] Public acceptability is best promoted when programmes are funded by user contributions rather than relying upon general taxation. Hence, the proposal for a subsistence insurance. I do not wish to criticize the assessment that user charges are more acceptable because benefit levels in these programmes rise more rapidly and benefit is less stigmatizing than in programmes to which only the employers contribute or the funds come from the general budget. But it should be recognized that social insurance is based on the implicit assumption that the regressive tax structure in insurance programmes, where the poor pay higher proportions of their incomes, is the price that must be paid to assure the programme's wide public and legislative acceptance. Here it is the general approach, rather than the substantive argument, that is instructive. Etzioni's research calls for a systematic analysis of public opinion attitudes toward various social policies. He hopes that by drawing together empirical studies of public opinion over time, patterns showing which types of programmes are most acceptable to the community will emerge. The dangers are a mechanistic translation of public opinion into public policy, or a selective interpretation of the data from a position arrived at independently.

Conclusions

This chapter has identified the terrain of policy not by its subject matter but by its procedures of analysis. I have tried to illu-

32. J. S. Mill, *On Liberty*.
33. Amati Etzioni, 'Job and Subsistence Insurance', 1968 (mimeograph).

strate how values inform analysis in every aspect of the procedure.
What implications follow from this interpretation of policy
analysis? Policy analysis is not invalidated by the close relationship between values and modes of analysis, but it does seem that
there will never be one 'true analysis'. We cannot conclude that
every analysis must simply be *judged good or bad within the framework of its value assumptions*. On the contrary, the study of policy
can be most perceptive when it examines afresh the critical-values
assumptions on which action proceeds. And the assumption
about the context within which the analysis is framed is often
most important, including the definitions and the choices between constraints and options, which are typically based on belief
or opportunity or both.

This also suggests, at least implicitly, what might be the stance
of those who undertake policy analysis. Their most demanding
task is identification of their own values, along with an understanding of how these values blatantly and subtly bias analysis.
'The excessive involvement in one's own value preferences may
inhibit accurate observation ... [the analyst] will do his job
better if he is personally capable of a measure of temporary
suspension of passions in the process of achieving his highly
valued goals.'[34] I believe that this temporary detachment can be
encouraged by the recognition that many of the values we most
strongly cherish may at least partially conflict. But, in the end, detachment is not a substitute for action. We must make choices, and
these are finally based on brute preference. To search for some
Olympian platform supposedly detached from values is illusory.

Even if the analyst is successful in discovering his values, he
soon faces the ethical problem of how to act on his prejudices. An
explicit statement of values may weaken the political case for
reform. The concealment of values, by tactical ambiguity or
denial – which takes the form of a retreat into an impartial, dispassionate, value-free scientific stand – threatens moral integrity.

A review of the interplay of beliefs and analysis by its nature
poses more questions than it can resolve and frustrates efforts to

34. Ithiel de Sola Pool, 'Some Facts About Values', *PS*, newsletter of
the American Political Science Association), vol. III, no. 2, spring 1970,
p. 103.

develop policy analysis as a discipline. This happens because each of the terms of reference for conducting a policy analysis is insufficient by itself. We need a combined standard for judging the desirability of policies able to pass the tests of what is politically feasible, ideologically acceptable, and rationally compelling; and such a common standard can never be developed. So we return to the problem with which we began – how can we advance the study of the analysis of social policy when its basic subject matter and its modes of analysis are informed by an interpretation of beliefs? In the search for answers we have embraced eclecticism (or is it faddism?) as a substitute for disillusionment.

Chapter 5

Stratification and Social Policy

Ideologically both Britain and America are egalitarian societies, where political and civil rights are in principle the same for all, the equal worth of every citizen is accepted as a fundamental article of faith, and the inheritance of privilege broadly condemned. As secular democracies, they have rejected the notion of any divinely ordained hierarchy of privilege, while they hold to the Christian insistence on the unique value of each human experience. Yet both societies are, in practice, obviously stratified in ways which seem incompatible with these values.

I suggest in this chapter that the difficulty of defining a just and workable stratification policy reflects a pervasive confusion and conflict of values, which inhibit and distort every attempt to alter the prevailing distribution of rewards. Between uncompromising radical arguments for complete equality and conservative arguments for the protection of the poor from increasing hardships, it is hard to establish any consistent principles of intervention; and so egalitarian social policies, as much as income policies, tend to argue from elusive and vulnerable value premises, which lack the moral authority to challenge the established order.

My basic argument can be briefly summarized as follows:

(1) Equality is a difficult ideal to rationalize coherently;

(2) policies to reduce stratification are also confused and often mutually incompatible – partly because of the incoherence of egalitarian principles, but also from the complexity of the pressures which influence them;

(3) hence the efforts to reform stratification are, on the whole, at best only marginally successful. (We do not claim that ideo-

logical confusion itself is a major cause of the persistence of stratification, except in the sense that it weakens the argument for change.)

(4) In these circumstances a more widely accepted interpretation of equality might be more influential – such as the principle of equal respect and the equal right to be treated with dignity.

Stratification in Industrial Societies

I shall not attempt to review here the findings of contemporary studies – of the distribution of prestige and status by income and occupation, of the life-styles associated with class and status, or of the extent of occupational mobility among generations – which confirm the persistence of stratification. But three broad conclusions can be drawn from them:

(1) Class stratification exists in society. Although it is doubtful whether class itself can be characterized simply in one-dimensional terms, occupations are generally regarded as the most useful method of defining stratification. (Income, education and occupation are, however, only loosely related to one another, and we know very little about the distribution of occupations and earnings around a given level of educational achievement.)

(2) Stratification, however defined, tends to remain relatively stable over time, despite considerable mobility of individuals and occupational or income groups. Society cannot be characterized as rigidly class bound and income constrained. But some groups, for example Negroes and other minorities, remain persistently at a disadvantage at the lower income levels. The broad framework of inequalities is retained.

(3) Social class positions (income, occupation and education) are closely related to life-styles. In a democratic society these life-styles are valued, especially when they are measures of personal preferences. Moreover, these class differences are important because we derive our sense of social worth and personal identity from them.

It is not difficult to document the uncertain nature of evidence in this field, and each of these general conclusions can be modified in a number of ways. But when the main threads are drawn together we can conclude that a stable stratification system exists, offering some opportunities for mobility within an unequal society; these class differences are also reflected by life-styles on which identity and social worth depend.

The Rationalization of Inequality

How is such obvious stratification tolerated, in societies whose democratic ideology seems to repudiate the unequal treatment of their citizens? As John Goldthorpe asks of Britain, 'Why is it that, given the prevailing degree of social inequality, there is no widely supported and radical opposition to the existing socio-political order, and that at all levels of the stratification hierarchy attitudes of acceptance, if not of approval, are those most commonly found?'[1] It would not be surprising to find egalitarian ideals defeated by the self-protection of the privileged. But it is, surely, puzzling that inequality – apart from racial inequality[2] – should be so generally accepted; especially when, as we shall try to show, it can appeal only to the most doubtful moral rationalizations.

In societies where inequalities are so persistent and so firmly supported by custom and institutions, we would expect to find them explicitly justified by a set of countervailing principles, which challenge the egalitarianism of democracy by other values claiming equal moral authority. Yet these countervailing principles seem curiously uncertain, and the more clearly they are stated, the less they justify the pattern of stratification as it appears in practice. We suggest that for this reason people turn to egali-

1. John H. Goldthorpe, 'Social Inequality and Social Integration in Britain', *Advancement of Science*, December 1969.
2. The argument I present here does not take account of racial inequality, although in practice social stratification nearly always includes a racial bias. By ignoring this, I have simplified somewhat artificially – but it makes the point clearer. It would, of course, be possible to achieve perfect equality between races – collectively – without altering social stratification as such at all.

tarian arguments, even in defence of inequality; and, indeed, paradoxically, some of the rationalizations of inequality are more used by reformers seeking to help the poor than by the protectors of privilege. But first, let us look at the kind of arguments which seek to make inequality respectable.

The most explicit, perhaps, is the ideal of rewarding achievement, within a society where the opportunities for all are equal. Its crucial moral principle is the Puritan faith in hard work, thrift and prudence as signs of grace, and deserving of reward. So reward for achievement is advanced as a principle to legitimate inequality in the distribution of income, status and social class. But the argument depends on the assumption that the opportunities for all are indeed equal. Since, clearly, they are not, equality of opportunity becomes a slogan of reform, not a justification of things as they are: it appears regularly in the preambles to the proposals of Community Action and Model Cities Agencies in the United States.

Even as a radical proposition, the doctrine of equalizing opportunities runs into difficulties. If ability is partly innate, why should those fortunate enough to inherit the genes of talent be rewarded for their luck? We do not accept the corollary that those born with mental or physical defects should be left to their fate. And as Michael Young showed in his *Rise of the Meritocracy*,[3] the achievement of a perfect correspondence between talent and status could institute a hierarchy in which the self-assurance and security of those at the top would be appallingly absolute.

Apart from the rewards of achievement, the only other moral principle much in fashion seems to be the notion of compensation. It is a variation of the first: if hard work and talent deserve reward, the reward can be seen as compensation for the effort and expense of acquiring valuable skills. Hence wages should reflect the length and cost of training; the burden of risk and responsibility borne; the hardships incurred. Thus Adam Smith proposed a list of five 'principle circumstances' which he believed would account for the net wage advantage of a particular occupation: 'Agreeableness or disagreeableness, easiness or difficulty of performance,

3. Michael Young, *The Rise of the Meritocracy*, Thames and Hudson, 1958. Penguin Books, 1961.

expense of learning, degree of trust reposed in those who follow it and the probability of success or failure.'[4] But obviously enough, compensation is awarded on those terms only capriciously. University professors, who at least until recently were not thought to be exposed to much risk or hardship, are quite generously rewarded for their comfortable lives, while coal miners had to make do with much less until outside economic forces gave them greater bargaining power. No doubt film stars and corporation presidents suffer heroically, but is their work really ten or twenty times more exacting than teaching in a slum school, or collecting garbage in all weathers? However one may try to relate rewards to skill, training, risk, responsibility, hardship, danger or unpleasantness, the anomalies are so gross in reality that the exercise can only end up as a satirical tract.

Both of these moral arguments, whatever their inherent weaknesses, would radically challenge the present pattern of stratification if they were pressed – and so they are used more as arguments for reform than in support of what is. The defence of inequality seems to depend less on rationalization of its intrinsic justice than on the belief that it lies beyond the reach of value judgements. The labour market, like the weather, works by natural laws which can only be respected. People are paid according to the net marginal productivity of their labour, the scarcest skills in most demand command the highest price, and so it must be – just or not – if the economy is to maintain its vitality. On the whole, so the argument implies, the result will be for the greatest benefit of all: some will be much better off than others, but everyone will be better off than under an economy that constrained the market by moral prejudice and thereby inhibited its capacity to grow. The moral principle here is a utilitarianism as old-fashioned as the image of the economy on which it is based.

But here again the actual distribution of rewards is clearly not the outcome of a free market in skills. Trade unions, professional guilds, the control of entry to vocational training, restrictions on certification, conventions of status everywhere intrude to create artificial scarcities and isolate wages from the influence of demand.

4. Quoted in Guy Routh, *Occupation and Pay in Great Britain, 1906–60*, Cambridge University Press, 1965, pp. 136–7.

Hence this argument, too, turns out to be radical: if a free market is the way to recruit the talent to run a vigorous society, then a country like Britain is doing very badly, recruiting three quarters of its senior civil servants from the mere $2\frac{1}{2}$ per cent of the population privately educated in fee-paying grammar and public schools. Surely so small an élite cannot contain so high a proportion of the available talent?

If, then, we have fairly interpreted the plausible arguments for inequality, they all imply radical reform before their principles of justice can be realized – the abolition of inherited privilege, redistribution of educational resources from rich to poor, outlawing of restrictive trade practices and professional guilds, downgrading of safe, secure, irresponsible occupations and the upgrading of dangerous or responsible skills at present wretchedly paid. In practice, reformist political parties do draw upon these abuses, attacking privileged education, selective schooling, the class-bound recruitment of managerial talent, and (as far as they dare) the self-interest of restrictive occupational groups. Indeed, in recent years, British socialist leaders have presented political ideals less in terms of equality than of a rational inequality, distributing rewards according to the needs of a dynamic, modern, technically sophisticated economy, from whose rising productivity the poor would gain a generous share. In America, too, it is reformers concerned to help the poor and minorities who stress the justice of rewarding individual achievement and creating a more competitive society, in which the disadvantaged will enjoy a fair start in the race.

Inequality cannot, therefore, be rationalized to justify the stratification that exists in both Britain and America nor, especially, the ways in which the differences are maintained. The rationalizations characteristically refer to rewards to individuals for their particular contribution: but in practice, inequalities are defended far more by collective bargaining and the organized self-interest of professional groups; individual claims are rarely at issue. So we are left with the puzzle that an obvious and persistent stratification maintains itself in the face of our egalitarian ideology without any apparent legitimacy, and yet arouses remarkably little hostility. No major political party in either country believes it can win an election by appealing unambiguously for equality: rather, election campaigns seek a delicate balance between humanity towards the poor and reassurances that no one's position in society will be seriously disturbed.

The relative status groups enjoy in society is, of course, a crucial factor in maintaining inequalities. Social stratification represents much more than a pattern in the distribution of resources: it broadly defines our social identities. Where we live, how we spend our leisure, our relationship to family and friends; the way we teach our children, eat our meals, make love, argue about politics; our loyalties and tastes and sense of worth are all bound up with the status of our occupations. We are what our education, the work it led to and the income it earned have made us. And we are profoundly dependent on the stability of this identity, since it embodies the meaning of our lives. If it were radically threatened, we would lose the familiar purposes, the reliable relationships and comfortable routines on which our ability to make sense of our social environment rests. Certainly, we would like to be better off, promoted perhaps, or offered more interesting work; but we imagine the same self enjoying the extra margin of prosperity and prestige. Those who win an unexpected fortune and exploit all its material possibilities are often destroyed by their luck. We might like to make the neighbours jealous by displaying a new car; but if we also move away to a smart new neighbourhood, it becomes an empty triumph. There is a profound, protective conservative impulse in us all, which grasps at the familiar – not merely from cowardice, but because it contains the meaning of our lives. Radical change appeals only to those too young or too unfortunate to have acquired a secure sense of their social identity – and those who have incorporated a radical ideology as part of their interpretation of life. These are, and seem likely to remain in the near future, a minority in both Britain and America. Hence the politics of social stratification are, we believe, bounded by an underlying conservative premise: that each of us has a right to maintain the essential quality of his life – to be himself. And that self is defined by complex conventions of social differentiation.

Within these boundaries, the adjustment of status seems to

proceed by two kinds of argument. The first relates the present to the past, demanding that a given position be restored. The second relates an occupation or status to others which it claims to resemble and demands equal treatment. Both appeal to highly selective reference groups, by which one's own rightful position is defined. Characteristically, the arguments turn on the real value of incomes relative to what an occupation earned in the past, or to the earnings of one's peers. But much more than money is involved. If, for instance, school teachers see their income decline, compared with occupations they believe to be of similar status, they feel not merely impoverished, but dishonoured. They take their salary as a symbol of the value society places on their vocation: are they to accept that their work matters less than it used to? Thus wage claims may become involved in a passionate defence of social worth. Conversely, an occupational group on the make begins by redefining the reference group against which its wages are to be judged, and so the way it claims to be regarded by society. If it succeeds, it may threaten other occupations, who see their status encroached upon and then seek to restore the difference. When rubbish collectors in England won a claim for a thousand pounds a year, many people were shocked – not because they would gladly have done the job themselves for less – but because it raised dustmen's income to the level of occupations with much higher status pretentions. Thus, while there are marginal changes, especially where a job changes its character, the net effect of all these adjustments is to restore a familiar conception of social differences. When American university students try to repudiate their élite position and identify with the most disadvantaged, borrowing the vernacular style of the ghetto, they make nonsense of the whole system in a way which most people bitterly resent because their sense of their own worth is deeply involved in it.

It is not, of course, surprising that people use their economic and political power to protect whatever advantages they hold. But equally it would be surprising if they did so without appeal to any principle but self-interest. After all, the distribution of income is a matter of frequent public debate. Whenever there is a wage claim in a major industry, or a conspicuous strike, the dispute is discussed in the newspapers, spokesmen for management and labour put their case on television, the government does not hesitate to state its view, and independent arbitrators may be called in. Such a debate would be irrelevant if nothing but bargaining strength were at issue. And even more clearly, any proposal to shift the burden of taxation or reform social benefits raises questions of justice which must be decided somehow.

In the last few years, the distribution of incomes has become a growing issue, not only of social welfare policy, but of the management of the economy. Between 1964 and 1970, the Labour government in Britain tried hard to institute a policy for the regulation of wage claims as it struggled to solve the country's economic crisis. The White Paper on income policy in April 1965 gives special attention to raising the position of those workers who have 'fallen seriously out of line with the level of remuneration for similar work'.[5] By 1967 this principle of horizontal equity was subordinated to the principle that 'Improvements of the standard of living of the worst-off members of the community is a primary social objective . . . It will be necessary to ensure that any pay increases justified on this ground are genuinely confined to the lowest paid workers and not passed on to other workers.'[6] After several years of confusion, frustration, and inconsistency the Labour government abandoned its prices and income policy. The continued inflation which followed the policy's failure may have cost Labour the election in 1970.

After the election of the new government, a reluctant Conservative Prime Minister was forced to impose wage and price controls and to accept as well egalitarian ideals. A White Paper issued in March 1973 announced the intention of paying 'full regard to the objective of improving the relative position of the low paid'.[7] Of course, intention must not be confused with performance.

The miners' strike of 1974, and the general election it provoked, dramatized how crucial to stability of governments are the issues of who controls wage differentials, and what differentials are

5. *Prices and Incomes Policy* (Cmnd 2639), H.M.S.O., 1965.

6. *Prices and Incomes Standstill: Period of Severe Restraint* (Cmnd 3150), H.M.S.O., 1966.

7. *The Counter Inflation Programme: The Operation of Stage Two* (Cmnd 5267), H.M.S.O., 1973.

right. But the election did not settle these questions. I believe that, however pragmatic, flexible and complex a wage policy is likely to be, it cannot succeed unless it is fundamentally egalitarian in tendency. In the end no other principle will prove politically acceptable.

American policy also reluctantly accepted the view that only deliberate wage and price control is likely to restrain inflation. Despite President Nixon's declaration of faith in the operation of a free market, when he first came to office, in the face of a year of unprecedented price rises in a sluggish economy he was forced to pursue price controls. And, as in Britain, the Economic Stabilization Act of 1971, which created the authority to impose control, also accepted the principle that 'wage increases to an individual whose earnings are substandard or who is a member of the working poor shall not be limited in any manner, until such time as his earnings are no longer substandard or he is no longer a member of the working class'. When it came to implementation, the Cost of Living Council wished to exempt wage controls only for those who had a very low poverty wage of $1·90 per hour. Reducing inequalities was for the Council a secondary goal to that of reducing inflation. However the Council was required to increase the poverty wage to $2·75 under sustained pressure from Congress and the Courts.[8]

Wage control policy in the United States is based on the view that the structure of wages is governed by conventional expectations, reinforced by protective institutions, which prevent both an absolute fall in money wages, and any ready transfer of labour from one sector to another. From this point of view, therefore, an anti-inflationary policy of wage control should seek to restore the equilibrium. Rather than set any overall limit to increases, it needs to hold back leading key wage rates, while it permits lagging wages to catch up. Such a policy may have to tolerate a considerable short-term inflation while the structure recovers its balance. But once the balance is restored,

8. Robert H. Haverman and T. W. Mirer, *Price Controls and Income Redistribution in an Expanding Economy* (a Joint Economic Committee Print, 92nd Congress, 2nd Session), U.S. Government Printing Office, 1972, p. 308.

people will be receiving what they expect: their pay will reflect the occupational status they recognize. The policy assumes an inherent conservatism, which leads people to identify with these familiar expectations.

The government in Britain, as we have seen, put forward a principle of higher increases for the lowest paid. But, against this, it also tried to tie the increases to higher productivity, discriminating against all whose output could not be improved by technical aids, or measured in these terms. The British and American experiences show how difficult it is to define any principle of wage restraint that will be accepted as fair. Neither could withstand the pressure from occupational groups in a strong position to bargain.

It is easy to assert the principles on which a rational wage policy might be forged at a very general level, but this formulation neglects the inherent conflicts which emerge when the policy is put into operation:

We know indeed what a rational wage policy should achieve. It should give the worker the highest possible wage over the business cycle that is compatible with the highest possible employment over the business cycle. It should give the enterprise a predictable wage burden that would combine flexibility of labour costs over the business cycle with efficiency for each wage dollar spent. It should give the economy a maximum of stability. It should provide a wage burden neither so high as to make impossible the proper provision for the costs of the future, nor so low as to deprive the economy of the consumer purchasing power it needs. It should not push up the break-even point of industrial production to a level at which even a minor setback could produce widespread unemployment. But at the same time it should establish the principle that wages should go up in definite relation to an increase in productivity and efficiency.

But none of these is clear, objective or measurable. All attempts to arrive at objective yardsticks of the 'right' wage have been utterly futile. The objective and impartial determination of wages is sheer illusion.[9]

How then do we argue about these things? Plausible arguments for the justice of inequality are doubtful weapons in defence of present differences. No one knows, for example, at what level of

9. Peter Drucker, *The New Society: the Anatomy of Industrial Order*, New York, Harper Torchbooks, 1962, pp. 317–18.

taxation, if any, executive skill becomes discouraged from further effort; and it would be difficult to convince anyone that tax and income bear much relationship to any rational inducement of crucial skills. Indeed people seem to sense the subversive nature of these arguments and do not press them. Instead inequalities in society as a whole are sustained by piecemeal claims to equality within a much narrower frame of reference, as the egalitarian aims of price controls clearly indicate.

Arguments about the allocation of social welfare benefits are forced into the same context. In the past we have been able to appeal to physical suffering as the criterion, and indeed we still can, but this redefines the problem as one of poverty rather than inequality. But once the argument is divorced from absolute want, it becomes purely an argument about relative deprivation within a generally prosperous society.[10] If the arguments appeal to general principles of equality, or even to the rationalization of inequalities, they can only succeed if society is prepared for radical change – as, for instance, in Britain after the Second World War. At any other time, the conservative impulse will repudiate any serious attempt to implement these principles as Utopian and politically unrealistic. So if anything is to be done immediately for those in need, the argument falls back upon much the same principles of equity that inform the debates about wages. The assumptions are almost as conservative, and the range of comparisons equally narrow. If you can show the value of a benefit has fallen in relation to the cost of living or, more ambitiously, in relation to average income; if you can demonstrate that people in one category are differently treated from those in another, where the needs seem similar; or if you can establish anomalies in policies towards people in essentially similar circumstances – then your case is persuasive, because it does not threaten conventional expectations. Thus arguments about the equitable treatment of

10. Public policy in the U.S., however, still does not accept a relative conception of poverty. Here the poverty line relative to median income has steadily declined from 46% in 1959 to 38% in 1968 and about 33% in 1972. Poverty is stubbornly defined as a subsistence concept rather than in terms of the acceptable limits of inequalities. But inequalities are not altogether rejected. In the past as the poverty line fell in relation to median income, poverty was redefined and rediscovered.

specific groups seem politically more practical than idealistic arguments for equality.

But reducing inequities in this way tends to introduce complementary inequities elsewhere. Most European societies for instance have instituted earnings-related pension schemes, which try to sustain the relative value of retirement benefits in spite of inflation and rising living standards. As a principle of equity, people should neither suffer a sharp decline in their standard of life when they retire, nor lose their relative position in old age through rising costs. Their present circumstances should bear a close relationship to their past. Ideally, then, the public pension should fully replace lost wages: in practice, most countries compromise, accepting replacement rates from one half to two thirds as the highest current financial outlay they can afford. The efforts to promote equity between different stages of the life-cycle, through wage-related superannuation schemes, conflict with the aim of creating equity within an age group, which was embodied in the principle of flat-rate benefits. Thus equity between the active and retired creates inequities among those in retirement. Swedish social policy has since 1959 recognized this dilemma and created a new principle of paying benefits to reduce the differentials between those receiving wage-related pensions and those who only receive flat-rate benefits or benefits related to a very low wage.

Consider another example of interdependency in welfare reform: income-tested programmes which distribute benefits selectively by some criterion of economic need. These programmes are closely interrelated, so that an improvement in one benefit can effect entitlement to others, both within and outside the family of means-tested programmes, and these readjustments can nullify the value of the initial improvement in net terms.

So when arguments about the distribution of welfare benefits are narrowed to specific questions of equity, each reform tends to achieve more equal treatment in one respect only at the cost of instituting inequities in another. Nor do these marginal adjustments seriously challenge the overall distribution of rewards. Simply, the emphasis is shifted from one concept of disadvantage to another within the limits of an established pattern of stratification. Such arguments are certainly an important part of the process by which the disadvantaged are defended against gradual impoverishment and neglect. But their persuasiveness, even to conservative governments, rests on a tacit acceptance of a familiar order of differentiation.

We suggest, then, that any arguments for egalitarian social policies which fall short of revolutionary absoluteness suffer from the uncertainty of the principles on which they rest. Where they are not trapped by implicitly conservative assumptions, they tend to argue for a more rational inequality which, if it were ever achieved, would probably offend those who propose it as much as does the incoherent injustice of things as they are. Against this background of moral and intellectual confusion, how do the recognized strategies for intervening in the process of stratification make out?

The Reform of Stratification

Broadly speaking, policy to modify stratification can follow two alternative approaches. Firstly, it can encourage individual occupational mobility. But a coherent strategy of individual mobility requires that other conditions be satisfied. Recruitment and downward mobility need to be contained, so that fewer people enter jobs of low income and prestige. If the demand for these jobs remains constant, the growing scarcity of applicants should raise the wages and working conditions of those who remain behind, or draw more of the unemployed into work. Such a position must also assume that there is a growth in the demand for higher occupational skills which substantially exceeds the supply of new job entrants and can therefore absorb those in lower skilled occupations seeking mobility. This theory presupposes an underlying change in the structure of society, producing more middle-class occupations while eroding the demand for unskilled labour. But even if there is evidence to support such a broad trend at a national level, the pattern in particular areas or cities may be quite different. Moreover, we must assume that the distribution of occupations is roughly linear.

Mobility does not take place typically by great leaps from one end of the spectrum to the other. Improvement in status and earning is more gradual. Thus cities which attract the rich and the poor, but not the middle, would find that those at the bottom have little place to move. Heroic assumptions about the low costs of geographic mobility to achieve occupational mobility are obviously required if this awkward problem is to be avoided. The increased marginal costs of housing which accompany each geographic movement may alone offset economic gains achieved by a change of occupation. These difficulties complicate the task but do not alter the essential line of argument.

The ability to achieve is a combination of genetic, personal and environmental forces. While it is necessary to alter those aspects of the environment which inhibit the capacity to achieve, simply providing educational opportunity will not be enough. Increasingly we have moved in the direction of creating a whole range of supportive social services to enable economically deprived groups to alter their economic position. These services are most efficiently organized when they are directed at a group in a relatively homogeneous residential area.

Alternatively, policy can try to encourage collective rather than individual mobility. This will not eliminate stratification, but it can change the degree of inequality by shifting the position of the groups at the bottom relative to those at the middle or top. This could be accomplished by raising the prestige level, working conditions, salary levels, fringe benefits or some combination of these approaches. We might alter the wage levels of the low income groups so that they accelerate more rapidly than those of other occupational groupings. In principle, a wages or incomes policy can be geared to do this. The market itself could be used as a mechanism by massive government purchases of the goods and services in those sectors which employ low-income and low-occupational groups. More direct intervention could also be pursued, through policies directed at reducing the number of levels of differentiation within a given industry. If each separate level demands some wage differentiation from the level above or below it, then the fewer the number of levels the less the spread of income.

While raising relative wage levels can alter the prestige of an occupation, other policies may also be pursued. For example, in the United States the poverty programme has sought to upgrade the prestige associated with service occupations, such as housework, by encouraging men to enter this field and helping them to form a business enterprise to reduce the personal relationship between helper and employer. Or the difference in economic security between wage and salary earners can be narrowed when those who are paid on an hourly or weekly basis receive an annual income. Automobile workers in the United States have narrowed the differentials between white- and blue-collar workers by winning an annual income.

Policies that attempt to reduce differentials by taxation also work towards collective mobility. Groups may be permitted to retain more of the earnings they command, and social benefits may also augment the value even of modest earnings. Differentials in economic well-being and prestige can be narrowed directly and indirectly through such strategies. For example, occupational pensions, once limited largely to managerial groups, have now been extended to other levels within the occupational hierarchy.[11]

Perhaps the most acceptable way of achieving equality, since it does not affect the stratification of rewards or the preservation of differentials, is to remove a sector of life from the class of rewards for which people compete; by expanding the range of public provision. The National Health Service in Britain is a prototype of a public policy designed to provide an important service for all, irrespective of income and occupational position. The principle can be extended to education, housing, food consumption, etc. Such a policy can narrow the impact that income differentials have on the level of well-being, if there is no class bias in the use of these services. This may be the case in Britain, at least for medical care.[12]

11. The quality of these pensions may differ in terms of their benefit levels, transferability and vesting. This example illustrates both the way in which the position of a total group can be raised relative to other occupational groups, and how difficult achieving these aims may be.

12. Martin Rein, 'Social Class and the Health Service', *New Society*, 20 November 1969.

Why Choose between Occupational Up-Grading and Individual Mobility?

It is difficult to pursue both policies simultaneously because they are in conflict with each other. If the most talented individuals are 'creamed off', the group left behind would be less competent to negotiate its demands for improved conditions. All policies designed to encourage individual mobility within occupations, within communities, or within regionally depressed areas suffer from this difficulty. In public housing projects where an income ceiling is placed on the eligibility of tenants, an individual who improves his position will exceed the income limit and be forced out. The more vulnerable and less competent tenants are left behind, creating a community continually impoverished of its likeliest leaders, and those who could best protect it from stigma. But if we try to improve the position of the group as a whole, then policies must be designed to encourage individuals to stay behind and to provide leadership and cohesion to the group. Such a policy discourages individual mobility, on the grounds that the improvement of the group as a whole depends on the continued identification of its strongest members. But this distinction should not be drawn too sharply. For example, a trade union official is individually mobile but still works for the group from which he came. It is possible to make leadership of a depressed class a relatively higher status job.

The Difficulties in Altering Stratification

Neither of the theories for altering stratification seem to be very effective. A variety of studies conducted in the United States, Britain and the Continent all suggest the difficulty of equalizing educational opportunities and encouraging individual mobility through education. Equality of opportunity is an elusive concept and there is less than full agreement on what empirical evidence would support or refute the claim that inequalities have been reduced. But the evidence available in three broad areas is discouraging. Despite dramatic increases in the absolute number attending school at all levels and despite increased proportional expenditures for compensatory education, we find that the social class disparities have persisted in (a) educational achievement, (b) educational participation rates, and (c) the economic benefits of education.

Social class differences in educational achievement have been identified as the child enters school. A recent report in the U.S. Office of Education concluded that a deprived child needs about 0·43 years of additional educational effort for each school year to catch up with the non-deprived child. In other words, when children enter school there is about half a year's difference in educational achievement by social class as measured by maths and reading achievement scores. The difference in achievement then widens by a little less than half a year for each additional year of schooling, so that by the time the children enter High School there is a three- to four-year achievement gap. Such findings may, however, be an artifact of the testing procedure, since tests are constructed to measure greater variability in performance among older children. A different way to look at achievement is suggested by the U.S. Census, which reports that only 4 per cent of the children of high-income families ($10,000 or more) were in grades below the modal grade for their age, as contrasted with 37 per cent of children in lower-income families ($3,000 or below).[13] This gap in educational achievement has not been reduced through compensatory educational programmes directed at the school and teachers. To cite just one example, an evaluation of Title 1 of the Elementary and Secondary Education Act in 1967 and 1968 concluded that 'one-fifth of the participants achieved a significant gain in reading, roughly two-thirds showed no change, and the rest showed some loss'.[14] Despite our efforts,

13. 'The Role of Education in Promoting Social Mobility and Equality of Income', the Paris Centre for Educational Research and Innovation, 12 December 1969, p. 3 (mimeograph).

14. 'Educational Growth and Educational Opportunity', O.E.C.D., for the Paris Centre for Educational Research and Innovation, 26 September 1969, p. 10 (mimeograph).

we have not discovered ways to narrow significantly the gap in relative educational achievement among the social classes.

There is, of course, a continuing debate about how best to account for these discouraging findings. When the Coleman report was issued, it was fashionable to relate achievement to the social and economic background of the pupils and to discount the contribution of education resources as a causal agent in educational deprivation. One re-analysis of the original data reached a far more cautious conclusion, arguing essentially that very little is known about what produces achievement outcomes because of the large number of factors that comes into play. In an attempt to simplify the multivariable problem, the report concludes that the socio-economic background of students alone can account for 12 per cent of the differences in pupil achievement, while the characteristics of schools and teachers account for only 6 per cent. The remaining 82 per cent depends on a combination of these factors which cannot be isolated.[15] Thus the issue is muted.

Social class disparities in educational participation rates have also persisted, despite the increase in the length of time that all groups remain in school. But this conclusion largely depends on the measure of participation used – *enrolment rates* at a given level of formal education or in terms of total years of study; *attrition rates*, which take account of drop-outs; or *transition rates*, which measure movement between grades or levels of education, for example, from secondary school to college. By our first measure, class difference appears to be narrowing slightly in the United States. The bottom quintile had 8·6 per cent of the total number of years of education in 1950 and 10·7 per cent by 1970. By contrast, the top quintile had 31 per cent in 1950 and its share declined modestly to 29·3 per cent by 1970.[16] But when we consider the attrition rates we find that the drop-out rate between the tenth and twelfth grades was six times as high for the lowest socio-economic group as compared with the highest. Nor are

15. 'Teachers Do Make a Difference', *American Education*, May 1970.
16. Lester Thurow and Robert Lucas, 'The American Distribution of Income: A Structural Problem', *Joint Economic Committee*, March 1972, p. 15.

these differentials simply attributable to a close relationship between ability and social class. When the bottom half of the ability distribution is examined, we find that the drop-out rate for children in the lower socio-economic group is twice as high as for the better off. But in the top half of the ability distribution, poorer children have five times the drop-out rate of the more prosperous children.[17] Low ability is, at best, only partly related to the number of years people stay at school.

The persistence of social disparities in educational participation is evident everywhere. A review based on evidence from nineteen member countries of O.E.C.D. concludes:

Social differences in educational participation is a universal phenomenon. In country after country, the chances of being in school are distinctly superior for those with higher status origins, somewhat advantageous for those with 'middle class' backgrounds, and inferior for those from the lower strata or with agricultural backgrounds. Only the magnitude of differences varies among countries, and even here the similarities among nations are more impressive than the dissimilarities.[18]

When the transition between secondary school and college is studied, similar findings emerge. In the United States and Britain the working class comprise about one-quarter of the population of those receiving higher education. Cross-national comparisons are filled with hazards, because the definitions are so treacherous. For example, teacher education is part of university training in the United States, but not in Britain. On the assumption that educational expansion is a precondition for equalization of educational opportunities, it was a great shock when the Robbins Report on university education in Britain reported that despite the substantial growth of university enrolment, the likelihood of manual workers' sons going to university between 1925 and 1961 had changed very little, while the chances of non-manual workers' sons increased very substantially during this period of growth.

An American study, Project Talent, tried to relate transition rates to ability and class. This report found that among those who

17. For a review of this and other studies see Thorsten Husen, *Social Background and Educational Careers*, Paris, O.E.C.D., 1972, p. 72.
18. 'Educational Growth and Educational Opportunity', op. cit., p. 6.

scored in the top 10 per cent on academic aptitude tests, 14 per cent of the children did not go on to college if their fathers were blue-collar workers or failed to complete high schooling, as compared with 3 to 4 per cent of children whose fathers were white-collar workers or high-school graduates.

Equalizing educational achievement, participation and transition rates is, after all, only a means to the end of equalizing incomes and that still more elusive aim of well-being, which income is presumed to crudely measure. While it is very difficult to isolate the relative importance of length and quality of schooling, personal ability, academic achievement and market demand forces associated with labour-market conditions, all studies consistently report that rates of return from education differ by social class and race. Even when ability is taken into account, earnings differentials are not simply accounted for by different investments in education. Thus investment in human capital is an insufficient explanation of inequality in earnings.

Jencks reports that after the association between schooling, initial ability, and family background are taken into account, 'an extra year of elementary or secondary schooling really boosts future income less than 4 per cent, an extra year of college boosts it about 7 per cent and a year of graduate school boosts it about 4 per cent'. Note however that these figures are, of course, averages. A comparison of mean differences between groups do show that education and income are related.

Moreover, these averages affect groups differently. Thus, 'An extra year of schooling . . . seems to do about twice as much for a student from a middle-class background as for a student from a working-class background. It is more valuable for white than for black' (although Jencks observes that racial disparity appears to be declining).[19] These findings were to some extent obscured by the main thrust of Jencks's analysis, which is designed to show that dispersion within a group is as wide as the spread between groups. There is almost as much economic inequality among those who score high in academic aptitude tests as in the general population. His main conclusion is that inequality is recreated a new in each

19. Christopher Jencks, *Inequality*, New York, Basic Books, 1972, p. 223; Penguin Books, 1973.

generation, even when people start off in more or less similar circumstances. The statements are not contradictory, they are simply different ways of looking at the same data.

Husen's study in Sweden, a country deeply committed to egalitarian policies, shows that individuals from working-class backgrounds with a similar level of educational achievement to workers from middle-class and upper-class backgrounds secure only half the pay of their middle-class counterparts. When I.Q. and scholastic achievement are taken into account, social-background factors still give children of middle-class origins one-third more income. Unfortunately the study did not take into account whether the students had gone into fields which pay significantly different wages. Nevertheless the findings do suggest that social class still contributes to differentials in pay. There is only a weak correlation between investment in human capital through education and inequality of earnings.[20]

As we have noted earlier, education has become somewhat more equally distributed among white males in the United States. Between 1949 and 1969 the share of the total number of years of education received by the bottom quintile rose from 8·6 to 10·7 per cent, while the share of the top quintile fell from 31·1 to 29·3 per cent. So we might expect that supply and demand of different types of labour would seek a long-range equilibrium and that the wages of the more poorly educated would rise, assuming that demand for their labour remained unchanged. Yet, as Thurow notes, 'Education has been becoming more equally distributed yet income has been becoming more unequally distributed'.[21] He explains that what may be happening is that individuals are competing against one another for jobs on the basis of personal background characteristics, which he calls 'job competition', instead of competing against each other on the basis of the wages that they are willing to accept, which he calls 'wage competition'. Those with unwanted characteristics are at the end of the queue and get the worst jobs; that is, those which pay the lowest wages, are most vulnerable to economic fluctuations, and therefore to

20. Husen, op. cit.
21. Lester Thurow, *Generating Inequality*, New York, Basic Books, 1975, p. 16.

higher unemployment.[22] Such an interpretation does not deny that individuals who have improved their education also improve their earning levels. It does call attention to the neglected fact that increased education does not improve relative income position.

Despite vigorous efforts to promote mobility through education, class differences in academic achievement, in educational participation, and in the contribution of education to later earnings have persisted in the United States and in European countries. In an effort to account for these failures, much attention has been given to the difficulties which educational policies confront in overcoming the initial handicaps of low income and the related culture of poverty which is presumed to encourage indifference and an incapacity to exploit available educational opportunities. But even when education is equalized, income inequalities persist. And the differential importance of education for later income continues to vary for different subgroups, even after ability is taken into account. Moreover, the confusion and conflict of principles continuously inhibits the development of policies committed to equalizing income opportunities through education. As a result of this, interpretations of the limits of education are incomplete.

The more uncompromisingly we pursue the goal of equalizing individual opportunity, the more it appears to conflict with the theory of democratic pluralism. There is an ambiguity in the American value system which tries, on the one hand, to promote conformity to an American way of life, and, on the other, to demand of those who work at the bottom, that they alter their position within the social structure. Anthropologists, protective of cultural diversity, have in particular been distressed by what they regard as an arrogant desire by well-meaning reformers to impose one cultural norm upon another. In this tradition Walter Miller regards the war on poverty as an insensitive effort to homogenize the low-income population.

But the issue becomes even more complex when we recognize that mobility may be purchased at the cost of family loyalties and even personal freedom. Individuals want to pass on to their

22. ibid., p. 20.

children the advantages they have won, and they seek to protect them from failure. This is the obligation of a kinship system. To insist on reducing the advantages of heredity so that each generation sets out with an equal opportunity for achievement must conflict with these ideals of family responsibility.

Inequalities of opportunity are sustained even in principle by the conflict between democratic ideals and family loyalties. Parents socialize their children in such a fashion that they are aware of these differentials and try to maintain them. Middle-class parents protect their children from downward social mobility, even when their intellectual ability is only average or below. Upper income groups are much more likely to send their lower-than-average children on to higher education than are other groups. Policies designated to promote individual mobility are thwarted by micro-processes in which class privileges are preserved. Parents are unwilling to make their children pay the price for their ideals of equalizing opportunity. In his caustic criticism about liberal dissatisfaction with the extent of social mobility in the United States, Kristol notes that no one,

envisages a society that is utterly mobile – in which *all* the sons and daughters of the middle and upper classes ended up in the very lowest social stratum, where they can live in anticipation of *their* sons and daughters rising again toward the top – and then of their grandsons and granddaughters moving downward once again.[23]

The contradiction cannot readily be resolved. Equal opportunity is accepted as a doctrine on which public policy must proceed in an open, democratic society, yet the argument is not secure, for the principle is accepted while its implications are rejected.

Other policies directed at improving the relative position of groups in society seem equally equivocal. Taxation and direct government expenditures are accepted as instruments for the distribution of 'social income', yet analysis of the receipt of social benefits and the incidence of taxes proves that the contribution of

23. Irving Kristol, 'About Equality', *Commentary*, vol. 54, no. 5, November 1972, p. 41.

these outlays towards the narrowing of income differentials is slight for the majority of households. The studies show that lower income groups tend to pay proportionately more tax than upper income groups, because the progressive income tax is offset by the regressive effects of indirect taxes and social security contributions. So the tax system appears to counteract much of the redistributive policies on the expenditure side of the budget; and when the combined effects of taxation and benefits are considered only a small increase in vertical redistribution has been achieved. Lampman's study in the United States indicates that only about 6 to 7 per cent of total personal income is involved in transfers. Nevertheless, these programmes do move some families out of poverty, because they improve the net income resources of those who were poor before they received the transfers. Who are the major beneficiaries? The aged and other groups outside the labour force.

So, while there is evidence that some redistribution on behalf of the poor does take place, there are persistent ambiguities about the meaning of these findings. One difficulty centres on the problem of how to treat social security transfers, which, after all, comprise the largest segment of the income of those outside the labour force. Social Insurance is a puzzle because individuals pay the tax, when at work, through compulsory contributions, for benefits they receive later in retirement. Smolensky considers that these transfers should be treated as annuities, paid for in the form of contributions during one's working life, while only some specific groups who are not very large in numbers are getting out of the system more than they put in. He estimates that when we exclude the social security income from the bottom quintile, then the share of the income received by the bottom quintile drops from 5 per cent to an estimated 2 or 3 per cent.

A United Nations' study of incomes in post-war Europe lends further support to the conclusion that the rate of reduction of inequality has not been impressive.

The degree in the pattern of income redistribution varies between countries; but broadly speaking, the reduction in income dispersion appears to be very modest among the bulk of households deriving their income from employment, self-employment and property. The reduction which has occurred is largely in favour of non-active persons (principally pensioners) and has been largely financed by their own payments in the past, either by social insurance contributions or by general taxes.

On the whole, therefore, it seems legitimate to conclude that for the bulk of the population the pattern of primary income distribution is only slightly modified by government action.[24]

The report argues that even the income redistribution that has taken place is largely a result of the falling manpower in agriculture and the reduction in self-employment. The reduction of these traditional low-wage sectors has had more influence on the distribution of net household income than government policies.

We conclude therefore that the lack of any generally accepted principles about income redistribution makes it difficult to coordinate government programmes into a consistent policy. In a muddled way, we undo with one hand what we do with the other. Even when expenditures for social services are directed towards the lower occupational groupings, the tax system, including direct and indirect taxes, tends to work in the opposite direction, producing in its net effect little redistribution. In the end, people pay for what they get. The broader the definition of the subsidy system, the more nearly does it serve to multiply privileges rather than reduce disadvantages. High expenditure benefits tend to go to middle and upper income groups, as in the case of higher education, and so too do most indirect subsidies, such as tax concessions for medical care, mortgage loans, etc. Seen in these terms, public expenditure may have exacerbated rather than reduced inequalities.

We need not accept the provocative thesis that social policy multiplies inequalities to recognize that, with the exception of special groups like pensioners and families with large numbers of children, social policy has made only a minor contribution to the reduction of income inequalities.

The redistributive impacts of tax and social benefits cannot be isolated from the broader economic context in which they are

24. United Nations Study of Income in Post War Europe, *Studies of Policies, Growth and Distribution*, Geneva, 1967, p. 40.

contained. Inflation is one such example, because it has a differential effect on the standard of living of various income groups. Inflation always presents a government with moral choices: it can let it alone, hurting those dependent on fixed incomes; create more unemployment; subsidize prices; or increase interest rates. The fairness of any policy depends, of course, on whom inflation harms; but the consequences are not necessarily obvious. An American analysis, by Hollister and Palmer, using information from the 1961 survey of consumer expenditures, concluded that price changes were about the same for all products; hence rich and poor suffered alike from inflation, although their patterns of expenditure were different. The analysis implied that a deflationary policy would harm the poor disproportionately, since they would lose more income by higher levels of unemployment and a slack labour market than they lost in purchasing power by inflation. A 'tax on employment' was worse than the 'tax of inflation'; the cure worse than the disease. But a more recent staff report of the Joint Economic Committee, using the same differentiated indices of consumption, concluded that between August 1971 and December 1973 'low income persons suffered about one fourth more from inflation than did middle and upper income consumers'[25] largely because of disproportionate rises in food, housing and fuel costs. If this is so, the social justice of letting inflation take its course is much weaker. But we are faced now with inflationary trends which seem to defy regulation by traditional means. Unemployment and inflation have risen together, and regulators which assume an inverse relationship between levels of unemployment above 4 per cent and rates of inflation seem less and less reliable.

In Britain the Child Poverty Action Group – a pressure group concerned with improving the conditions of poor families with children – argued during the election campaign of 1970 that under a Labour government the economic position of the low-wage

25. R. G. Hollister and J. L. Palmer, 'The Impact of Inflation on the Poor', in K. E. Boulding and M. Pfaff, *Redistribution to the Rich and the Poor*, Belmont, Wadsworth Publishers, 1973; 'Inflation and the Consumer in 1972', staff report prepared for the Joint Economic Committee, 92nd Congress, 1st Session, 14 January 1974.

sector actually declined. The government denied the charge, pointing to the large increases in family allowances, public assistance, rent rebates, etc., that it had initiated, and claiming that the position of the poor had, in fact, slightly improved. Labour lost the election but the debate emerged again under a Conservative government. On 2 March 1973, the *Guardian* reported, in an article entitled 'The Widening Poverty Gap', that in 1971, within 'eight of the twelve family or household groups into which the population is divided for the Government's analysis of the incidence of taxation and social benefits, the poorest 20 per cent of eight of the groups lost ground relative to the average in 1970, while the poorest of the remaining four groups managed only to hold their relative position'. We wonder why, despite the action of both the Labour and Conservative governments to improve the well-being of the poor, they have only been able to preserve existing differentials or (as they are charged by their critics) to permit differentials to widen. One interpretation is that more powerful economic forces such as inflation undermined the effects of redistributive social policy. It is the effort to fight inflation which erodes the economic position of the low-wage sector, because it threatens their employment. But the main point of these observations is to show that social policy appears unable to compete against broader economic forces and policies whose impact undermines the relative economic position of the poor. The distributional effects of policies which are not directed at distributional questions appears to offset the distributional effects of policies which are more explicitly concerned with redistribution.

Our policies towards social stratification appear, then, as a confusion of pragmatic adjustments. We appeal now to one principle of justice, now another; frustrate reform by inconsistent and uncoordinated economic regulation; enforce on some a wage restraint which we abandon elsewhere. We neither altogether accept things as they are, nor put forward any coherent alternative. Issues of social justice seem to be manageable only when they are presented in a specific and narrow context, where equity can be defined by reference to some comparable group in society. As soon as the issue is broadened to the overall distribution of rewards, we no longer know how to confront it. Only the uncompromising egalitarian, who believes that each of us should take what he needs and contribute what he can, or the laissez-faire economist who believes in perfect competition, can take an unequivocal stand. For the rest, the issue resolves itself into an uneasy compromise between the meaning of justice and the impulse to conservatism. If the failure to reform stratification stems, in part, from the incoherence of policy, and not only from indifference; and if a more coherent policy depends upon assessing the outcome of a complex of interdependent actions, then the clarity and authority of ideals are crucially important, since without them the most sophisticated, informed and far-reaching of analyses ends once again in confusion.

Equality as Equal Dignity

Most of us, at heart, seem to accept social stratification more or less in these terms: that inequality is natural, because it corresponds to the necessarily unequal distribution of power and skills, and to expect otherwise is unrealistic; but given this, everyone is entitled to respect – both for himself, as a citizen, and for the work he does. The first concept specifies the limits of equality and the second the limits of inequality. Inequality becomes intolerable when it leaves some so poorly provided for that their condition is humiliating to them; and conversely, changes in the conventional order of stratification are unfair when they threaten to deprive anyone of their self-respect.

The impulse towards stratification can be seen, then, as a morbid expression of anxiety about one's worth – morbid in the sense that it ignores the underlying source of the anxiety, and cannot resolve it. Just as a neurotic cannot respond to blunt appeals to pull himself together and behave more rationally, a stratified society cannot respond to the preaching of equality. We have to deal first with all those conditions of work and life which rob people of their self-respect – the denigration of individual worth, conscious or unconscious, blatant or subtle, by which our personal dignity is continually affronted. The contempt implied by failing to keep people informed, by impersonal communication, discourtesy, indifference to the surroundings in which people live or work, the reduction of work itself to meaningless repetitions, the segregation of responsibility, the perversion of ambition into status competition and the nagging exploitation of these anxieties by crass advertisement – all this demeans people, creating a society where self-respect is pervasively corrupted and insecure.

Egalitarian social policies can best argue their purposes in terms of equalizing personal dignity. Rawls assigns self-respect a central position in his theory of justice. He distinguishes:

> between equality as it is invoked in connection with the distribution of goods ... and equality as it applies to the respect which is owed to persons irrespective of their social position ... equality of the second kind is fundamental. It is defined by the first principle of justice ... it is owed to human beings as moral persons.[26]

This appeal to a more equal society avoids doing violence to the prejudices of most citizens and is least threatening to the definition of their own self-esteem. Though there are still many people who wish to see the poor or the black humiliated, they are surely now a minority. So too are those who find some comfort in punishing the weak for the grudging respect with which they themselves are treated. The right to equal treatment and equal dignity is a universally recognized human need, and a widely accepted principle of reform. Note, however, that this concept of equality concerns the quality of relationships rather than the distribution of rewards. This interpretation of equality is commonly held by the average citizen, as Rainwater's Social Standards Survey, based on a random sample of Boston residents, makes clear:

> The most broadly-based model of equality among our respondents is one in which equality means equal treatment despite resource inequality. For our respondents American egalitarianism means that everyone is treated the same regardless of what he has. Their comments reflect a strong desire to ignore resources, to treat them as irrelevant from a social interactional point of view ... Everyone has the right to

pursue his own life-style and to be treated as a person of equal merit and value by those around him.[27]

By rejecting the importance of resource inequalities this popular view avoids two awkward problems – of rationalizing the prevailing unequal distribution of income and wealth, or of declaring that all differences are illegitimate. It changes the emphasis of policy from the institutions of stratification to the way we treat one another, at work, in services, and in the social surroundings we create.

Parenthetically we note that a corollary to this conception of equal treatment is that it elevates participation to an important new place in policy. What makes a democratic society is not only the denial of unearned privilege but the acceptance of the principle of equal respect and the equal chance for involvement in decision-making which derives from it. If the idea of citizen participation were no more than a grudging delegation of control over some neighbourhood resources, it would not mean very much. But if it is part of a much broader attempt to restore to people a sense of control over their own lives, to respect their right to be heard on every issue that concerns them, at work as much as at home, then it may grow into a persuasive principle of reform.

Equal respect can be seen, then, as a condition to which everyone has a right and as a principle whose value is generally recognized. This proposition has many versions, whose terms are more or less interchangeable. Whether you speak of self-respect, dignity, liberty, enjoyment or equal treatment, the argument asserts that the redistribution of resources is only a means to some more fundamental quality of life which we all have a right to share. This quality is characteristically unlimited, in the sense that to enhance it in the experience of others does not diminish one's own enjoyment of it. It is not a zero-sum game, where those who gain dignity can only do so by the loss of the dignity of others. Rather, like love, the more one gives, the more one has. The argument has an obvious drawback: it tends to treat con-

27. Lee Rainwater, *What Money Buys: Inequality and the Social Meaning of Income*, New York, Basic Books, 1974, p. 170.

flicts over the distribution of scarce resources as finally trivial. But can we, as it is widely assumed, really ignore the redistribution of resources if we wish to bring about equal dignity, equal respect and equal treatment to which all human beings are entitled? Seen in these terms, we have shifted our argument from a normative question, of what we mean by equality, to a factual question of how to achieve equal dignity. We can now test empirically whether equalized dignity and self-respect can be brought about without a redistribution of resources. The average citizen in Boston believes the one can be achieved without the other. But is he right?

Rainwater's analysis shows that those who do not enjoy the mainstream of resources (whatever median income can buy) suffer as well from a lack of membership in society, on which the sense of dignity and respect depends. Ethnographic accounts of low-income families report consistently that those who lack resources, lack as well self-respect and self-confidence, and view themselves as helpless victims without the power to control the events which influence their lives. This is, of course, the existential agony that some social critics have argued is an endemic characteristic of all men in modern industrial society. It is not only the poor who suffer from profound anxieties of personal impotence and isolation. We are all victims of alienation. This is not the place to debate this widely held view. We should, however, point out that there is consistent empirical evidence to suggest that those who do have resources feel more integrated in society and enjoy a greater sense of control, satisfaction, respect and dignity than those who do not.

It is not unreasonable to assume that if those who lack resources had them, they too would enjoy a greater sense of dignity and respect. This conclusion is, of course, only an inference from available information; it has not been confirmed experimentally. We cannot specify how much of this shift in esteem is brought about as resources increase; or what is the time-lag between acquiring resources and experiencing enhanced dignity; or what level and form of resources are necessary to achieve this aim. If, however, it can be demonstrated that dignity can be achieved without a redistribution of resources then we would be prepared to accept the former without the latter. We strongly doubt that this is the case.

If narrowing resource inequality is necessary to equalize dignity, we may discover that the two principles are in conflict. Will equalizing resources also erode the self-esteem of those who already have them? That is to say, if the relative economic and political position of those at present declassed by society improves, will those who enjoy the position in society just above them become threatened? Since self-respect is bound up with differences of status, we do not think it fair that, for instance, university professors should be expected to put themselves on a footing with school teachers, or secretaries with waitresses. They have learned to think of themselves as enjoying a superior social status, and this sense of social honour is a necessary part of their self-respect. In the same way, we accept that a middle-class child would suffer hardship if he had to accept a life of substantially lower status from that of his parents; but we do not regard the child born into a family of that lower status as badly off at all. It is what you are used to that counts. The Chinese Communists have developed a 'sending down' system which requires that white collar and managerial workers spend some time during the year in the factory or fields. Note, however, that they continue to receive their customary salary. Thus their self-esteem is not threatened by this procedure; indeed, this system of job rotation reinforces the social obligation of élites to mix with other social groups.

If this interpretation is right, the determined impulse to preserve inequalities arises largely from anxiety about the respect in which one's occupation is held. The differentiation of rewards embodies the conventional symbols of respect, so that wage claims become claims for recognition of worth. These wage claims sometimes represent a desperate attempt to force society to reaffirm the worth of an occupation whose real contribution is declining.

So, for instance, doctors in general practice in Britain have insisted, with much bitter wrangling, on substantial increases in pay. But their sense of grievance seems to arise more fundamentally from the downgrading of the skills they practise. The older men who still work in solo practice cannot afford the diagnostic equipment of modern medicine. With long lists of patients to care for, they tend to refer all but the simplest cases to hospitals. Their own practice begins to look like little more than a referral service, passing patients on to specialists, and filling out medical certificates for sickness benefits. Hence doctors complain of the triviality of the complaints they deal with, the lack of respect in which their patients hold them, the long, tedious hours of work; and they resent increasingly the disparity between themselves and the specialists. Their resentment expresses itself in salary claims; but the deeper grievance is the disparity in skills. If doctors worked in group practices large enough to install diagnostic equipment, allow for specialization among partners, and provide more assistants, their work would be more satisfying: doctors who have already organized such practices do seem substantially more content. Thus the heart of the grievance lies not in the hierarchy of medical salaries, but in the nature of the work.[28]

In a stratified society many people use the position of those at the bottom as a basis for comparison with their own harsh circumstances, and hope by this invidious contrast to shore up their fragile or shattered esteem. They try, in other words, to achieve secondary personal gains by comparing their position with those worse off than themselves. But we are not prepared to conclude from this observation that we must maintain a permanent underclass to preserve the prestige of the blue-collar workers.

People adjust to the realities they confront. But this is not the only way, or even perhaps the most important way, in which people derive a sense of value in their lives. If their work is purposeful and interesting, if the people they work with respect them, if they have some control over their work and responsibility for its success, if their contribution is recognized – then they are likely to feel secure in their self-respect. And if, outside their work, they have leisure and means to pursue their interests – a physical and temporal space in which they are autonomous – they possess a fundamental equality with everyone else. Defences against humiliation and self-doubt need not depend upon strati-

28. See Ann Cartwright, *Patients and Their Doctors*, Routledge & Kegan Paul, 1967, especially chapters 4 and 9.

fication at all; they are not defined by differences, but by rights which everyone can claim. Hence the more self-respect is assured in these ways, the less anxiety there may be to sustain differentiation by status.

How much of a political stake have people in trying to bring about a more equal distribution of resources, or a wider range of resources to which everyone is entitled, in medical care, housing, and income, for example? There seems to be only mild political support for such egalitarian ideals, perhaps because few feel they have much to gain from the venture.

The ideal of equalizing resources to equalize dignity seems to take hold, for the most part, only when a crisis in the history of a society – a war or its aftermath, an economic collapse – has already undermined conventional expectations. At other times we tend to fall back on narrower principles of equity, which can lever this group or that to a slightly better level; but the adjustments seem marginal and in continual danger of slipping. Only the claims to equality between races and between the sexes provide a moral force powerful enough to sustain reform: and even here, progress is slow.

Clearly the politics of equity dominate the politics of equality and redistribution, but this situation is neither inevitable or irreversable. At the time of the debate about a guaranteed income in the United States political scientists like Wildavsky predicted that Congress would not accept a serious income redistribution proposal. But Congressional opinion shifted after President Nixon proposed the Family Assistance Plan (F.A.P.). Where there is no strong support for income redistribution, leadership can overcome political indifference when the idea is proposed by a President in office. F.A.P. failed to pass Congress, but this was largely because economic changes such as inflation and other factors led the President to abandon the initiative for reform. This example illustrates not a ground swell for equality, or that F.A.P. was in fact an important redistribution programme, but only that an opposition believed to be deeply embedded in the values of society can be modified by executive initiative. Interest groups follow as well as lead; they may support redistribution even if they would not initiate it.

Can equal dignity, treatment, and self-respect ever be brought about by any means other than the equalization of resources? The Second World War made Britain a more egalitarian society because nearly everyone had a greater sense of purpose; even dull, routine work was enhanced by its contribution to national defence.[29] And everyone was able to acknowledge the value of another's work, without feeling that the status of his own was threatened. Afterwards, as the war and the problems of reconstruction receded, so the egalitarian mood faded; no new sense of purpose took its place. It seems, from the experience of the kibbutzim in Israel, that a radically egalitarian society can survive indefinitely if it sustains an ideology which dignifies the work of all its members. But the opportunities for such reforms in most advanced industrial societies seem limited, and we may have no alternative but to promote equal dignity by a fairer distribution of resources.

Conclusion

In the pursuit of equality as a goal we need first to specify the dimensions or meaning of equality rather than treat it as an abstraction. The ideal of equal dignity, equal treatment and equal respect provides a moral principle which is generally honoured. Moreover, this view conforms closely to what most people mean by the concept of equality. They value equal treatment more than equal opportunity, and they believe that equal dignity and equal treatment can be achieved by endeavours less sacrificial than the

29. Peter Drucker offers a similar observation about the effect of the war in Britain: 'Equally startling was what happened after the war. Instead of making door hinges for cockpits, the worker was again making door hinges for passenger cars. They were the same hinges, and the worker performed the same operations. But the meaning had gone out of the work. The result was a let-down or deep feeling of frustration and dissatisfaction – perhaps even more noticeable in Great Britain than in this country. What is usually explained as "fatigue" – the sudden drop in productive efficiency after the war – was probably largely this disappointment, this feeling of being deprived of the satisfaction and meaning which the worker and the work had had during the war. The wave of postwar strikes in this country may have had a similar origin.' (op. cit., p. 179.)

equalizing of resources and the surrender of privilege. There is a broad agreement in attitude or values – men may favour equal dignity – but disagreement about whether a more equal distribution of resources is necessary to achieve this end. We believe that those who enjoy resources (median income or better) enjoy more dignity than those who lack it, and, from the available evidence, which is admittedly fragmentary, have inferred that if those who have less were to get more, then in time these added resources would also enhance their dignity. This argument may be false. There may be industrial societies where resources are as unequally distributed as in the United States and Britain (where, for example, one-quarter or more of the population commands less than half the median income), but where nevertheless dignity and respect are equally distributed. This is a matter for empirical study. It affects the truth of our premisses, but not the acceptability of our conclusions.

If we can establish that it is necessary to redistribute resources to achieve equal dignity, do the means then conflict with the ends, because raising the position of those at the bottom threatens people's sense of their social worth? In a stratified society with an underclass, people need to protect their social worth not only by the intrinsic satisfaction of what they do, but by comparing their position with those worse off than themselves. People play the game they face, but that does not imply that they would not accept other options if they were confronted with a different set of equity rules. We believe that to spread most widely what is most valuable in life, namely dignity, self-esteem, and self-worth, does not necessarily imply an exchange of gains and losses. In the long run, we may all win by a more equal enjoyment of life and a more equal distribution of dignity.

But it does not follow that there is a strong incentive to promote a change of rules. This accounts for the weak political support for egalitarian aims. McGovern's failure to promote the ideals of redistribution does not discredit the ideals. His campaign was inept, when running against a presidential incumbent. When Nixon proposed F.A.P. as a President in office the idea received considerable support. Statesmen may lead as well as follow public opinion.

Is there any other way that equal dignity can be achieved? If everyone had a secure place in society and felt that their efforts contributed to a public purpose they supported, then dignity might be won despite unequal resources. Some societies, like Cuba, China, Israel, do maintain this sense of moral purpose, but it seems doubtful that countries like Britain and the United States can discover a compelling moral mission that will win the allegiance of all its citizens. Modern wars, like that in Vietnam, are not integrative, but divisive. Moreover, to assure a secure place for everyone in a complex, industrial society may reduce freedom and mobility. In the end, resource redistribution may be the only or the least costly means.

Our present social policies seem on the whole to be mutually frustrating, incoherent in both thought and action. What new direction might we seek? We need some broader direction of policy by which to coordinate our interventions. This master policy requires a criterion against which to judge the achievement of our purposes – some common coin of value. It does not perhaps matter too much whether we call this coin equal liberty, equal self-realization, or equal enjoyment – the currencies are mutually exchangeable, because you can derive one social ethic from another in all sorts of ways – liberty from equality, equality from dignity or both from justice. We can accept Rawls's equality principle, that the only justification for increasing inequalities in any of these dimensions is if it can be demonstrated that such policies would have the effect of increasing the dignity, self-respect or liberty of the weakest members of society. Unfortunately the principle 'permits indefinitely large inequalities in return for small gains to the less favoured',[30] and this weakens the usefulness of the principle as a guide to public policy.

By translating equality into a question about the distribution of unlimited resources, such as dignity, we obscure the question about the distribution of finite resources (freedom of action,

30. John Rawls, *A Theory of Justice*, Cambridge, Mass., Harvard University Press, 1971, p. 536. Such a concession undermines the principle. In an effort to rescue the principle he goes on to say that 'the spread of income and wealth should not be excessive in practice, given the requisite background institutions'.

income, power). This makes it seem less threatening, because no one need lose dignity by giving it to another. However, once we argue that dignity implies equality, the threat returns, and the apparent consensus about the equality of the right to respect breaks down. The readiness to concede the right to respect is only as widespread as it is because it does not seem to imply equality. People may accept the principle and reject the implication.

And so we are left with the question of how we might bridge the gap between equity and the broader concerns of egalitarianism.

Chapter 6
Social Science and Health

The categories of description and analysis used in scientific inquiry are infused with value implications which provide the researcher with the moral premises from which his policy conclusions can be drawn. March explains this in an interesting way:

> The point is simple. Independent of its truth value, a model has a justice value. Different models suggest different actions, and the attractiveness of the social and moral consequences of those actions do not depend entirely upon the degree to which the models are correct. Nor is this problem solved in any significant way by producing a more correct model. Since two equally correct models may have radically different action implications and radically different moral force, we can easily imagine a circumstance in which we would be willing to forego some truth in order to achieve some justice.[1]

March has over-extended his position. We may get some 'justice' by abandoning 'truth', i.e., by engaging in demagoguery, but this will lead to some injustice as well. His main thesis is nevertheless central for policy-oriented research. The view of the world we hold, that is, the model of reality we carry about with us and the categories for description it contains, not only has implications for action, but also serves as a guide for empirical analysis. It is because value premises are embedded in descriptive accounts that empirical study can lead to policy conclusions. A 'normative leap' from a factual analysis to a prescription for action is possible precisely because values enter analysis. And it is because normative statements are embedded in both descriptive and

1. James G. March, 'Model Bias in Social Action', *Review of Educational Research*, vol. 42, no. 4.

analytic categories that the social scientist can make policy recommendations from empirical research findings. Yet much of the discussion about the relationship between ideology and policy analysis has been pejorative, designed to show that social science provides only an ideological defence of the status quo. I use the term 'ideology' for a set of beliefs and assumptions concerning not only what is morally right and politically desirable, but how the processes of society function. To show how values enter theory, it has sometimes been amusingly suggested that when the smallest box in Parsons's functional analysis is opened, it contains a tiny American flag.

My purpose in this essay is different. I do not wish to deride, but to demonstrate by specific examples how the categories of description and analysis contain moral implications. Those who sponsor research frequently also have value commitments to what they regard as the right thing to do in a given situation. What they lack is better information about how to get where they want to go. They hope that a systematic understanding of the processes will contribute towards realizing their commitments. Here researchers can help when they accept these commitments, for under such circumstances research can provide a rationale for action or inaction and discipline in selecting alternative directions within the terms of a value commitment.

What research typically fails to do is provide a method for selecting among alternative commitments and a set of rules for choosing among competing frameworks of thought. Data are seldom convincing enough in the social field to settle questions about contrasting world views. More factual information alone will not settle the question of how the world works and how to intervene in it. When there are many causes for a single event, and the causes are interdependent, we may truthfully say that everything is in some sense causally linked to everything else. However, it is extremely difficult to isolate the independent contribution of these interrelated events. Even if this task could be accomplished, it does not necessarily follow that by altering the isolated factor we will bring about the desired state of affairs. Social science fails in practice to provide a single, synthetic sophisticated regression model which parcels out the independent contribution of each variable and assigns a rating to each which can be accepted as a general law, faithfully capturing reality as it is, and predicting future outcomes as well. But since the ideal is still accepted in principle, each disappointment leads to a renewed call for further inquiry which can rescue the earlier studies from their methodological weakness.

When we focus on practice we find that different social scientists may select different categories of description (naming) and explanation based on different theories about how the world works (framing). *Knowledge becomes partisan in the policy struggle from which it presumes itself detached.* As a result available scientific evidence typically supports several competing modes of thought, as an analysis of the literature on virtually any given problem will reveal. Broad societal commitments, i.e., moral and political ideals in good currency, provide the shared framework for the selected use of evidence, and thus a dominant analysis is forged in which a course of action can be intellectually defended. In addition alternative scientific interpretations which challenge the consensus are always to hand, although they naturally do not enjoy the popularity of the dominant analysis. These competing views may, however, provide the insights on which alternative value frameworks can be built. Of course, a dominant analysis presupposes a basic consensus. But even when this exists we still need to understand what the actual societal commitments are and how they are determined. For it is the social and political context which gives weight, support and acceptability to one view rather than another.

Research on the cause and consequences of poverty and ill health provide a good arena in which this general theme can be concretely explored, and this chapter examines competing frameworks of thought among social scientists. It does not try to answer the related question of how research findings are used in the political process. It attempts to clarify the nature of the interdependence between evidence, interpretation, and the initial research perspective. Three different frames for linking poverty and ill health – resource allocation, personal and social theory and institutional performance – can be found in the literature. One cannot isolate the findings of empirical studies from the theoretical and policy perspective that shapes the research. Yet a review of social science literature shows most strikingly the failure to confront the conflict among these perspectives. When considered individually, each frame leads to quite different priorities for action. While this state of affairs is unsatisfactory, it is not disastrous, because there is not necessarily any contradiction in maintaining all three positions at the same time. They may all be valid in different places and different circumstances. What research has failed to do is to specify when and where they apply so that differentiated policies can be developed to capture the diversity to real-life situations.

As one examines this literature, it also becomes evident that not only is there a lack of consensus on an appropriate framework within which to examine social problems, but also that conflicting findings even within the same terms of reference are seldom identified or reconciled. There are few attempts to bring together or acknowledge contradictory evidence or to reconcile systematically differences in fact and interpretation.

It is with these problems in mind, then, that this chapter sets out first to discuss the rationale behind each perspective, and to review the contributions from selected areas of social science theory and research that primarily focus on the subject of health and its relationship to income, and then to explore the implications of findings within each perspective for the development of social policy. My purpose is to illustrate how problem setting shapes the meaning of the findings obtained and determines their implication for policy.

Resource Allocation

The basic hypothesis underlying this perspective is that material insufficiency in housing, in nutritional levels and in income itself is not only an attribute of poverty and ill health, but an independent variable contributing to the creation and perpetuation of poverty and illness. Alvin Schorr has suggestively labelled this approach the 'non-culture of poverty' in order to contrast it with the current preoccupation with life-style and social structure, motivation and culture.[2] Although this perspective admits a circularity of causes – resource inadequacies are responsible for the way of life, while at the same time the way of life sponsors these insufficiencies – it nevertheless places the initiation of the cycle on the lack of resources. If this view is correct, the policy implications are clear-cut and quite different from those of other attributions of the causes of poverty.

The first set of hypotheses locates a strong biological link between malfunctioning of the body and serious organic and social consequences. For example, pre-natal nutritional deficiencies in mothers can lead to organic and mental defects in their children, leaving them physically and mentally disadvantaged and thereby increasing the likelihood that they will be unable to maintain an independent income in their adult life.[3] They are also more likely to produce children who are handicapped at birth. Thus, the legacy of poverty and malnutrition in one generation is passed on.

The cluster of hypotheses consistent with this biological frame of reference assume that inadequate nutritional levels, clinically identifiable by a symptom such as low haemoglobin count, alter the capacity of the body to function by affecting energy levels. When a nutritional deficiency is sustained over a long period of time, it can lead to a chronic state of depression, apathy, lethargy and low motivation. These psychological responses prevent individuals from participating in the world of work and from carrying out their functions as heads of families. This line of reasoning suggests that low income produces dietary inadequacies which, in turn, contribute to greater illness, and that the incapacities

2. Alvin L. Schorr, 'The Non-Culture of Poverty', *American Journal of Ortho Psychiatry*, XXXIV, 1964, pp. 907–12.

3. See, for example, the research of A. Keys, 'Caloric Deficiency and Starvation', and Frederick Tisdall, 'The Relation of Nutrition to Health', reported in Norman Jolliffee, F. F. Tisdall and Paul R. Canon, eds., *Clinical Nutrition*, New York, Harber and Brothers, 1950, and Benjamin Pasamanick, Abraham Lilienfeld and Martha E. Rogers, *Prenatal and Paranatal Factors in the Development of Childhood Behavior Disorders*, Baltimore, The Johns Hopkins University School of Hygiene and Public Health, n.d.

created by illness handicap the family's earning capacity while pressing it with high medical expenditures. The process has the effect of inhibiting upward social class mobility and increasing the likelihood of downward mobility.

There is also a set of hypotheses concerning the use of medical care services. According to this view, lacking adequate financial resources to acquire the necessities of life, such as food, clothing and shelter, the poor will often delay seeking medical care when symptoms of illness appear and will rarely make use of preventative health services. Thus they fail to avert some diseases that are amenable to prevention, and the diseases that are contracted tend to reach a more severe state because of the failure to use medical care appropriately. The poor experience more preventable illness, and suffer more from all illnesses because the illness conditions are allowed to reach a more serious state before being treated. Inadequate use of medical services has an even more damaging effect than nutritional inadequacies and lowered resistance to disease, and largely accounts for the high level of activity impairment as a result of illness among the poor – considerably greater than that of other classes.

These arguments all appear reasonable, but surprisingly, when we examine data on the relationships between morbidity and income, we find persistent ambiguities: are the poor sicker than other income groups; in what direction is the causal link between illness and poverty; and what are the processes by which class and morbidity are related? I shall review the evidence in each of these areas.

Class and Illness, Disability and Mortality

Are the poor indeed sicker as the resource argument implies? Some investigators challenge the commonly accepted assumption that there is a positive relationship between poverty and illness. The strongest evidence which casts doubt upon the link is data from the National Examination Survey on specific disease prevalences (age and sex adjusted) by income. Clinical diagnoses of coronary heart disease,[4] hypertension and hypertensive heart disease,[5] rheumatoid arthritis[6] and osteoarthritis[7] were obtained from physical examination of a sample of U.S. adults in 1965–6. These diagnoses indicate very little relationship between income level and ill health prevalence. Only prevalence rates for hearing and vision deficiencies display the expected inverse relationship to income. The best conclusion to be drawn from this sample of diseases is that some diseases are related to income levels while others are not. And it is important to point out that a very limited selection of diseases was investigated, although they do account for about 40 per cent of the disability in the United States.[8] Further complicating the task of sorting out how class and illness are related is the elusive question of the severity of the conditions. The national survey on which these clinical diagnoses were developed was designed to take account of even relatively mild cases of the diseases; but it did not identify differences in the severity of illness, nor the limiting effect of the diseases on customary activity.

How then is severity of illness linked to class? To answer this question we turn to information on the use of hospital facilities. This data does indeed suggest that the poor have more serious

4. National Center for Health Statistics, *Coronary Heart Disease in Adults, U.S. 1960–62* (U.S. Department of Health, Education, and Welfare, Public Health Service publication no. 1000, series 11, no. 10), Washington, D.C., U.S. Government Printing Office, 1965.

5. National Center for Health Statistics, *Hypertension and Hypertensive Heart Disease in Adults, U.S. 1960–62* (U.S. Department of Health, Education, and Welfare, Public Health Service publication no. 1000, series 11, no. 13), Washington, D.C., U.S. Government Printing Office, 1966.

6. National Center for Health Statistics, *Rheumatoid Arthritis in Adults, U.S. 1960–62* (U.S. Department of Health, Education, and Welfare, Public Health Service publication no. 1000, series 11, no. 17), Washington, D.C., U.S. Government Printing Office, 1966.

7. National Center for Health Statistics, *Osteoarthritis in Adults by Selected Demographic Characteristics, U.S. 1960–62* (U.S. Department of Health, Education, and Welfare, Public Health Service publication no. 1000, series 11, no. 20), Washington, D.C., U.S. Government Printing Office, 1966.

8. Harold S. Luft, 'Poverty and Health: An Empirical Investigation of Their Economic Interactions' (Ph.D. thesis in economics), Harvard University, Cambridge, Mass., July 1972, p. 363.

conditions when they do seek care – the poor are hospitalized more frequently than the non-poor, their average length of hospital stay is longer, and they have a much higher rate of multiple hospital visits (the number of persons per 1000 with three or more hospital visits per year is almost three times as high among families with incomes under $3000 a year as among families with annual incomes over $10,000).[9] But how shall we interpret these findings? The poor may tend to delay longer before seeking care both because of cost barriers and social class differences in the recognition of and response to symptoms.[10] Or perhaps the poor are less able to afford expensive treatment methods or intensive care that might speed up the recovery process. Better care is more readily available to the non-poor for financial and cultural reasons. Members of the upper classes are more likely to take aggressive action and to manipulate their environment in combating an illness condition – by seeking out the most efficient care processes, for example, and by working half days or at a reduced pace to ensure a rapid recovery. This line of argument does not suggest that the poor are sicker, but that the consequences of illness vary by social class.

It is important then to distinguish between health status *per se*, as measured by the prevalence of specific illnesses and the impact or consequences of health status on the ability to function, as measured by the number of activity-restricted days caused by ill health.[11] The age specific mortality rate is also important. When we turn from disease to disability we find very little evidence that the poor are sicker but abundant evidence in support of the

9. National Center for Health Statistics: *Hospital Discharges and Length of Stay: Short-Stay Hospitals, U.S. July 1963–June 1964* (U.S. Department of Health, Education, and Welfare, Public Health Service publication no. 1000, series 10, no. 30), Washington, D.C., U.S. Government Printing Office, 1966, pp. 10, 37.

10. Barbara Blackwell, *The Literature of Delay in Seeking Medical Care for Chronic Illness* (Health Education Monographs no. 16), Society of Public Health Educators, Inc., 1963, pp. 3–31; Ann Cartwright, *Patients and Their Doctors: A Study of General Practice*, Routledge & Kegan Paul, 1967.

11. Diana D. Mitchell, 'Review of the Literature on the Use of Health Services' (preliminary paper), M.I.T., Cambridge, Massachusetts, 1972, p. 12.

thesis that the effects of ill health are more burdensome on lower-income people. Families with incomes below $3000 a year incur 50 per cent more disability each year from accident and other causes than families with incomes of $10,000 a year or over. The days in the year lost from work were 7·9 and 4·8 respectively.[12] There is also considerable evidence to suggest that a greater proportion of persons in low-income as compared with upper-income families have activity-limiting chronic conditions.[13,14]

The discrepancy between clinically-measured disease prevalence rates and the various measures of impact or disability has been attributed to differences among classes in their 'reaction' to illness. However the evidence regarding these alleged differences in reactions is ambiguous. During the 1950s a number of studies reported findings which suggested that lower-class persons were more 'tolerant' of symptoms of ill health and less 'concerned' about the state of their health in general.[15] However, more recent research disputes this view, finding little difference among socio-economic groups in the interpretation of symptoms as indicating illness or in the amount of concern expressed about symptoms.[16] Other studies have found evidence that lower-class people are *more* concerned than upper-class people about their health, and perceive themselves to be *sicker*, given apparently similar states of

12. Dorothy Rice, 'Health Needs of the Poor' (unpublished paper), Social Security Administration, 29 January 1972, p. 3.

13. ibid., p. 1.

14. Harold S. Luft, 'Review of the Literature on the Economics of Poverty and Health' (preliminary paper), Harvard University, Cambridge, Massachusetts, 1971, p. 50.

15. Earl Koos, *The Health of Regionville*, New York, Columbia University Press, 1954; August B. Hollingshead and Frederick C Redlich, *Social Class and Mental Illness*, New York, John Wiley, 1958; Mark Zborowski, 'Cultural Components in Response to Pain', in E. Gartly Jaco, ed., *Patients, Physicians, and Illness*, New York, Free Press of Glencoe, 1958, pp. 256–68.

16. Edward A. Suchman, 'Stages of Illness and Medical Care', *Journal of Health and Human Behavior*, VI, 1965, pp. 114–28; David Mechanic, 'Illness and Cure', in John Kosa, Aavon Antonovsky and Irving Zola, eds., *Poverty and Health*, Cambridge, Mass., Harvard University Press, 1969, pp. 191–214; William H. McBroom, 'Illness, Illness Behavior and Socio-economic Status', *Journal of Health and Social Behavior*, XI, December 1970.

health. Comparisons of self-reported hypertension and heart disease prevalences from the Department of Health Survey with medical examinations for these diseases revealed that the self-reported disease prevalences were slightly exaggerated at the lower income and lower educational levels. Lower-income individuals apparently tended to perceive themselves as more ill than (as measured by clinical examination) they actually were. Similar findings have also been reported in a study of maternity patients which found that lower-class women tended to regard themselves as more 'sick' during pregnancy than women of middle and upper classes.[17] Kadushin, in a provocative, but not rigorous, discussion, asserts that 'a review of the evidence . . . leads to the conclusion that in recent years there is a very little association between getting a disease and social class, although the *lower class still feel sicker*'.[18] (Emphasis added.)

It may be that if the chronic conditions of the poor are more serious (as other evidence suggests) or if they are more numerous, then fewer of the poor survive until age 65. Higher mortality among the poor would explain the reversal of the relationship between income level and chronic conditions. Although this is only an hypothesis, data on income-specific death rates do suggest that it might have some validity. Luft estimates death rates by income level, using National Center for Health Statistics figures (and working out approximate figures for the number of persons in each age–sex–income category).[19] These rates reveal the effects both of health on income and also of income on health. The difference between the death rates of the lowest income group (under $2000) and the highest income group (over $8000) is greatest for working-age men – there are ten times as many deaths

17. William R. Rosengren, 'Social Class and Becoming Ill', in Arthur Shostak and William Gomberg, eds., *Studies of the American Worker*, Englewood Cliffs, New Jersey, Prentice-Hall, 1964.

18. Charles Kadushin, 'Health and Social Class', *New Society*, 24 December 1964, p. 14. See also Thomas Arie, 'Class and Disease', *New Society*, 27 January 1966. Arie tries to refute Kadushin's thesis by the argument that if mortality rates are higher among the poor, sickness rates must also be higher.

19. Luft, 'Poverty and Health: An Empirical Investigation of the Economic Interactions', op. cit., p. 78.

in the lowest income group as in the highest. Data from Britain project an even grimmer picture. When we examine trends between 1930 and 1961 in the standardized mortality ratio for males we find an 'apparent deterioration in social class V. . . . Whilst the mortality of all men fell at all ages, except 70–74, that for social class V men . . . rose at all ages except 25–34. . . . It is clear that class V men fared much worse than average.'[20] (Class V are the unskilled.)

These findings of a strong positive class-related mortality gradient must reflect, at least in large part, loss of income due to ill health. But the young, and especially young females, do not contribute significantly to family income in most cases. If we compare death rates for those under 25, we still find substantial discrepancies between high- and low-income groups. Among females under 25 there were 41 deaths per ten thousand in families with incomes under $2000, while there were only 5 deaths per ten thousand in families with incomes of $8000 and over – an eight-fold difference in death rates between these two income levels. And there is a more than five-fold difference in death rates for males under 25 between these two income levels.

The Causal Link Between Poverty and Illness

If we are to proceed on the assumption either that income and illness or that income and the impact of illness on social functioning are closely related to each other, we need to specify the nature of the causal relationship between them. Is poverty the cause or the consequence of ill health? Here we encounter considerable disagreement among social scientists who have studied the question. Some believe that poverty breeds sickness through mechanisms such as improper nutrition, poor health practices and inadequate medical care. But others take the position that the relationship is the other way round – that, through lowered earnings and increased medical expenses, poor health is actually the cause of poverty. Victor Fuchs observed:

20. The Registrar General's Decennial Supplement, *Occupational Mortality Tables England and Wales, 1961*, H.M.S.O., 1971, p. 25.

One possible reason for the effect of income levels on health having been over-estimated is that investigators often find a very high correlation between income and the health status in individuals ... There has been a tendency to assume that the latter was the result of the former, but some recent studies of schizophrenia and bronchitis suggest that the causal relationship may run the other way. There is evidence that illness causes a deterioration in occupational status (from a skilled job to an unskilled job and from an unskilled job into unemployment). The evidence relates to the decline in occupational status from father to son (where the latter is a victim of the disease) and also within the patient's own history.[21]

Two early longitudinal studies support this view. The first examined the relationship between changes in income levels and illness rates among urban California families during the Depression.[22] The second study provides evidence of illness causing a downward drift in economic level over the years based on data of families in Hagerstown, Maryland, gathered in an original survey in 1923 and a follow-up survey in 1943.[23]

More recently Luft analysed new data from the Survey of Economic Opportunity and the Survey of Disabled Adults. He concludes that

the evidence points to a fairly minor role of income in the likelihood of disability. Factors correlated with income, however, especially the characteristics of jobs associated with different income levels, do have an important influence on disability. The influence of disability on poverty, however, is much greater. At least 20 per cent of the poor are poor because they are disabled; for white men, the figure is close to 50 per cent. In addition, nearly 70 per cent of all non-elderly poor families include at least one disabled adult.[24]

21. Victor Fuchs, 'The Contribution of Health Services to the American Economy', in John B. McKinley (ed.), *Economic Aspects of Health Care*, New York, Milbank Resource Books, 1973, p. 31.
22. Margaret C. Klem, *Medical Care and Costs in California Families in Relation to Economic Status, 1933–34*, San Francisco, State Relief Administration, 1935.
23 P. S. Lawrence, 'Chronic Illness and Socioeconomic Status', in Jaco, ed., op. cit., pp. 37–49.
24. Luft, 'Poverty and Health: an Empirical Investigation of the Economic Interactions', pp. 383–4.

This is a very important conclusion. If disability is identified as a major cause of poverty, a specific policy is needed to deal with the disabled poor. Meanwhile the causal link between income and disability remains illusive.

The impact of illness on income may occur through a number of ways: physical disability may necessitate a reduction in the number of hours worked per week, in the number of weeks per year, or in the ability to work at all; it may also result in a decline in the hourly wage rate if this rate is related to job productivity, or if the disabled person is forced to find a job with a lower wage rate which will accommodate his disability. Luft's investigation shows how race and sex interact to determine the actual impact of illness on income level:

> The outcomes ... are not the same for all; blacks are much more likely to drop out of the labor force or work fewer weeks per year, while whites are more likely to shift to jobs requiring a cut in hourly wage but still enabling them to be employed. Women are also more likely to have to drop out of the labor force, probably because of more restricted occupational choice and greater availability of alternative income sources. All of these changes tend to have an effect on earnings. This, in turn, influences other family earnings, as does disability directly through the need for home care. Finally, transfer payments are usually dependent on the level of earnings or income of the family. Thus, the various aspects of 'poverty' not only have an effect on the likelihood of disability, but they also affect the ways in which disability produces further changes in income and occupation.[25]

The Processes which Link Poverty and Illness

Meanwhile the search for an explanation of the assumed link between class and illness goes on. Consider a line of reasoning which, taking as given the association between income and illness, explores a possible mechanism through which the effects of poverty may be transmitted to health status. The argument can be stated as follows: deprivation (adversity, hardship) produces stress and emotional instability as suggested by the physical analogy of a 'heavy and unpleasant load applied to the body'.

25. ibid., p. 383.

Low income as a state of deprivation is assumed, often uncritically, to be inherently 'stressful' regardless of the context of surrounding events. So stress created by the circumstances of a harsh
environment is treated as an intervening variable to help account
for poor physical and mental health. 'The hypothesis that "stress"
is associated with disease is one of the most pervasive and
tenaciously held in current thought.'[26]

The literature abounds with studies of stress due to: major
changes in life situation,[27] overcrowding, inconsistency or ambiguity in tasks or roles, changes in customary activities,[28] low
status,[29] status inconsistency[30] and 'socio-environmental conditions'.[31] These various sources of stress are presumed to affect
health by generating anxiety, discomfort and emotional tension.

Two sources of stress that have been studied in some detail
are status inconsistency and lower-class status. The findings in
general suggest that both are (independently) associated with
higher-than-average stress symptoms. In several studies evidence
was found that the number and seriousness of stress symptoms
experienced were related to the number and type of status inconsistencies.[32] In their study of mental disease in the urban population, Pasamanik and his colleagues find that the prevalence of

26. Sol Levine and Norman A. Scotch, eds., *Social Stress*, Chicago,
Aldine Press, 1970.

27. Richard Rahe, Robert Biersner, David Ryman and Ranson Arthur,
'Psychosocial Predictors of Illness Behavior and Failure in Stressful
Training', *Journal of Health and Social Behavior*, III, December 1972,
pp. 393–7.

28. Joseph E. McGrath, ed., *Social and Psychological Factors in Stress*,
New York, Holt, Rinehart & Winston, 1970.

29. Richard J. Jeile and Philip N. Haese, 'Social Status, Status Incon-
gruence and Symptoms of Stress', *Journal of Health and Social Behavior*,
vol. X, September 1969, pp. 237–44.

30. Elton F. Jackson, 'Status Inconsistency and Symptoms of Stress',
American Sociological Review, XXVII, August 1972.

31. Joseph R. Hochstim, 'Poverty Area under the Microscope', *American
Journal of Public Health*, LVIII, 1968, pp. 1815–27.

32. Elton F. Jackson and Peter J. Burke, 'Status and Symptoms of Stress:
Additive and Interaction Effects', *American Sociological Review*, August
1965, pp. 556–64; Walter T. Martin, *Social Stress and Chronic Illness:
Mortality Patterns in Industrial Society*, Notre Dame, Indiana, University
of Notre Dame Press, 1970.

psycho-neurosis is concentrated in the lowest and highest income groups. They account for this as follows:

On the face it would appear that stress is greatest in the lowest and highest social economic strata, in the former due to deprivation and the frustrations consequent to deprivation and in the latter possibly due to various social and cultural inconsistencies and stress consequent to attempt to maintain status.[33]

Scattered evidence supports the hypothesis that the lower economic classes experience the greatest amount of stress. Adversity saps the morale so that those who suffer most can take suffering the least.[34] Studies contrasting the stress experience of people living in poverty areas with those comparable in other regards but living in relatively better-off neighbourhoods find that the conditions of the poverty neighbourhood itself constitute a source of stress, creating greater than average experience of illness, injury and psychological disruption.[35]

Hylan Lewis, from an intensive study of sixty-six families, fifty-seven of whom were low income, asserts that deprivation is the source of stress and life-style is a protective, adjustive reaction to stress. Lewis is one of the few writers to single out deprivation as an independent variable which 'causes' life-style. Unfortunately, the report does not demonstrate how 'adjustment' is achieved, nor how deprivation leads to the selection of a life-style. Crucial to Lewis's argument is the normative conclusion that 'programming might best focus on the facts of deprivation, rather than by intervening in life style'.[36]

33. Benjamin Pasamanik and others, 'A Survey of Mental Disease in an Urban Population: Prevalence by Race and Income', reprinted in Frank Riessman and others, *Mental Health of the Poor*, New York, Free Press of Glencoe, 1964, p. 47.

34. Philip Eisenberg and Paul Lazarsfeld, 'The Psychological Effects of Unemployment', *Psychological Bulletin*, 35, 1953, pp. 358–90.

35. Rodney M. Coe, John M. Goering, Marvin Cummins and others, *Health Status of Low Income Families in an Urban Area* (Final Report for the Bi-state Regional Medical Program), St Louis, Missouri, Medical Care Research Center, 1969, and Hochstim, op. cit.

36. Hylan Lewis, 'Child Rearing Practices Among Low Income Families in the District of Columbia' (paper presented at the National Conference on Social Welfare, 1961), p. 9.

We find that the literature is dominated by the view that deprivation, adversity and economic insufficiency are conditions promoting physical and psychological stress, which in turn cause
breakdown of health. But there is also literature which suggests
that hardship seems to lead to stress only under certain social
situations. Poverty alone may have little adverse effect. According
to this argument, man can withstand substantial adversity; it is
the sense of deprivation relative to the situation of others that
produces stress. Scotch, in a study of the relationship between
stress and hypertension among the Zulu, observed that while
people were poorer in the rural as compared to the urban areas,
stress and hypertension were higher in the urban setting. 'Stress
is not inherent in a given social situation or behavior pattern.'
The social context is crucial. Stress in urban areas is associated
with 'not only poverty, but degradation and humiliation in the
treatment of Africans by Europeans . . .'[37]

In this review of the literature on the relationship between
income and health status, we encounter ambiguity in the data
and basic disagreement over its interpretation. Some argue that
there is a positive causal relationship between poverty and illness
incidence, created by stress, hardship and malnutrition; while
others take the opposite position, arguing that illness creates
poverty by inhibiting the capacity to work. Some call attention to
a weak link between class and illness, while others stress how
class influences the impact of illness on the ability to function and
on mortality. The disagreement stems in part from the particular
data on which conclusions are based and in part from the types
of factors which are 'controlled for' in examining the data. The
disagreement also arises because of bias as the investigator
selectively seeks evidence to support a preconceived idea. Yet
even in the absence of conscious partisanship, resolution of the
apparent conflicts in the relevant available information is prob-

37. See Norman A. Scotch and H. Jack Geiger, 'The Epidemiology of
Essential Hypertension', *Journal of Chronic Diseases*, 16 November 1963.
The classic work on relative deprivation is found in Stouffer's study of the
American soldier and Merton's re-analysis of his findings and study of the
development of reference group theory: Robert K. Merton, *Social Theory
and Social Structure*, New York, Free Press of Glencoe, 1961.

ably impossible – the data is too fragmented and incomplete, and the explanations of conflicting findings lie buried in the unrecorded details of completed research projects.

Policy Implications

So far as it can be demonstrated that insufficient economic resources promote inadequate nutritional levels and poor medical care, and that these conditions are not only attributes of poverty but contribute to its perpetuation, then it is argued that an improvement in these circumstances may lead to the reduction of economic poverty. According to this formulation, increased attention to health can effectively reduce poverty by changing certain key circumstances of deprivation which reinforce and perpetuate the poverty cycle.

But in many respects this review of the literature is profoundly disturbing. It challenges some traditional views and suggests that the causal link between poverty and health is not uni-directional, and that we may have overestimated the extent that the poor are ill. It forces us to recognize that the relationship between physical illness, disability and medical care is extremely complex, and that a policy which recommends improved medical care as a means of cutting poverty through a reduction in physical illness is inadequate. There is little doubt that in the early stages of industrial development, health was more closely associated with poverty than it is today. In part, then, the problem is one of historical lag, for we have failed to change our assumptions as the data have changed.

We may also be relying on a rationale to support the provision of medical and social services which is becoming outdated, but which, since it usually remains implicit, is rarely questioned. This rationale is based on the principle that through the provision of adequate health resources and other services to the poor, poverty can ultimately be eliminated. Social policy is thus seen as self-liquidating. Spending money on services for the poor is justified as an economy in the long run, since it is assumed that these services will aid in lifting the poor out of poverty by increasing their capacity to maintain an independent income.

It is useful to make explicit this rationale underlying the provision of medical and social services, for it allows us to judge the accuracy of the assumptions about the causes and consequences of poverty on which it is based and also to evaluate the social priorities and goals which it implies. Since social priorities reflect the developing and evolving conditions of society, social policy should be continually re-evaluated as these goals and priorities change. The provision of resources to the poor, while undoubtedly a necessary pre-condition, will certainly not be a sufficient condition for the elimination of poverty. Economists like Kenneth Boulding have questioned the relevance of a poverty elimination policy; for some groups permanent subsidization is the only way out, as for the chronically disabled. Adequate social provision in an affluent society is a legitimate goal in itself, without considering its contribution to reducing poverty. Medical and social services should be rethought not in terms of their remedial, therapeutic and instrumental value for reducing poverty, but as an extension of income, as amenities in their own right. Certainly the poor need money if they are to command the resources which affect the quality of their lives. But increasingly poverty is viewed not only as a lack of income, but as a lack of the goods and services necessary to support a desired level of well-being. Medical care is a service that is becoming increasingly difficult to obtain easily and satisfactorily, even for the affluent. This is, in part, because the providers of these services enjoy certain monopoly privileges over the consumer. Moreover, the consumer is largely unable to evaluate the quality of the services he receives. For these reasons, there is a growing trend in the United States toward the provision of medical care services through some form of financial intervention which softens the impact of a competitive market. Although this will benefit all consumers, it will be especially important for the poor, since they are at the greatest disadvantage in obtaining these services under current free market conditions.

Even if we accept that there is an inequitable distribution of quality medical care resources, it is not at all clear, from available data, that improved medical services for low-income families would augment income sufficiently to reduce poverty. While inadequate use of medical services probably does contribute to the greater impact of illness and disability on the poor, it is likely that this is only one factor, and probably a minor one. We lack sufficient knowledge about the causes of illness and disability and the most effective ways to combat them. Environmental deprivation, housing insufficiency, poor nutrition and poor home health practices are also involved and probably dominate the role of medical care. In addition, even if improved medical care were a guaranteed route to improved health status, some of the poor are poor for reasons other than ill health. For these people, improved health would certainly improve their net personal welfare, but might not change their economic status. Thus the provision of medical care services should really be viewed as an end in itself, grounded in principles of equity, and not as a tool for reducing poverty. People are poor when they lack adequate access to health services; by definition, adequate amenities means reduced poverty.

Personal and Social Causes of Ill-Health

The bulk of social science research deals with hypotheses which are derived from personal and social frames of reference. This literature is readily available to most readers and a less extensive review seems necessary. However, ordering so vast a body of information, even for a brief review, is a formidable task. Selection is only one problem; equally difficult from a policy perspective is how to reconcile, or at least to understand, the conflicting evidence and theories.

The common theme of research grounded in personal and social theory is its emphasis on characteristics of the individual or of the individual's social group as the key elements responsible for the link between income and mental health. But there are two rather different strands in this body of research. The first sees the causes of poverty and illness as a pathology located in various characteristics of the poor, while the second deals with the role of critical stages of life-cycle development in increasing the likelihood of falling into emotional distress. These two views, while both focusing on the responsibility of the individual for his economic status, have rather different policy implications, as will be seen. This distinction between pathology, i.e., physical, emotional and social malfunctioning, and normal developmental needs, which all individuals confront at each stage of the life cycle, serves as a convenient, although admittedly arbitrary, way of organizing the main trends of thought within the general framework of social and personal theory.

Pathology

A pathological approach accepts uncritically the assumption that mental illness is concentrated among the poor, and proceeds to develop hypotheses to account for this relationship. However, the assumed relationship between poverty and mental illness is questionable and even less documented than the physical illness–poverty relationship. Here, as before, we encounter various theories, often similar in form to those concerning the relationship between poverty and physical illness. The drift hypothesis argues that people owe their poverty to their pathology. Emotionally sick individuals drift through the class structure and eventually are concentrated in the core of centre cities – Skid Row and the ghetto.

In their study of schizophrenia, Brown and his colleagues offer evidence of the downward drift in occupational position and income caused by mental illness. When we examine the occupational level of the patients before their first admission into a mental hospital, we find there is a disproportionate concentration in the semi-skilled and unskilled categories in comparison with the occupations of their fathers. But this is what one would assume on a common-sense basis. It is not surprising if schizophrenics cannot hold their jobs. When, however, one examines the highest occupation these patients ever attained, the distribution is very similar to the usual occupation of their fathers. The implication is clear. The illness which has eventually brought about their entry into the hospital was also responsible for reducing their occupational positions below what could be expected on the basis of their fathers' occupational level. Besides, at the end of a five-year period, following a first admission to hospital, over half the professional, clerical and skilled workers had declined in their occupational level or were unemployed, and a third of the semi-skilled and unskilled were unemployed.[38] How indeed could it be otherwise, given social prejudices against people with a record of mental illness, and possible actual deterioration of personality and performance. In the examples given above ill-health is the cause of poverty and not its consequence.

An alternative position is that when individuals strive to break out of poverty with limited resources, the odds against them are so great that they succumb to mental illness in the course of the struggle. Upward mobility strivings, which are, of course, not limited to the poor, are associated with mental illness. In support of this view, one study found vertical mobility 'to be a factor in both schizophrenia and psycho-neurosis', but cautiously added that 'this does not necessarily mean that mobility is the only or even the principal causative factor'.[39] One can attempt to side-step the difficult question of causality by defining low income and unemployment as attributes of mental illness, components of an 'inadequacy syndrome'. In a study of families applying for help from major social agencies in Syracuse, Cumming, a well-known psychiatrist, finds that the majority of men in this study show a long-term inability to maintain a job or an adequate income.

These evidences of social inadequacy [are] viewed as symptoms of mental illness. The long term unemployed and those with insufficient income are defined as having inadequately organized egos, i.e., the executive portion of the ego which develops independent of the conflict between id and superego.[40]

This argument declares that the tangle of pathology prevents people from responding to opportunities available to them and therefore serves as a cause of their present and future circum-

38. George Brown and others, *Schizophrenia and Social Care: A Comparative Follow-up Study of 339 Schizophrenic Patients*, Oxford University Press, 1966, pp. 86–7.

39. Evelyn Ellis, 'Social Psychological Correlates of Upward Mobility Among Unmarried Career Women', *American Sociological Review*, XVII, 1952, p. 563.

40. John Cumming, 'The Inadequacy Syndrome', 1968 (mimeograph).

stances. This approach is highly questionable. Poor people are not mentally ill by definition. Many who are not poor also have inadequately organized personalities and many poor are normal.

The concept of the pathological life-style with its cultural deficiency is strongly held, for the view that such deficiencies set in motion a self-perpetuating cycle of poverty has great appeal. This theory of the poverty cycle or the inter-generation transmission of dependency tends, with some variation, to take the following form: Poverty is seen as self-perpetuating; deprivation in one generation leads, through cultural impoverishment, indifference, or misunderstanding of their children's educational needs, to deprivation in the next; lacking the self-respect that comes from earning an adequate living, the young men cannot sustain the responsibilities of marriage and so they hand down to their children the same burden of ignorance, broken homes and apathy by which they were themselves crippled.

The theory of the poverty cycle stresses the *effects* of poverty on the poor – apathy and social disengagement – which prevent the poor from being able to exploit available opportunities. Once the cycle has begun, blame for its continuation is placed on the social–psychological effects of poverty, that is, on the personal characteristics of the poor, and it is assumed that the only way to break the cycle is by treating these personal characteristics. But the attribution of a causal link is unsupported, and the poverty cycle, as its name implies, is circular; thus the order of priority which places personal rehabilitation before attack on the inequalities in the distribution of resources seems arbitrary. Many believe that it is mistaken. According to their view the main question is whether there are significant opportunities. While we cannot create a world in which everybody holds equally attractive jobs, it is also a mistake to believe that if the poor were less apathetic, discouraged, etc., they would rise out of poverty and obtain highly regarded jobs.

In addition to questions about the empirical and theoretical bases for this view, the emphasis on deficiency, disorganization and disruption as the central theme of poverty has been sharply criticized as value-laden and reflecting middle-class bias. Broadly speaking, these critics share a more positive view of the values of lower-class sub-culture. Frank Riessman views the thesis of the culture of poverty as a packaging of negative attributes, the negative character of which is derived from an invidious comparison with presumably better middle-class standards. The resulting portrait is incomplete because it fails to take into account, for example, the rich and imaginative language of the poor. The focus on the limitations of the poor leads to a neglect of opportunities for constructive action based on their positive qualities.[41] Riessman's emphasis on the neglected strength of the poor directs attention to the need for reform in the techniques of teaching.

Policy Implications

Themes of apathy, impotence, incapacity and incompetence underlie much of the research discussed in this section, which focuses on personal and social causes of the poverty cycle and mental illness. The thesis is that the root cause of poverty and mental illness lies in some form of personal or social inadequacy. Its advocates regard the conflicting evidence as a challenge rather than a repudiation, believing that more research is needed to determine the specific causal link between poverty and social pathology.

These various themes of personal and social inadequacy all lead to strategies of intervention involving personal rehabilitation. Although the major assumptions seem to be drawn from many different fields of social science – psychology, anthropology, education and sociology – rehabilitative strategies share a common if implicit conception of social services. As in the case of resource allocation policies, services here are also intended to be ultimately self-liquidating. According to this perspective, however, it is the personal and social inadequacies of the poor which are the key to breaking the poverty cycle; thus services must be directed towards changing the competence of people rather than simply providing them with greater resources. People must be made sufficiently independent to be able to use established institutions effectively in the arenas of education, health, employment

41. Frank Riessman, 'Lower Income Culture: The Strengths of the Poor', *Journal of Marriage and the Family*, November 1964.

and politics. It is people's capacity to use institutions that is at issue, rather than the relevance of the functions which these institutions carry out.

Some of the policy implications of the personal and social view of the poverty cycle are illustrated by the types of programmes stimulated by Community Mental Health and Community Action Programmes. If the causes of poverty are circular and self-perpetuating, then there is no necessary order of priority in strategies attempting to break the cycle. Intervention at any point may be effective, and the more the better. Community-based programmes encourage variety rather than concentration on one preferred programme. Coordination of these multiple interventions then becomes crucial. At the same time, neglect of any one aspect of the programme could be excused by the claim that it was indirectly influenced by other interrelated programmes.

Remedial programmes are another important concern. The logic of the poverty cycle argument leads to an emphasis on preparatory training programmes which are less concerned with technical skills than with adjustment of individuals to the demands of living and work. Compensatory education programmes were another example of the remedial strategy. In these programmes, the school acts as a substitute family to the child, compensating him for earlier stimulus deprivation. Programmes like Operation Headstart try to reach the child early in his development through an enriched programme outside the home which will permit him to negotiate the school system better. Change in the school is assumed to be less crucial than increasing the competence of the child to use the school.

Another major concern of community-based programmes is to provide families with a stake in society by encouraging their participation in social action. As individuals go through the process of seeking to change their work, they change as well. Social action is thus a form of social therapy to treat apathy and social disintegration through self-help.

The goals of such programmes may be characterized as efforts to take poverty out of the people rather than merely taking people out of poverty by providing them with adequate resources. The assumption that poverty is 'in the people' rather than in the society is very significant – it not only places the blame for poverty squarely on the poor, but in so doing it characterizes them as incompetent, pathological or morally deficient. It is difficult to disguise the assumptions which underlie the provision of a service from those for whom the service is intended – and many community mental health programmes have had the unintended effect of reinforcing a sense of failure, futility and inadequacy. It is obviously unfair to blame poverty and mental illness on the poor. But we cannot solve the problem easily by putting the blame on society without a theory of what specific societal forces have produced the condition.

Developmental Needs

Scheduling

A rather different approach to the attempt to understand the nature and causes of poverty and associated illness is represented by research into the role played by stages of development. Instead of viewing poverty as the result of various psycho-social characteristics or deficiencies, this approach focuses on the effects of the timing of major events on the likelihood of succumbing to pathology. The timing of work and family cycles, for example, is critical if the family is to maintain itself financially and function effectively. Beyond purely economic considerations, it has been suggested that emotional well-being is best promoted when the preferred order for timing significant life events is followed. For example, in the relationship between work and family formation it is widely believed that occupational identity should precede psycho-social intimacy in marriage, and that early marriage is to be discouraged as a premature assumption of responsibility. Schorr's analysis of the relationship between family cycle and income illustrates the kind of process which may take place, at least for low income groups. Early marriage seems to affect the number and spacing of children, producing more children both early and late. (This does not seem to apply to blacks.) Husbands are pressed to take the first job they can secure, and with limited educational achievement the first job affects future jobs and determines a chaotic pattern of employment. Moreover, since the husband is young, the risk of unemployment is high and the likelihood of a low income seems assured. And these risks come at the very time when family needs are outstripping resources. Frustration leads to the abandonment of the roles of husband and breadwinner as family break-up and an unstable work history follow with disturbing regularity.[42]

It will come as no surprise that the case for scheduling life-cycle transitions to prevent pathology and emotional breakdown is not clear-cut. Recent studies of college marriages suggest that 'early marriers tend to be more mature, to be better academic performers, and to display fewer indications of marital disruptions than students who were single or married after graduating from college'.[43] The studies imply that the order in which the events are scheduled is *not* as significant as the capacity to cope with the circumstances surrounding simultaneous status transitions. Geismar's study of stable and unstable families in a housing project challenge the view that there is a similar behaviour pattern in the spheres of work and family. He reports that malfunctioning in intra-familial relations does not appear to be related to malfunctioning in the world of work.[45] Economic stability – earning a low income but having the ability to hold a job – does not significantly distinguish between problem and stable families.

If we set aside the negative findings and accept the view about the importance of scheduling, it follows that there are critical stages in the life cycle when intervention is most effective – the birth of a child, adolescence, retirement, death. In addition to normal developmental changes such as these, transitional crises

42. This argument is presented as a rationale in support of a children's allowance programme in Alvin Schorr, *Poor Kids*, New York. Basic Books, 1967.

43. Robert and Rhona Rappaport, 'Work and Family in Contemporary Society', *American Sociological Review*, XXX, no. 3, June 1965.

45. Ludwig L. Geismar and Michael A. La Sorte, *Understanding the Multi-Problem Family: A Conceptual Analysis and Exploration in Early Identification*, New York, Association Press, 1964.

may be brought about by: (1) traumatic events, such as premature birth, surgery, loss of income; and (2) points of re-socialization such as entry or release from prison or a mental hospital.[46] Psychiatrists and sociologists have developed the hypothesis that status transition points provide the greatest point of leverage for intervention. Old patterns of adjustment are being challenged, while new forms of adaptation have not yet emerged. It is during such transitional periods that the potential for growth is greatest.[47] Observers who have studied this process have suggested that the period of 'heightened susceptibility' is quite short, lasting only a few weeks or at most two months before new patterns are crystallized.[48]

The transition from school to work is very important, since the first job strongly influences a life's career. This transition falls most heavily on those who leave school early, for they are at their least mature and are least prepared to compete successfully in the work world. Adequate preparation and guidance for this transition period are critical. Adulthood is also characterized by continuing transitions. Women usually complete the task of raising their children when they are still relatively young, and so are in search of new careers as they experience the transition from home to work. In a period of rapid technological change, occupational shifts are common to both men and women – this dramatizes the need for continuous education, retraining and counselling throughout the life cycle. But while we are chasing after opportunities by acquiring new skills, the demand pattern may change again. If the discoveries of modern science make recovery from long-term illness more likely, then many will experience transitions from dependency to self-care. Finally, in the transition from work to retirement we are catapulted into a crisis when the

46. The importance of crisis and transition as normal events experienced during the life cycle has been proposed by a number of investigators. See, for example, Orville Brim, 'Socialization Through the Life Cycle' (mimeograph); Rhona Rappaport, 'Normal Crisis, Family Structure, and Mental Health', *Family Process*, II, March 1963; and Gerald Caplan, *Principles of Preventive Psychiatry*, Tavistock Press, 1964.

47. Bertram Gross, *The Managing of Organization*, New York, Free Press of Glencoe, 1964, p. 792.

48. Robert and Rhona Rappaport, 'Work and Family in Contemporary Society', *American Sociological Review*, XXX, no. 3, June 1965, p. 389.

activity which provides meaning and dignity to life must be found in areas other than work.

Policy Implications

The focus on scheduling and life-cycle transitions suggests that intervention is possible at any stage of development. This perspective permits us to abandon the demanding principle that early intervention is always preferred for the more flexible view that the occurrence of a significant event rather than age is the crucial factor in promoting change and nurturing health.

The risk of falling into poverty is probably greater at each of the critical transition points. The role of the family in facilitating transition over the life cycle is decreasing, and society is indifferent or unable to create the kind of personal service needed. As we have suggested, new social inventions are needed to extend and enrich the quality of life in an affluent society. Seen in this light, social services take on a new role as universal provision to expand choices rather than specific resources to reduce pathology as now.

When maturation and developmental change rather than pathology and alienation serve as the terms of reference for policy development, a new set of assumptions concerning the nature and purpose of social services seems to be necessary. Remedial strategies for the disengaged, apathetic and sick are replaced by strategies which facilitate crisis and transition, risks which all people encounter over the course of the life cycle. Thus, universal mental health services, broadly defined and for all citizens, are appropriate, rather than isolated services for the alienated, neurotic and mentally ill.

Periods of transition can be sustained by a variety of direct and indirect policies: intervention outside the family, increasing job stability, educational opportunity or the size and stability of income transfers. Universal student stipends have been proposed, which in effect would pay students to continue in school, where they can mature at low risk. The success of this postponement approach for low-income groups will depend on our inventing new forms of socially approved dependency. Student subsidies will need to be justified on some new principle, such as the right to emotional development through broadening and deepening life experiences. The educational curriculum need not be bound by tradition – travel as well as reading can be stressed.

Another approach discounts the issues of scheduling and attempts to reduce the pressure from the family squeeze – the divergence of income and family growth.[49] It is directed not at the future generation but at the mental health of parents and their young children. Three programmes are illustrative: the expansion of income through a family or children's allowance, the reduction of need by a programme of birth control and abortion, increase in disposable income made possible by altering the family's level of expenditures for basic necessities through low cost subsidized housing, saving food costs by building supermarkets in the slums and developing more effective protection against salary garnishing (fringe benefits) and loan sharking.

Finally, we can concentrate on the relationship between employment and the capacity to fulfil the adult role of wage earner. In his interesting analysis of the policy implications of the problem of identity in lower-class youth Rainwater suggests how work and growth affect each other. He argues that a loss of identity comes about when the self we presented to others fails to be acknowledged or accepted.

The major validation of self for men is expected to stem from performance in the occupational world. For the blue collar worker, career opportunities are limited. He must rely on the goal of being a good provider, oriented to providing adequate income rather than occupational mobility. Lower class youth tend to reject both the career and the provider roles and rely for their identity on a life style variously called action-seeking, cats and kicks syndrome, or expressive style. The available rewards of the expressive life style are greatest for the young and seem to decrease rapidly with age.[50]

49. See Alvin L. Schorr, *Slums and Social Insecurity* (Research Report no. 1, Division of Research and Statistics, Social Security Administration), Washington, D.C., U.S. Government Printing Office, 1963, pp. 31–2, for an analysis of how different types of income transfer schemes affect the family squeeze.

50. Lee Rainwater, 'Work and Identity in the Lower Class', in Sam Warner, ed., *Planning for a Nation of Cities*, Cambridge, Mass., M.I.T. Press, 1966.

At this point, since earlier forms of adaptation no longer suffice, we would expect the personality system to be most fluid and open for change. Rainwater suggests that job continuity – holding a job without being fired – can validate the role of good provider. But during the period of transition from school to work, employers will need to tolerate behaviour which interferes with job performance. A tight labour market for unskilled workers naturally lowers the performance standards of employers. It is chiefly in a labour surplus market that new devices are needed, both in and outside the market, such as work experience programmes to ease youth from one stage of development to another. Job continuity can only be achieved by significantly expanding the volume of low-skilled jobs. Economic and social policy cannot be arbitrarily isolated from each other. And both are relevant as strategies to encourage mental health and to prevent pathology.

Institutional Performance

In the nineteenth century it was often assumed that organized charity encouraged people to become paupers by interfering with the functioning of the market and destroying the incentive system. These ideas about the relationship between institutional performance and individual behaviour still influence our thinking. We tend to believe that social institutions nurture poverty and ill health.

Perhaps the most influential theory about the consequences of institutional performance on personal well-being is that public and private institutions benefit most those people who need them least. Consider the use of medical care in relation to need: there is abundant evidence to show that the poor, who suffer the most disability from illness, have the least access to medical care services. This is shown by statistics on the average number of physician visits per year in the United States, the likelihood of having a 'regular' source of care and the likelihood of receiving any care at all during a year; all of these are positively related to income level.[51] Other social institutions also operate on an implicit double standard, blocking the access of the poor to quality care.

Many aspects of the health-care system discriminate, perhaps unintentionally, against the poor. The traditional method of allocating health services has been to set a price on their use, with the result that those who use them most pay the highest total price. Since the poor suffer the most disabling illnesses and at the same time have the least income, this system discriminates against the poor. But the health-care system also has non-financial methods of discouraging use by the poor: physicians and health-care facilities are less likely to be found in areas where the poor live, such as urban ghettoes and rural areas; hospital out-patient departments and emergency rooms, which have become the predominant sources of medical care for the urban poor, are less likely to provide comprehensive care or to emphasize screening and follow-up procedures; and the impersonality, fragmentation and inconvenience of these large clinics are discouraging to everyone, but especially to the poor. Very often, use of these facilities requires long waits. A survey of a poor area in Baltimore found that 42 per cent of those surveyed stated that they had to wait more than an hour to receive services at their usual source of care.[52] Financial aid programmes for medical care, intended to remove the economic barrier, often themselves constitute a psychological barrier. These programmes often involve requirements perceived to be demeaning, or participation in the programme itself is seen as an admission of social inadequacy and acquires a social stigma.[53] Finally, the attitudes and training of

51. See, for example, National Center for Health Statistics, *Volume of Physician Visits, U.S. July 1966–June 1967* (U.S. Department of Health, Education and Welfare, Public Health Service publication no. 1000, series 10, no. 49), Washington, D.C., U.S. Government Printing Office, 1968, pp. 19, 38; and Coe, Goering, Cummins and others. op. cit.

52. Peter Densen and others, 'Primary Medical Care for the Urban Population: A Survey of Present and Potential Utilization', *Journal of Medical Education*, XIII, 1968, pp. 1244–9.

53. Lawrence L. Bergner and Alonzo A. Yerby, 'Low Income and Barriers to Use of Health Services', *New England Journal of Medicine*, CCLXXVIII, no. 10, 1968, pp. 541–6.

the professional providers of health services can discourage the poor from using the services. There is considerable evidence that a wide social and cultural gulf often exists between patients and professionals. Willie reports in a survey of a sample of public health nurses that a majority expressed a preference for treating persons of relatively high socio-economic status.[54] Other studies, controlled for frequency of contact, show that the social class and race of the patient were significantly associated with how well the doctors felt they knew him or her, lower-class Negroes being the least well-known by their doctors.[55] These professional attitudes are not effectively disguised. In Koos' well-known study of Regionville, the lower-class patients were much more likely to consider physicians to be uninterested in their cases than upper-class patients were.[56]

The true effects of these and other barriers to utilization can only be fully appreciated when they are removed – when a group of people is provided for the first time with medical care which is truly accessible, physically, economically and socially. Such was the case when medical clinics providing free medical care were introduced into six migrant workers' camps in California.[57] The clinics were located in the camps, they were free, and they were open during non-working hours. Utilization patterns before and after introduction of these clinics were studied in order to challenge the assumption that use of health services is primarily determined by social, cultural and educational factors – the thesis of the personal and social research orientation. The percentage of reported illnesses for which medical care was received rose from 43 per cent before the introduction of the clinics to 70 per cent. Increases in the use of preventive services were even more striking.

54. Charles Willie, 'The Social Class of Patients that Public Health Nurses Prefer to Serve', *American Journal of Public Health*, vol. L, 1960, pp. 1126–36.

55. Richard I. Feinbloom and others, 'The Physician's Knowledge of Low Income Families' (paper presented at the meeting of the American Public Health Association, 1967).

56. Koos, op. cit.

57. Howard Snyder and others, 'The Effect of Medical Facilities on Use by the Migrant Workers of California', *Medical Care*, VI, no. 5, 1968, pp. 394–400.

The authors concluded that the migrant workers' low rates of utilization prior to the introduction of these clinics had been primarily due to problems of accessibility and other barriers.

A similar conclusion was reached in a study comparing the use of health-care services by poverty and non-poverty groups within the Kaiser prepaid group-practice plan in Portland, Oregon.[58] Most of the major barriers to care were eliminated by giving the poverty group free access (as a demonstration, the cost was paid by the Office of Economic Opportunity) to services and facilities similar to those used by the rest of the Plan members. Under these conditions, there was a striking degree of similarity between the utilization patterns of the poverty and non-poverty groups. Seventy-five per cent of each group used at least one medical-care service (although there were some differences in the age–sex distribution of users in each group, and also in the timing of the visits). The investigators concluded that 'much of the reported difference in the behaviour of poverty populations relates to differential access to medical care'.[59]

These examples of localized efforts to equalize access to medical care suggest that the removal of financial and institutional barriers often results in increased utilization by the poor. Would this same effect prevail if access were enlarged more broadly, say on a national scale? The experience of the British National Health Service suggests that it might. 'Utilization of medical services by different status groups, by the acute and chronic sick or mentally ill and handicapped, and by adults below and above pensionable age, is more unequal in the United States than in Britain.'[60] A review of recent data (1971) suggests that among the poorer classes in Britain there is a pattern of relatively low utilization for males and for children under five, higher rela-

58. Merwyn R. Greenlick, Donald K. Freeborn, Theodore J. Colombo and others, 'Comparing the Use of Medical Care Services by a Medically Indigent and a General Membership Population in a Comprehensive Prepaid Group Practice Program' (paper presented at a meeting of the American Public Health Association, 26–30 October 1970).

59. Ibid., p. 21.

60. Peter Townsend, 'Inequality and the Health Service', February 1974, p. 14 (mimeograph).

tive utilization as they grow up with noticeably higher rates in late middle years (ages 45–64), and then a slight under-utilization for the aged (over 65). Except for the very young, the lowest social classes appear to make more use of medical services than the better off. While detailed information on type, length and content of consultations with doctors is lacking, there is some support for the view that the care they receive may be as good as that secured by the other social classes. While the question of quality is sur-rounded by controversy, several features of the British system support an optimistic view. First, the self-diagnosis which is so characteristic of American specialist-oriented medical care is replaced in Britain by a system where a patient's access to special-ists is screened by the general practitioner, and while this limited role of the general practitioner has been criticized, it may contri-bute to the equalization of class use of medical services. But the most crucial factor in reducing class inequalities in use in Britain is the availability of universal, free-on-demand, comprehensive services. (Private medical care is also available, but is relatively little used.) The 'market' mechanism in the field of health is neither a law of nature nor a law of society. The lack of charges for use plus the truly accessible and acceptable system of care re-sults in a pattern of use by social class quite different from that found in the United States. However, it is not clear that even the British pattern of use is truly equitable, since its relationship to need, or illness, is unknown. But it does seem reasonable to con-clude that medical care is more equitably distributed in Britain, under their system of universal, free services, than in the United States under the private fee-for-service system.[61]

Why has opportunity been blocked in medical care and other institutional areas in the United States? A great many theories have been advanced. Among them are: professional technology and ideology support the middle-class client and reject the poor; bureaucratic rigidity acts to prevent institutions from adapting rapidly to changing social and economic conditions. A harsher explanation is found in the conflict of interests between classes

61. For a fuller discussion see Martin Rein, 'Social Class and the Health Services', *New Society*, 20 November 1969.

and races: the status of the middle class requires that 'the poor be kept in their place'; or racial discrimination blocks opportunity.[62]

Policy Implications

If the structure of various institutions bears major responsibility for the creation and perpetuation of poverty and ill health, two broad approaches can be identified: resource redistribution and institutional reform. The former is different from those redistributive policies discussed earlier, in that here resources are provided to institutions rather than directly to people, on the assumption that increasing the funding and competence to carry out their mission will eliminate unintended discriminatory practices. But in many large urban areas it is not enough only to allocate more resources to social service institutions. Where they have ceased to be responsive to the needs of their clientele their purposes, assumptions and practice must change as well.

Thus institutional reform calls for the form and practices of institutions or even their basic structure to be altered in such a way that they no longer discriminate against the poor, but perhaps even favour them.

... if we are effectively to reach the poor ... we must differentiate and discriminate, individually and collectively. We have to do so if we wish to channel proportionately more economic resources to aid the poor and the handicapped ...

The problem then is not whether to differentiate in access, treatment, giving, and outcome but *how* to differentiate; ... how in some respects to treat equals unequally and in other respects unequals equally. We cannot now disengage ourselves from the challenge of distributing social rights without stigma.[63]

This might be accomplished in many ways, ranging from minor reforms of particular features of institutions which affect only the

62. The literature on this perspective is fragmented. Research and analysis of how institutional defects affect poverty are not readily available. It is for this reason that I have only presented the arguments without reference to the literature.

63. Richard Titmuss, 'Social Policy and Economic Progress' (paper presented at the National Conference on Social Welfare, Chicago, June 1966), p. 12.

poor to major structural changes which have a universal impact. Reform in the medical care system illustrates both poles: the discriminatory effect of the fee-for-service pricing system is countered conservatively by categorical, income-tested programmes sponsored by the federal government, such as Medicaid; but the more radical position is that the entire pricing structure needs to be changed to a lump-sum prepayment system with services free at the time of use. Of course, medical services, medical training, etc., are costly. They must be paid for somehow. This requires the creation of public funds for the purpose. Although such a change would affect all users of medical care, its effect would nevertheless be more beneficial to the poor since it would eliminate the present direct relationship between amount of illness and cost of care.

However, institutional change is not an easy route – witness the medical profession's strong resistance to the incremental changes in the role of the federal government in the provision of medical care over the years. Institutions are composed of large numbers of people, and in order to function must develop formal and informal rules and patterns of behaviour. As these patterns become more ingrained and are passed on to new employees in the institutional system, they acquire something of an independent existence. Change proceeds at the pace of those most resistant to it, since the cooperation of all parts of the institution is required in implementing any new procedures. And we know much less about the processes by which institutions change than we do about the source of resistance to change. The literature on purposive social change has been built largely on an educational model which assumed that communication failures are a major source of institutional resistance. More recently the limitations of this view have been recognized, and change is being examined in terms of interest groups and conflict. It has become clear that the policies of promoting change need to be separated from the agenda of change – the specific institutional reforms which are necessary.

The Community Action Program provides one example of an attempt to change medical care institutions as a means of reducing poverty on the assumption that the institutions ought to become more relevant to the needs of the poor. It devised a strategy to fit its theory that social service bureaucracies had become preoccupied with loyalty procedure at the expense of their functions, and had drifted into a self-regarding posture which made them insensitive to the needs of those they served. Disturbed about lack of professional interest in serving the poor, it insisted that programmes make use of non-professionals. Not only did this provide employment opportunities for the poor, but the intrusion of indigenous personnel into a rigid bureaucracy could force self-examination and propel the organization change. But the heart of the strategy assumed that the problem was the arbitrary jurisdictional boundaries established by agencies and that the crucial reform was reorganization of the total framework of splintered and unrelated social services. The whole medical care delivery system needed to be integrated and made more coherent through coordination.

The financing, organization and distribution of health services have continued to be topics of concern. Innovative forms of health care delivery are becoming increasingly common – prepayment, which does away with fee-for-service payment, organized group practices, consumer representation in the management of health-care facilities. Decentralized community-controlled medical-care systems accountable to local citizens who are the direct consumers of these social services have been developed. National reform of the entire medical care system is no longer in doubt; the current debate concerns the type and extent of the reform. But there are no panaceas. All these strategies are very problematic. The idea of a fully nationalized medical-care system, based on the British model, is receiving increasingly favourable attention as the inadequacies and inequities of the present system become more glaring.

Concluding Observations

In this review I have arbitrarily excluded the economic literature and have treated the social factors in a selective way, examining each of three perspectives separately and without consideration of national economic policy. But clearly this is insufficient, for the task is more complex. If we accept the view that each perspective contributes something to our understanding about the causes of poverty and ill-health and the means to overcome them, then all of these factors must somehow be related to one another and brought together into some coherent national policy. But how are we to assess the relative importance of each perspective – resource redistribution, personal intervention, institutional reform – and then reconcile these with the competing goals of economic growth? It is not only a question of priority, for the simultaneous pursuit of these strategies may conflict.

One of the central, but neglected, issues is how, in constructing policy to integrate the three perspectives. It seems easier to draw on findings framed in terms of each of them. Research conducted within one frame rarely considers factors deemed critical under another. To some extent, this problem is analogous to the failure of communication among disciplines. While it is of course efficient to have some division of labour in the treatment of different issues by different disciplines, this often results in an excessively narrow point of view and ignorance of important extra-disciplinary substantive concerns and methodologies. With the increasing emphasis on interdisciplinary work in many fields, especially for complex social issues where many considerations and forces are in fact at work, this disciplinary isolationism will probably diminish.

In considering different disciplines and different research perspectives within one discipline we should recognize that if we set out to find out what is the part played by, for example, economic forces in a particular social behaviour pattern, we are likely to discover a relationship which can be interpreted as a 'role'. But if we then explore the impact of various institutional characteristics on the same behaviour, we will find yet another relationship. The explanation is straightforward – a large number of different models can be used to 'explain' the same observations. But my point is that one perspective fails to take into account other interpretations of the same evidence. Some approaches lend themselves to the simultaneous consideration of numerous factors fairly easily – for example, under the personal and social perspective, many different personal characteristics can be examined and their relative contribution to the explanation of the phenomenon in question assessed. But the possible impact of institutional reform can only be inferred from the fragmentary evidence of such reforms as have occurred, and these are often minor and inapplicable, requiring questionable inferences. And more difficult still is the assessment of major redistribution policies; there is little evidence available from which to understand their effect. We lack the data and the tools to reach an objective reconciliation of the competing claims of the different perspectives.

But even with the benefit of better information, we must in the end make brute personal, political and value choices about what we regard as desirable public policy. These choices cannot be made without some conception of the good society. Thus, the more ruthlessly we pursue the path of technology the more we come to acknowledge the role of ideology in the choice between policy alternatives. Public policy must inevitably involve the resolution of conflicting goals both within the same group and among different groups. The main safeguard against bias lies in insuring that different perspectives are heard, and that much more systematic attention be given to problem setting.[64] This requires that research be organized not in terms of method but of outlook. In short, multi-paradigmatic research must be sponsored. The contribution of social science to the choice of a value framework is likely to be modest, but it can have a broader role in the management of conflicting goals pursued by those who share similar value judgements.

64. For a discussion see Martin Rein and Sheldon White in Carol Weiss (ed.), *Problem Setting in Policy Research* (forthcoming).

Chapter 7

Social Science for Social Policy

The Contribution of Objective Inquiry to Normative Issues

How does an understanding of reality, or of what Mannheim described as 'what has already become', contribute to the clarification and the choice of a direction of 'what is in the process of becoming'?[1] In other words, how do questions of fact and the issues of understanding which are the central concerns of social science, enter into deliberations about normative and value questions, which are the accepted language of politics? This is perhaps the major issue underlying efforts to develop a social science which can contribute to policy questions. But it is a difficult question because understanding of why things are as they are may contribute to a sense of bafflement, confusion and complexity which can inhibit the capacity to act, even though it is inspired by the desire for action.

I want in this essay to set out my views about the interplay between values and objective knowledge, and also to suggest the kind of social science knowledge which I believe most clearly reflects that interplay. The views I will develop are somewhat controversial, for they run counter to much of the received wisdom about what men of action request of social science and what social scientists feel they can contribute to those who must make decisions. Before examining this question I want to explore how

1. Karl Mannheim, *Ideology and Utopia*, New York, Harcourt Brace (Harvest Books), 1936, p. 112.

knowledge and value questions interact. Three approaches are reviewed.

Values Organize Facts

The first perspective holds that it is concern for values that makes objectivity important. When the consequences of action matter, the truth or falsity of predictions about these consequences seems urgent; and so objectivity or truthfulness is especially valued when a person is committed. Again, if the consequences are important, the quality of the understanding on which the predictions are based also seems essential. Hence, if a person is rational (in the sense of wanting to accomplish purposes in the real world), the stronger his attachment to certain values that he wishes to realize through action, the greater his concern with evidence which permits him to assess whether he is achieving the aims he intends by the course of action he has chosen. According to this perspective, then, we need objective knowledge, because it will enable us to control and manipulate our environment so that it is congruent with the values we espouse. Accordingly, the more passionately we hold our values, the more deeply committed we are to objectivity in predicting the consequences of our action on those values.

Unfortunately, this logically attractive argument – that truth aids in bringing about values we cherish, and hence objective knowledge is essential to action – encounters some stubborn, practical difficulties which makes it difficult to realize. The main difficulty arises because the values we passionately hold often inhibit our capacity to understand reality and to pursue objective knowledge. Man is, after all, interested not only in controlling, manipulating and predicting the consequences for his environment so that it falls in with his purposes, but also in creating and maintaining a sense of order, continuity and meaning in life. Our concern for order, both in nature and in human affairs, derives from a fundamental inability to tolerate too much confusion and disarray. Structure and meaning are essential to our existence. Therefore, when objective facts threaten the orderly framework which assigns meaning to events, we tend to repudiate the facts rather than abandon the framework. In fact the quest for order and meaning may be more compelling than the search for truth, which can threaten the order we have created. So, when values determine the direction of inquiry, we risk distorting reality in the interests of maintaining our value system.

Facts are Compatible with Different Values

The second perspective holds that there are many different ways of looking at reality, all of which may be valid, and that there is no means of deciding among these views. There are no true facts which can be isolated from the framework of belief that gives these facts meaning and context. That is to say, truth is not inherent in the objective events themselves, but in the way in which we order these events in relation to some framework of interpretation. Values must necessarily intrude into inquiry. I do not wish to carry the argument too far, since constructions of reality are open to criticism and some frameworks are difficult to defend. In this sense observation can provide some check on the truth of the framework, and logic can provide a check on its internal consistency. But while there is scope for debate there is no definitive way to determine which of the competing frameworks or ideologies is the most true. As Popper points out, '. . . no conclusive disproof of a theory can ever be produced; for it is always possible to say that the experimental results are not reliable or that the discrepancies which are asserted to exist between the experimental results and the theory are only apparent and that they will disappear with the advance of our understanding'.[2] Kuhn develops this thesis when he explains that 'the criteria with which scientists determine the validity of . . . and application of existing theory, are not by themselves sufficient to determine the choice between competing theories'.[3] It appears

2. Karl Popper, *The Logic of Scientific Discovery*, 1959, p. 50, as quoted in Thomas S. Kuhn, 'Logic of Discovery or Psychology of Research?', in I. Lakatose and A. Musgrave, eds., *Criticism and the Growth of Knowledge*, Cambridge University Press, 1970, p. 14.

3. ibid., p. 19.

then that there is no 'truth' which is independent of the framework of interpretation which directed the search for facts and which gives them meaning. We must rely upon ideology which contains announcements of values worth striving for, theories of why things work as they do, and strategies of how to achieve these values in a given circumstance if we are to impose order on the facts we observe. Often we find that the same facts are compatible with quite different interpretations of reality, order, and meaning.

Mannheim eloquently developed this argument in his study of how we deal with the problems of knowing when our ability to know is bounded by our position in time and society. But he was deeply troubled by this insight, which he regarded as a great obstacle to a science of politics. He argued that according to ordinary expectations a science of conduct would be possible only when the fundamental structure of thought was independent of the different forms of conduct being studied. Even though the observer is perforce a participant in the struggle, the basis of this thinking, i.e., his operational apparatus and his method of settling intellectual differences, 'must be above the conflict'.[4] Of course, he found no solution to the dilemma he posed, except in the hope that the marginal position of the intellectual in society would enable him to rise above his class-bound interests, recognize the competing frameworks of argument, and create a true synthesis. This is a doubtful solution, but we have not found a better one. We must accept the position that objective evidence does not permit us to choose among competing ideologies or frameworks of thought.

Facts Organize Values

A third perspective holds that objective inquiry enables us to discover the crucial underlying values. Here the argument is turned on its head, for it makes reality the master of values rather than their servant. As reality unfolds in history it provides the ultimate source of authority for our values, because it informs us about what is 'true' and hence what is 'legitimate'.

4. Karl Mannheim, op. cit., p. 117.

Popper believed that all forms of historicism shared this view of history. 'I mean by "historicism" an approach to the social sciences which assumes that historical prediction is their principal aim, and which assumes that this aim is attainable by discovering the "rhythms" or the "patterns", the "laws" or the "trends" that underlie the evolution of history.' The main implication of this approach is that 'Only such plans as fit in with the main current of history can be effective.'[5] Of course Marxism sees the relationship between values, history and reality as implying a view of the world in which the normative and the intellectual are merged. To the Marxist, then, the normative position is derived from an interpretation of the movement of history and hence is grounded in an understanding of historical reality. According to this argument, socialism or communism is on the agenda of history, because an objective interpretation of historical events suggests that we are inexorably moving in this direction. Such a view of historically grounded objectivity leaves little room for moral dissent, because our cognitive grasp of reality leads to the belief that what is inevitable must also be desirable.

The argument that facts organize values is pressed not only by those on the political left but also by those who are conservative or take a middle course. For example, conservatives tend to argue that human beings are naturally competitive, aggressive and greedy for power. If you recognize these fundamental aspects of human nature as revealed through past history, then you must accept that certain kinds of utopian socialist goals are psychologically impossible, irrespective of how attractive we consider them from a moral point of view. In addition there has recently been a revival of historical thinking by those who see themselves politically as neither conservative nor radical. Goldthorpe describes the 'evolutionary' liberal as a theorist who holds that all modern economies inevitably develop a broadly similar pattern of social institutions and social life. The politics of this new form of technocratic historicism are of moderation and gradualism, in contrast

5. Karl Popper, *The Poverty of Historicism*, p. 3, as quoted in John Goldthorpe, 'Theories of Industrial Society: Reflections of the Recrudescence of Historicism in the Future of Futurology', *The Archives of European Sociology*, vol. XII, 1971, p. 264.

to nineteenth-century historicism which tended to embrace either a conservative laissez-faire ideology or a revolutionary one.[6]

Dilemmas of a Policy-Oriented Social Science

The arguments above can be briefly summarized: either (a) values determine the facts and therefore objective inquiry provides us with no means to reconcile policies which are based on different value frameworks; or (b) reality is distorted in the service of pre-conceived value positions; or (c) reality determines what values are realizable, thus reducing the scope for moral debate because reality contains and is master of value choices.

As indicated in Chapter 1, my own research derives from a sceptical outlook. In this concluding chapter I return to this and to other themes which I have discussed earlier. I reject the last view, but I acknowledge the problems inherent in subscribing to the first two. I do not easily commit myself to one value paradigm as the basis for my research on policy questions. I value empirical inquiry and believe that every ideology should be examined critically. In my approach to research on policy questions I am concerned with the way in which value positions distort reality; therefore I am interested in the way in which objective analysis permits one to explore this distortion. But I do not believe that such an analysis will usually lead to another value position, only to an alternative way of looking at things within the original one.

Although I believe that purposes are essential for policy analysis, I do not altogether know what my purposes are, because I cannot defend the meaning in my life in any way which is ultimately secure. Therefore, I do not know which purposes I should try to realize with any certainty. I hope that because I accept this position I am less inclined to distort reality to fit my purposes. Indeed, I restlessly search reality for a deeper understanding of what my purposes should be. I do not believe that reality ultimately shapes our values. But even so the lack of any certainty of purposes confuses my sense of what I should be looking for. On

6. Goldthorpe, ibid., p. 276.

the occasions when I look for the limits that reality imposes on purposes I do not look for data with the same insistence as when I start with the view that a particular course of action is desirable. While a lack of commitment, or an open perspective, protects me against distorting reality, it does not provide me with any guiding principle of what I am looking for and what is problematic in the situation. I am very aware of the dilemmas that arise when one is morally committed to a point of view, but also of the difficulties caused by a lack of commitment to any value perspective.

I also take the view that values must of necessity intrude into every mode of analysis. But I recognize that there are many different value frameworks for organizing reality, each of which has a validity of its own. My particular scepticism makes me especially interested in questions about these different paradigms. While you cannot do research without a paradigm, research will never lead you to choose among the paradigms in any final way.[7] Yet, if there is to be any action, there must be some choice among these paradigms. This leaves only limited scope for objective inquiry as an aid in policy choice.

In summary then, value-committed and value-critical perspectives are ways of searching for reality. In a value-committed perspective, I am interested in the consequences of possible action for the goals I cherish. However, from a value-critical point of view, I embark on a search for something in reality to which I may attach myself to make my purposes satisfying emotionally. While reality can challenge the value frameworks it cannot yield a value perspective. Of course, one way to cope with this question is to argue that commitment and doubt are both necessary at different stages of an inquiry. For example, I have a different attitude of mind when I am trying to define what the research problem is, when I do not know what is problematic in the situation, from when the problem is identified. At first I want to explore

7. In principle it is possible to create a critical experiment that might decide between two paradigms. If both can make sense of all previous events in the universe, but one predicts a different event from the other, we could then see which is confirmed. This kind of proof – as Popper says – is not absolutely convincing, but it is an objective way of choosing. However, these tests are much easier to design in the physical than in the social sciences, where you can hardly control all the relevant variables.

as many areas as possible, not systematically but in search of what is problematic. Of course, I can only know when I have found what is problematic if it resonates with, or is responsive to, the purposes I have in mind, which I recognize by the connotation of feelings which they evoke, and by that diffuse intuitive sense as to whether I care about what I have identified. But once I have committed myself to a definition of a problem and a perspective for interpreting it, then my attitude towards data changes. Now, I search for evidence unrelentingly and try to interpret facts and reconcile contradictions in the light of the framework of argument I have set out.

I want to be simultaneously committed to a moral position yet at the same time to doubt that position sufficiently to want to expose it to evidence and criticism. It is this wish to do both that leads me to the question of how we can reconcile the competing paradigms which arise from different ideological commitments. I have an intellectual commitment to questions about multi-paradigmatic frameworks of argument in the policy arena. While I recognize that I must make a commitment at some level, I firmly believe that reality can be constructed in different ways, that these constructions may be incompatible and that there is no final way to determine which is truer and no procedure for choosing among these constructions of reality, because they are ideologies – that is, frameworks of interpretation where knowledge, values and ways of organizing the world are inextricably interwoven. For me, this is the crucial question that a policy analysis must address. Politics is also largely about the problem of multiple definitions of the same events. In politics, and/or policies, there is no such thing as reality, but there is current reality which consists of those aspects of the contemporary situation which are salient for most people in a society (or most people in a sector of society which will be affected by policy making in this area). And it is the central question in the discussion about what contribution social science can make to policy. In fact, this is of increasing importance because of the 'pollution of information' syndrome, about which so much has been written. The positivists assume that one can separate the elements of inquiry and conduct an analysis which deals with values in isolation from the objective level of study. But such a separation is impossible and leads to unrealistic positions. In this sense we can say that there is no reality except that reality which is informed by value screens and ideological frames.

Policy Choice and Conflicting Paradigms

I take the view that there is both a bridge and a gulf between questions of values and questions of truth. If there were no gulf separating the world of the 'is' from the world of the 'ought' then there would be no room for moral debate and the most urgent normative questions about the meaning of life would surrender to a relentless search in reality and in history for the resolution of ethical issues. I reject this view. I think that the gulf is important in separating the two realms of discourse into what is morally right and objectively true. However, I believe that there is a bridge as well, and that if there were no bridge, then social science would have nothing to contribute to the ethical and normative questions which preoccupy government. But how can this bridge best be built? To consider this question we need to examine how we collectively act, given different perspectives. There are several possible answers.

One interpretation holds that in practice whatever group is dominant imposes its ideology upon others. Differing definitions and solutions of problems are resolved by power. The choice of a dominant ideology is thus determined by which interest group is most powerful in a particular situation. The competition between different schools of sociological thought is not merely a matter of intellectual debate but a political matter of some importance, because the survival of the interest groups they represent may be at stake. Academic debate is therefore much nastier than it might be if only intellectual disagreement were involved. Kuhn takes the view that this is both necessary and right in the field of scientific inquiry, because progress in science depends on everyone accepting a common paradigm, at least until the inconsistencies in the paradigm become visible and troublesome. Every ideology also sooner or later confronts events in a changing society which it cannot assimilate in its framework of thought and becomes self-contradictory, confused and ultimately irrelevant. Ideologies are often challenged by those who feel victimized by them. The alternative ideology contained in the challenge may become dominant if the other begins to disintegrate. But the mistrust of dominant ideologies does not arise from a fear that they are ultimately unadaptive – rather they may be too adaptive and perpetuate injustice. It is therefore a mistake to yield to a single dominant ideology imposed by power. If we accept this view, what other strategies remain?

Another approach simply accepts as natural and inevitable that there are multiple paradigms each directing a different line of inquiry and each providing a different system for interpreting truth, with only limited communication between those who sub-scribe to each of these different perspectives. Since these systems of thought are independent, one must make brute choice among them, without the benefit of objective criteria for choice. At its best social science can contribute a great deal to policy debates, because it can inform each ideological position, making each more realistic and capable of effective action. It thus strengthens the objective foundation on which ideology rests. It is doubtful whether social science can narrow the difference between the implications of each ideological interpretation, although this may be a strong motive for conducting the study. It surely cannot ultimately *decide* between the ideologies, but it can perhaps modify them. Hence, without being neutral or Olympian, social investigators have much to say that is relevant to policy debates. Unfortunately, many social analyses disagree, adding more con-fusion than clarity to policy debates, as the studies of the effects of schooling on income or the effect on I.Q. of race and class position illustrate.

My argument can now be briefly summarized. I have first set out three different interpretations of the interplay between objec-tive inquiry and normative choice: arguing that values can organ-ize facts; or facts are compatible with many different value-systems; or, finally, that facts organize values. Each perspective gives rise to its own special problems. When values are passionately held they provide a secure basis for the search for evidence but distort perception. A multi-paradigmatic perspective leads to many truths and no rules for choice; hence the scope for objective inquiry seems limited, because it bypasses the central question. If facts determine values then the scope of moral choice is severely constrained, as politics must surrender to necessity and value options foreclose other requirements of reality. I tend to follow a sceptical or value-critical position on each of these issues. I accept the importance of purpose and commitment, yet I cannot resolve the puzzle about the meaning of life and its converse, the fact of death, so I do not attempt to pass off unfounded positions as founded in either theology or reality. I accept the view that there are competing paradigms of policy interpretation and that there is no fundamental way to resolve the disagreements among these perspectives. I believe that there is no central, abiding, over-arching guiding principle that can fill the gaps in understanding, resolve the quandaries of action, order the conflicts of human purposes or resolve the conflicting interpretations of action which competing frameworks pose. In short, I do not think that there is a policy science which can rise above these conflicts and provide unity out of disorder. Finally, I reject the possibility of historical prediction as a guide for future moral action. In this sense I reject the view that values are inevitable in history, because I do not believe that history is on anyone's side. As we have seen, in Chapter 2, a value-critical approach does not accept values as self-evident or given and therefore not subject to further debate. Rather, we must argue for the values we espouse, because in a multi-paradigmatic world they are being challenged and we need to defend them against alternative perspectives and become anxious when the strategies we pursue to achieve our goals are not realized.

Increasingly, I am inclined to take the view that these dilemmas are desirable, because they pose moral choices and hence permit a debate about moral purposes.[8] If there were no dilemmas in social action, then there would be no opportunity for meaningful moral discourse on human affairs. This is important in a policy debate and should not be forsaken. Moral debate is both possible and

8. John Goldthorpe has called my attention to this interpretation.

necessary because there is a conflict of moral principles judged desirable by some standards. And it is the nature of this conflict which makes the debate between factual and normative questions most interesting. Thus, the search for objectivity, the yearning for empirical evidence to confirm or discount theories and beliefs does not foreclose debate about moral questions but only opens it for a deeper analysis.

The issue of competing frameworks, with no governing rules for choice among them, especially intrigues me. Actually, I have somewhat overstated the case, although the statement is basically correct. Some paradigms can be shown to be unsuccessful because they cannot explain what we know happens. Some explain little and have great internal contradictions and may therefore be discounted. Still, the broader competing frameworks of disciplines, and of methods, and of values, cannot be dismissed so easily, and this raises the question of what to do when more than one paradigm is important for action. If we rule out coercion, that is, the imposition of ideology as a solution, and if we rule out the Mannheimian search for a final synthesis by detached intellectuals, then we are faced with two choices. Either we can accept that there are different schools of thought and ignore the question of how society chooses, or we can pursue the question and search for a way in which the insights of paradigms can be assimilated without repudiating their structure. It is this latter question which I want to examine. Is there, then, an approach which lies between imposition by power and surrender by intellectual defeat? I think a middle course is possible. The argument can be briefly stated. Many paradigms contain stories which describe intrinsically good ways of looking at reality and drawing morals for action. These are persuasive whether or not we accept the whole paradigm of thought from which they come. It is possible to accept many Freudian insights such as the Oedipus complex without accepting Freudian methods of analysis and theory. Equally, the concept of class-conflict can be used to explain certain situations without embracing the whole of Marxist theory. Despite the debate about the rigid limits of functionalist perspective, we all use the theory of function, at least part of the time, to explain why institutions act as they do. Thus each paradigm offers valuable stories which can be accepted and are useful irrespective of the paradigm from which they emanated. Paradigms are valuable because they lead one to see things that otherwise one would not be looking for. The main task of a policy-oriented social science is to make use of these insights and apply them in specific situations to achieve specific values. It follows that an important role for a policy-responsive social science is that of advice giving and story-telling.

Advice giving is essentially a matter of choosing a relevant story which is about the circumstances and the particular values espoused by the person who needs to make decisions. This may take the form of supplying supporting evidence for what the policy makers want to do, or reassurance. More often the essential role of advice is to supply contradictory evidence, pointing out the limits of the policy makers' ideas or programmes, or speculating and, better still, supplying evidence, about the possibility of un-anticipated consequences. Story-telling extracts the insights of particular paradigms from the paradigm itself and thus makes possible a multi-paradigmatic approach to policy analysis. Of course, an attempt to use the insights of each paradigm does not settle the question of which paradigms are correct. The need for collective action requires that we abstract the stories from these different ideologies and use them in a way that does not commit the story-teller or the decision-maker to any particular paradigm. This provides a pragmatic solution for what is intellectually not reconcilable. This view is of course vulnerable to criticism as eclecticism, or as a surrender to the middle course and the repudiation of radical political alternatives, from both the right and left.

The Giving of Advice

In the remainder of this essay I want in a very preliminary way to sketch out some ideas about advice giving and to return to some of my earlier comments about story-telling. While one of the crucial tests of the objectivity of understanding about social events is the confirmation of predictions based upon it, this is seldom possible in the social sciences. Still, when someone consistently gives good advice, we trust their understanding of events and their capacity to translate their understanding into practical advice giving. Thus, if a person's predictions are generally realized, we believe that their understanding is objectively grounded.

Consider a non-political example of advice giving. One author advises the other that the argument in his essay is not clear: the first author re-reads the essay and confirms the second's opinion. Hence the advice seems good. If the first author often does this for the second author, and indeed, each provides similar advice for the other, in time they come to trust each other as good 'objective' critics. One important reason why they are good critics for each other is that they care about each other's work. It matters to each that his colleague's essay is successful. Because there is trust, and because there is concern about each other's work, each is careful to provide a most objectively grounded assessment of the other's work. The measure of objectivity is a combination of the critic's subjective assessment and his interpretation of the reception which the piece is likely to receive from others.

In everyday life, we trust advisers who are knowledgeable (those who have much experience of the consequences of relevant actions) or wise (those who have a good sense of what are the relevant questions – what needs to be predicted). It does not seem to matter to us how their understanding is arrived at, as long as it shows a consistent predictive power. Nor do we usually ask them to verify the sources of their information; we trust their understanding because it has been confirmed in our own or others' experience. It is only when we begin to doubt the validity of the advice that these questions arise. We do not usually trust advisers who do not share our values, because their understanding is irrelevant to us. Whatever the independent merit of the advice is, it tends, from the user's point of view, to be trivial or pernicious – that is to say, it strengthens the effectiveness of actions we do not want to take. Thus we seek advice which enables us to realize the values we cherish. Advice is best when we believe our advisers to share the same framework of values and when the adviser demonstrates that his predictions are generally realized.

In our example we have been concerned only with personal

values we hold as individuals and with a search for objectively grounded advice which can provide a guide for individual action to enable us to realize our values. But as we move from personal values to collective actions it is hard to know how these collective purposes were influenced by social analysis, and in what way, because it is difficult to trace the predictive power of understanding in the social sciences. In part this is so because it is hard to find out whether these collective actions were successful, or in what way. It is, perhaps, possible to evaluate the influence of social theory on nineteenth-century social policy and to determine its predictive power to some degree. But no one is now proposing these theories, and even if they were, the context of policy is different; and so we cannot use the evaluation of the past to determine the quality of contemporary social theory.

How then can we know when social understanding is good? Since we have no useful past record of the predictive power of social analysis, it is tempting to turn to another field of knowledge, which is known to be powerfully predictive, and imitate its techniques of analysis. That is, we know that natural science can predict reliably, so if social science can follow the method of natural science, it, too, could be predictive. The method of natural science seems to require neutrality about values as a condition of objectivity.[9]

I believe that efforts to imitate the analytic techniques of the natural sciences as a way of providing reliable predictions are based on a misleading analogy. First, pure science depends upon

9. A somewhat different view is taken by Karl R. Popper, who argues that 'all theoretical or generalizing sciences make use of the same method, whether they are natural sciences or social sciences ...' The essential method is that of testing deductive causal explanations. Science, he believes, is always concerned with explanations, predictions and tests. A hypothesis permits us to make some prognosis which is then compared with the results of either experimentation or observation. 'Agreement is taken as corroboration of the hypothesis, although not as final proof; clear disagreement is considered as refutation or falsification.' In this sense, the logical structure of hypothesis-testing is the same in all the sciences. How one first finds one's theory is an entirely private matter; the crucial aspect of science is how one tests one's theory. For a fuller discussion, see Karl R. Popper, *The Poverty of Historicism*, Routledge & Kegan Paul, 2nd ed., 1960, pp. 130–43.

analytic procedures which are not possible in the study of society; it deals with presumably stable and universal relationships between events, while social events are neither stable nor universal, and it can discriminate disaggregated factors and re-combine them in a way which seems beyond the reach of social analysis. But secondly, we are not, I think, ever really interested in 'pure' social science – a social science divorced from action, since the meaning of social events is inextricably bound up with the values we attach to them. I think that we accept the apparent relevance of pure science because the categories which define the natural world seem meaningful, irrespective of values. We assume that any understanding of the natural world is potentially useful, even if we cannot see how it might be used.

Perhaps social science can find a closer analogy in applied science. Applied science is primarily concerned with questions of design, that is to say, with the professional application of existing scientific knowledge and techniques to practical problems. This said, we begin to see that applied science has many problems in common with a policy-relevant social science. That is, it is hard to predict whether the application of scientific generalizations will be valuable in practical terms since purely scientific knowledge cannot predict with much reliability whether any application will achieve a desired result. More specifically, difficulties in applied science are encountered at two levels: (a) A great many physical factors are combined in a machine; it is hard to predict exactly how that machine will function in an environment. Therefore engineers build and modify prototypes, and even then, the production model may prove to have faults. (b) Even if the machine works, it may not be as valuable socially as expected – for instance, it may have unforeseen and undesirable social consequences. And indeed, these appear to be the very problems confronting social understanding – how to aggregate the overall effect of a great many factors (which are not, of course, as well understood as in the natural sciences), and help to foresee the overall social benefit.

A concrete example of the effort to apply this approach may be useful. Delinquency prevention programmes in the United States in the late 1960s were based on the proposition that crime was a function of blocked economic opportunity. The theory held that if youngsters had these blocks removed by making available education and job training, then delinquency in the ghettoes would be reduced. Social policy proceeded under the assumption that delinquency could be treated as an applied science problem and that the main task was to build prototypes of wider opportunity which would translate the scientific principle about the causes of juvenile crime into an operating programme. Once the design was debugged, it could be used in any community as a means of reducing juvenile crime.

The experience revealed the weakness of the approach. Why, in spite of its plausibility, is the analogy between applied science and social policy misplaced? First, because in the applied science situation usually a single value is being realized, such as profitability, whereas in public policy we cannot reconcile all the conflicting goals with a clear hierarchy of purpose. Second, since we cannot usually control the procedures thoroughly, we cannot tell where the prototype went wrong, or whether the problems are in the design or its implementation. Third, since we cannot measure the outcomes of the prototype easily, we cannot experiment with the interplay between the various factors involved. Finally, the steps between prototype and full-scale production are not clear in social programmes – there are the troublesome psychological questions of whether the same reactions by clients are likely (the Hawthorne effects), and an experiment has very different political implications from a general policy.[10]

I take the view that neither science nor applied science provides an adequate model for social understanding. What matters in social understanding is the overall effect of a complex of behaviour. This understanding cannot be reached by aggregating known regularities in the behaviour of discrete events. Rather, social understanding in this situation depends upon telling relevant stories: that is, deriving from past experience a narrative which

10. For a fuller elaboration of these points see Peter Marris, 'Experimenting in Social Reform', in *Community Work One*, edited by David Jones and Marjorie Mayo (Routledge & Kegan Paul, 1974).

interprets the events as they unfolded and draws a moral for future actions, suggesting, for example, how the future might unfold if certain steps were taken.

The giving of advice and the design of social programmes is like the telling of relevant stories. Such stories resemble proverbs and metaphors, for they seek to match reality to archetypical patterns of events by drawing analogies. That is to say, they provide an interpretation of a complex pattern of events with normative implications for action, and not with a universal law. Nor is the correspondence expected to be much more than a warning and a direction.

The simplest stories are proverbs and parables, used to justify policy relevant arguments. For example, we may argue that 'too many cooks spoil the broth', or that 'many hands make light work', or that 'a prophet is without honour in his own country' and so on. Of course, many proverbs are mutually contradictory, like the first two cited above. But the adviser's wisdom and understanding depend on his being able to see which proverbs apply in which context, that is, in discerning whether a given situation is, or is not, like cooking a broth. It does not matter that his analysis is subjective or intuitive. What does matter is whether the interpretation of the events is reasonable, or whether some other story is better able to account for what has happened or is likely to unfold. While one can check whether details in the story are accurate, the story as a whole cannot be refuted in any final sense because the very analysis itself, if acted upon, may influence action, and thus determine its own outcome. Nevertheless, the quality of stories can be compared because the best analysis is the one which can withstand critical questions about truth, interpretation and relevance. Story-telling which offers policy advice can be criticized by asking: Is the story true? If true, is it relevant? What we mean by 'objective' social understanding is that understanding which stands up best in the face of these criticisms. The techniques of social science have much to contribute here.

Objective knowledge is relevant to story-telling, because through it we can examine the fit between the story and the circumstances to which it is now being applied and assess whether the facts on which the story is premissed are true. In this sense, it is possible to argue objectively about the relevance of the story. An example may be useful here. One story-teller may argue that a social programme is defective because too many interest groups have had a say in its development and concessions were made to each group so that the results lacked internal coherence. Thus the analyst concludes that 'too many cooks' had spoiled the social 'broth'. The normative implication drawn from the proverb is that if fewer actors had participated and if less compromises had been required, we would have had a better social brew. This is a familiar élitist view of policy making. We need to inquire whether the story told is true. Is it factually accurate that many cooks, i.e., interest groups, were involved; and did they spoil the broth because there were too many of them, or, perhaps, just because they offered incompetent advice? The last question implies an alternative explanatory story – namely that it was not the number of cooks that was crucial, but their skill. To argue in favour of the theory about the number of cooks we need to challenge the rival theory about the competence of the chefs. In these ways normative explanatory theories can be subjected to objective analysis.

As discussed in Chapter 2 (p. 77 and pp. 87–8), the criticism of the truth of a story (did the events happen?) is not difficult: the explanation of what happened, that is, the interpretation advanced in the story, is much harder to evaluate. Unfortunately these interpretations are difficult to challenge with objective evidence, since the same facts can lead to quite different interpretations.

I have not fully reviewed in this book the role of the social scientist as story-teller, programme designer and social critic. I have only suggested the broad directions that a value-critical approach might follow. There are however at least three complementary paths that a social scientist interested in normative questions can pursue. There is first the task of freely speculating and developing imaginative stories with normative implications. The art of story-telling and advice-giving has only begun to be explored.[11] Secondly, there is the related task which explicitly tries to translate stories into a concrete course of programmatic action. Programme design is thus a form of social reform and social innovation. Design unashamedly postulates values and attempts to develop instruments for their fulfilment; indeed, this is the essence of a good design. Finally, there is the role of the social scientist as critic, with its value-critical, theoretically critical and empirically critical dimensions. To sum up, the task of the social scientist is to invent objectively grounded normative stories, to participate in designing programmes of intervention based upon them and to test the validity of stories that others commend. Invention, design and criticism are all crucial for story-telling. The theoretically critical and empirically critical tasks are widely accepted roles. We have, however, tended to neglect story-telling, design, and the value-critical approach. And these are the new directions in which a policy responsive social science should develop.

11. For example, Martin Krieger's thoughtful and provocative unpublished essay on 'Advice', which he revised while at the Center for Advanced Study in Behavioral Science, Stanford University.

Index